The Objectification Spectrum

THE OBJECTIFICATION SPECTRUM

Understanding and Transcending Our Diminishment and Dehumanization of Others

John M. Rector

OXFORD
UNIVERSITY PRESS

OXFORD
UNIVERSITY PRESS

Oxford University Press is a department of the University of
Oxford. It furthers the University's objective of excellence in research,
scholarship, and education by publishing worldwide.

Oxford   New York
Auckland   Cape Town   Dar es Salaam   Hong Kong   Karachi
Kuala Lumpur   Madrid   Melbourne   Mexico City   Nairobi
New Delhi   Shanghai   Taipei   Toronto

With offices in
Argentina   Austria   Brazil   Chile   Czech Republic   France   Greece
Guatemala   Hungary   Italy   Japan   Poland   Portugal   Singapore
South Korea   Switzerland   Thailand   Turkey   Ukraine   Vietnam

Oxford is a registered trademark of Oxford University Press
in the UK and certain other countries.

Published in the United States of America by
Oxford University Press
198 Madison Avenue, New York, NY 10016

Library of Congress Cataloging-in-Publication Data
Rector, John (John M.)
The objectification spectrum : understanding and transcending our diminishment and
dehumanization of others / John M. Rector.
    pages cm
ISBN 978–0–19–935541–9 (hardback)
1. Prejudices—Psychological aspects.   2. Other (Philosophy)   3. Social psychology.   I. Title.
HM1091.R43 2014
302—dc23
2014000964

9 8 7 6 5 4 3 2 1
Printed in the United States of America
on acid-free paper

To Ethan, Christian, and Garrett
and most of all, to Kirsten

CONTENTS

ACKNOWLEDGMENTS

Various individuals have played an indispensable role in making this book possible. First, I want to thank Dana Bliss, Senior Editor at Oxford University Press, for plucking this manuscript out of obscurity and giving it a chance with OUP. Second, I want to thank those who willingly took time out of their busy lives to read early drafts of the manuscript, providing invaluable feedback and encouragement along the way. These generous individuals include Jon Ivers, Dean of the College of Arts and Letters at BYU-I; Gwena Couliard, fellow psychologist and practitioner of mindfulness approaches to psychological health; Mike Farnworth, golfing buddy and courageous purveyor of deeper truths in the face of prevailing conventional wisdom; and my sister-in-law Lisa Mallory Rector, an ongoing influence for growth in the lives of her counseling clients in spite of the deep personal loses she has experienced over the years.

A special thank you goes to my collegiate son Ethan, whose close, painstaking reading of my revised manuscript can only be considered to be a labor of love, and whose thoughtfulness regarding ultimate matters became evident as he offered his clear, idealistic perspective on the problem of evil and the possibility of enlightenment. Finally, I wish to thank my wife Kirsten, my earliest and most devoted source of support, for providing countless hours of meticulous editing assistance and helping me communicate my ideas more clearly and effectively. I owe my ability to conceive of and finish such a project to you, my dear.

If there is no serious connection between education and hunger, injustice, alienation, poverty, and war, then we are wasting our time, deluding each other, and breaking faith.
—David E. Purpel (1989)

Introduction

Leaving Plato's Cave—Our Only Hope

On the cusp of my adolescence, I recall watching with some devotion the British-produced 1970s documentary series *The World at War* on Sunday afternoons. Sir Laurence Olivier's narration and the grave original musical score added a sense of solemnity to each episode that belied my casual repose on the plaid living room sofa. One episode in particular had as its central focus the legacy of the Holocaust and the liberation of the Nazi concentration camps at World War II's end. Even today, I recollect quite clearly the images from the surreal, grainy black-and-white newsreel depicting masses of decomposing, naked, Jewish bodies being bulldozed into mass graves. Like so many others, I was shocked and bewildered by what I saw and naively asked within myself, "How could this happen? What kind of a person could do such things to other people?" I wondered at the lives represented by each of the gnarled, decaying bodies. Who had they been? Boys like me? Girls like the ones at school? Men and women like my parents, and old people like my grandfather, who was living with us at the time?

And yet, seeing—from a great distance—the gruesome fate met by so many others in the past, while I was alive, young, healthy, and safely situated in the prosperous American present, allowed me not only to be indignant, but also transfixed by what I saw. Looking back now, I realize that in the midst of my youthful outrage and fascination, I was coming into contact with parts of my young self that I was unable to understand. One of these was what Carl Jung referred to as "the shadow" (Jung, 1975, p. 131)—that often denied, dark, yet potentially creative aspect of human nature that many of us prefer not to acknowledge. A second was what William James described as the human fascination with "the *strong* life; life in extremis," life at the edges of existence (James, 1906, p. 1). Most of us prefer to live our lives amid peace, societal stability, good health, and material prosperity. Nonetheless, we are captivated by stories and images of others caught in the crucible of mortal crisis, fighting for their very lives amid dire circumstances. This allows us to come into close but safe proximity to something primal within us—the desire to re-affirm our own fragile existence by witnessing others at the cusp of losing their own. Finally—and most important for the purposes of this book—a third element I experienced was my innate ability to emotionally distance myself from the suffering of other members of the species because, despite our common humanity, they were not members of my family; they were not my friends or acquaintances; indeed, they were compete strangers from another era and place.

Now, at the midpoint of my life, I'm still trying to come to terms with evil. This book began as a simple impulse to jot down some ideas I've been thinking and reading about since I was a graduate student in psychology during the 1990s. In addition to all the professional literature my professors assigned, I found myself being drawn again and again toward writers who addressed the extremities of human potential—both the very best and the very worst of which we are capable—and I wondered how to make sense of these glaring disparities. How could members of the same species be as different as Mahatma Gandhi and Jeffery Dahmer, or Nelson Mandela and Adolf Hitler, or Mother Teresa and Joseph Stalin? As I reflected on this, a few things became increasingly apparent. One was that such discrepancies had to represent a fundamental difference in how these individuals perceived or understood the reality of not only themselves, but of the world around them. Another was that *objectification*—the phenomenon of experiencing other human beings not as integrated wholes of psyche and soma, worthy of respect and even reverence, but more as objects—was a crucial concept for understanding the nature of these differences. The degree of objectification present in the psyches of each of these individuals had to vary greatly. For example, in someone like Saint Francis of Assisi—a man who saw the face of God in animals, in the beauties of nature, and in lepers and other social outcasts to the extent that he often embraced them and kissed them on the mouth—objectification seemed to be practically non-existent. For others such as Augusto Pinochet—a man who tortured, "disappeared," and killed thousands of his own fellow Chileans—it seemed a predominant characteristic.

This idea made even more sense to me when placed in the context of what is perhaps philosophy's best-known metaphor—Plato's Allegory of the Cave. In his *Republic* (380 B.C.E.), Plato, writing from the perspective of his great teacher, Socrates, asserts that human beings are like prisoners who have been in a deep cave since very early childhood; not only this, but we humans have been fixed in the same spot in the cave, with our necks and legs fettered so that we've only ever been able to see the cave wall directly in front of ourselves. Light inside the cave is provided by a large fire burning some distance behind us. Less far behind, but on higher ground, is a wall with a path running behind it. On this path other people walk (some speaking, some silent) while carrying a variety of artifacts—statues of humans, animals, and other objects made of stone, wood, and clay—above their heads. Thus, the path's wall acts as a sort of screen, similar to that employed by puppeteers as they hide while raising puppets into view. We prisoners, looking only straight ahead at the cave wall, never actually see the people who are carrying the objects, or even their human shadows. We see only moving shadows of the objects they carry and hear occasional voices bouncing off the wall in front of us. As a result, we begin to attribute forms to these shadows and assume that the shadows represent the entirety of the forms. Plato explains, "The prisoners in every way believe that the truth is nothing other than the shadows of those artifacts" (Cahn, 1995, p. 226; 515-C).

Imagine for a moment the degree of ignorance we would have—about ourselves, others, and the world—if we were stuck in such a predicament. This, Plato asserts, is the condition of almost all human beings at any given time during their lives. He goes on to proclaim that enlightening us prisoners to the reality of our situation is a difficult, gradual process at best—one that we are likely to resist. Nonetheless, this is the role of the philosopher. Picture yourself being suddenly released from your fetters and turned around so that you could see the fire, the path, the wall, even discovering the people behind the wall carrying items above their heads. You would likely be disoriented and incredulous that what you were now seeing was a truer, fuller representation of the facts than the mere shadows on the wall (this is to say nothing of actually being brought out of the cave itself). However, once these new realities set in, it would be nearly impossible to undo the impact of this new information about yourself and the world.

The problem of objectification is represented well by this depiction. We human beings see and experience many things, but we have a tendency to see surfaces, and then we go on to assume that this superficial understanding represents the truth about existence. To paraphrase the Apostle Paul, we see, but we do not see well, almost as if we were looking at the world through a dark, dingy glass. Seeing life in this way distorts the deeper truth of ourselves and others, making it possible for us to perpetrate evil in its many varieties not only upon our fellow human beings, but upon the planet as a whole. On the other hand, seeing others more as we see ourselves mitigates our willingness to knowingly inflict pain and suffering upon them, because we would not do such to ourselves, nor to those whom we love.

As I began to write about this problem, I came to realize that I was unpacking a phenomenon that ran much deeper than I had presumed. It became obvious to me that the human capacity to objectify others was not a yes-or-no, discrete proposition, but instead represented a vast continuum of psychology and attending behavior. To varying degrees, when we objectify others, we see them much as the shadows on the wall in Plato's cave. They are one-dimensional—lacking nuance, uniqueness, and most importantly, depth. Twentieth-century Jewish theologian and philosopher Martin Buber (1970) used the old English word *thou* to capture the essence of what human beings are and how they can be related to. We humans are self-aware, integrated beings of a corporeal and spiritual nature; we are capable of unspeakable acts of depravity and evil, but as Shakespeare's Hamlet proclaimed, we are also "... [so] noble in reason ... [so] infinite in faculty, in apprehension, how like a god!" Thus, we are worthy of rights, respect, and reverence, as is implied in the traditional Hindu greeting *namaste*. The *I-Thou* mode is one in which humans relate to one another with their full being, as Subject to Subject. However, human tendencies toward objectification often lead us to experience others as varying degrees of *it*; they amount to little more than shadows, objects in the periphery, and their psyche and soul are perceived to be irrelevant or nonexistent. This constitutes the problematic *I-it* mode—in which subject relates to object.

I also came to appreciate more fully that seeing others as objects is largely a boundary problem. Boundaries represent the natural and in many ways helpful human tendency to make distinctions between aspects of existence, thus perceiving the self as a separate and distinct entity. On the one hand, this capacity allows us to distinguish between our own experience and that of others, which is a crucial component of healthy emotional functioning. Indeed, individuals who cannot make this distinction consistently have a very difficult time thriving in personal relationships and in society in general. However, the paradox is that this very important capacity also contributes directly to the formation of what contemplatives have long considered to be the greatest of all stumbling blocks—the ego.

Attempting to think clearly about the ego is daunting—tantamount to being a fish deep in the ocean attempting to reflect critically upon the nature of the water that sustains it—but doing so also led me to give consideration to the ego's antidote: enlightenment. Unlike some of the authors of books I've referred to on the subject, I make no claims to enlightenment. According to Aldous Huxley (1970), the price to be paid for enlightenment is deceptively simple: "being loving, pure in heart, and poor in spirit" (p. x). The moment I think I've made substantial progress toward these ends, I see my equanimity evaporate rapidly before my eyes when an unforeseen irritant presents itself. In truth, the closest I come at this point in my life to such a blessed state might include some all-too-fleeting experiences of connecting to the present moment, a realization that external appearances can often be quite deceiving, an appreciation for the fact that truth can be found in many places, a healthy respect for my own and other's inner complexity, a desire to be more accepting of "what is," and intentions to live more for the benefit of others. While my own personal realizations and experiences do not constitute the condition of enlightenment, these moments have helped me to understand more about what enlightenment might mean, and I attempt to enumerate some of these insights in the last section of this book.

In the process of gathering my thoughts around these concepts, I became more convinced that objectification plays a primary role in evil's perpetuation, but I also realized that it is not the only source. For example, fear is a factor that can lead to the commission of evil without necessarily enhancing the amount of objectification occurring in the psyche. Because of his fear of authority, an otherwise sensitive, well-meaning man might be willing to do harm to another person not because he deeply objectifies that person, but because he fears authority more than he fears injuring someone else. But by the same token, fear can sometimes intensify the human propensity to objectify others in the service of self-perpetuation. This same sensitive, well-meaning man mentioned above has a limited capacity to connect to the reality of other persons in the first place, especially if those persons are strangers to him; toxic situations can catalyze whatever latent tendencies toward objectifying others this man might have *a priori*.

In addition to the problems of boundaries and the ego, it became clearer that other human tendencies contribute to our potential to objectify others. Among these are the problem of narcissism, an inherent part of human nature; the problem of death and the human need to deny this reality through a variety of means; the problem of heroism and the incessant need to make our lives matter; and the problem of toxic situations. Unfortunately, space does not provide me the opportunity to fully explore other contributing factors, such as systems of privilege—race, ethnicity, and gender—as well as hierarchical/patriarchal systems of power, such as corporations, governments, and other institutions. My level of analysis will largely be limited to the dispositional and immediately situational factors influencing the individual's tendencies to see others as objects. Later writers will be left to cover the broader systemic ground.

Finally, given the pessimistic cast of much of the topic at hand, I decided it would be beneficial to outline, in a very broad way, some of the various pathways leading out of Plato's cave. These represent differing routes toward the goal of enlightenment that human beings have discovered over the millennia. The existence of such paths and the fact that a few of our kind have actually left the cave successfully by walking them suggest that while the problem of objectification is ubiquitous and tenacious, it is not insoluble. Counterfeit spiritual growth attenuates or leaves unchanged our parochial perspective of those who count. It gives us the illusion that we are freed from our fetters, that we are in possession of *the* truth, and that we have found our way out of the cave. In reality, however, we haven't left the cave at all; we have simply moved from one inner chamber to another, still taking shadows to be the entire truth. Our worldview has hardened, our circle has rigidified or even diminished in size, and we have become more fearful and suspicious of others. As Plato knew, ultimately, such a limited perspective of reality leads to conflict, violence, and death. By contrast, the experience of true spiritual growth is always the same: symbolically, fetters come off our limbs; scales fall from our eyes; our freedom to perceive, choose, and act is enhanced; our perspective is broadened; and our "circle of those who count as neighbor" (Fowler, 1981) is expanded. We come to realize that what we have experienced previously have been mere shadows—one-dimensional versions of a much deeper reality.

Contemplatives through the ages have shown that by various means, the ego can be transcended to a substantial degree, and that the boundaries of our consciousness can be enlarged to include a domain of concern that encompasses the entire world. As renowned religious scholar Huston Smith (1991) puts it, shifting the nucleus of our empathic focus from ourselves to our family transcends selfishness, shifting the center from family to community transcends nepotism, shifting from community to country transcends parochialism, and shifting from country to the entire planet transcends nationalism. The bottom line, however, seems to be that there are no guaranteed methods, no easy paths to transcending the human condition, which is in many ways typified by the problem of objectification. Redemption from evil, if it is to occur, appears to be a gradual process, one that must be undertaken by individuals one at a time. While inspired collectives can be a support to realizing what is best in us as a species, history is replete with examples showing that such collectives tend to restrain and hinder as much as they facilitate growth. The worst in human nature tends to manifest itself when human beings come together in groups, especially when such groups are galvanized by the desire to proclaim and implement a new vision for what humankind is capable of being and should be.

I say nothing new when I claim that enlightenment—leaving Plato's cave—is our only hope as a species. Technology will undoubtedly continue to advance, and we may solve many of the problems that currently beset us, such as global hunger, global warming, over-reliance on fossil fuels, cancer, and so forth. However, human nature remains unchanged over many millennia. Any thoughtful adolescent is capable of realizing that the trajectory of human proliferation—exponential population growth, ever-increasing desire for and consumption of resources, and the nonstop production of waste, juxtaposed with the world's finite capacity to support human activity—will in the not-too-distant future reach a point at which we either adapt with more peaceful, sustainable, renewable ways of relating with each other and the rest of the world, or we experience what might be best described as cataclysmic collapse.

PART ONE

Shadows on the Cave Wall

The Many Faces of Objectification

CHAPTER 1
Preliminaries

After one ambush my men brought back the body of a North Vietnamese soldier. I later found the dead man propped against some C-ration boxes. He had on sunglasses, and a Playboy magazine lay open in his lap; a cigarette dangled jauntily from his mouth, and on his head was perched a large piece of excrement. I pretended to be outraged, since desecrating bodies was frowned on as un-American and counterproductive. But it wasn't outrage I felt. I kept my officer's face on, but inside I was . . . laughing. I laughed—I believe now—in part because of some subconscious appreciation of this obscene linkage of sex and excrement and death; and in part because of the exultant realization that he—whoever he had been—was dead and I—special, unique me—was alive.

William Broyles *(as quoted in Glover, 2001, p. 56)*

MAJOR SIGNPOSTS ALONG OBJECTIFICATION'S SPECTRUM

The commission of evil becomes much more likely when others are seen as mere shadows of themselves—objects, rather than as Subjects with interior depth, possessing both an immanent physical dimension of the body and a transcendent spiritual dimension of the psyche, integrated together as a whole. The psychological process of seeing human beings more as objects than as Subjects and treating them accordingly is *objectification*. Objectification is best understood not as a discrete variable, but as a *spectrum of misapprehension*. In other words, when we objectify others, we misperceive them as being less than what they are in their totality. This spectrum can range from mild to severe.

At the mild end, objectification is typified by *casual indifference*, in which individuals experience minimal affective connection between themselves and others, especially those outside their immediate circle of family and closest friends. When we experience little or no discernible emotional discomfort at the realization of some "distant" other's suffering, then we are exhibiting casual indifference. Most people experience this level of objectification most of the time.

Derivatization represents the vast midrange of the objectification spectrum and is itself best represented by a sub-spectrum of perceptions, feelings, and attendant behavior. To derivatize others is to perceive them as being primarily derivative of oneself—a reflection of one's own identity, desires, and fears. Other aspects of the other person's being or inner life are "disregarded, ignored, or under-valued" (Cahill, 2011, p. 32). Derivatization comes in many guises, from the relatively benign to the sadistically violent. At its most extreme, it is typified by *emotional hardening*. Jonathan Glover, a historian of twentieth-century atrocities, explains that "the human responses" (i.e., respect for humanity and sympathy for the experience of suffering) can be worn away by repeated exposure to violence (Glover, 2001, pp. 22–25).[1] Most human beings experience derivatization only in its mild to moderate varieties, either as victims or as perpetrators. The extremes of derivatization tend to occur in times of war, in cultures of violence, or as a byproduct of the incapacity to experience normal empathy (otherwise known as psychopathy).

Finally, at the extreme end of the objectification spectrum, *dehumanization* is the psychological phenomenon of viewing others as being completely devoid of a human essence, to the extent that they are seen not only as less than human, but other than human as well (Smith, 2011). Like the extreme end of derivatization, dehumanization also tends to occur in times of war and is thought by many experts to be a precursor to genocide (Bandurra, 2003; Chirot & McCauley, 2006; Goldhagen, 2009; Kelman, 1973; Kressel, 2002; Stanton, 2002). Each of these concepts and the territory they claim along objectification's spectrum will be explored in more depth in later chapters of this book.

TWO VANTAGE POINTS: WHAT AND WHO WE ARE

The nature of objectification and its contribution to the commission of evil can be explored from two broad perspectives: *what human beings are*, referencing factors endemic to our species that contribute to the problem of objectification; and *who human beings are*, referencing our situatedness in circumstantial and relational contexts contributing to the same problem. Historically, the attempt to understand human evil has been represented only by the dispositional perspective. For many centuries—indeed, over millennia—philosophy and theology were the only formalized channels of human thought which, as

---

1. This is somewhat different from Robert J. Lifton's term, "psychic numbing"—an involuntary defense mechanism in reaction to trauma characterized by a diminished inclination or capacity to feel (Lifton, 2011, pp. 102–103). While psychic numbing and emotional hardening share overlapping symptoms, psychic numbing is considered to be a response of *both* victims and perpetrators to trauma. Emotional hardening, on the other hand, is a response limited to perpetrators, and is believed to facilitate the ongoing commission of violent acts.

part of their realm of inquiry, attempted to understand the problem of human evil. The conclusions of the best minds of antiquity tended to locate the problem of evil within individuals themselves. In the present, the preponderance of psychiatric theory, heavily influenced by the medical model of disease, has tended to favor this same conservative, *dispositional* view, locating the pathology responsible for antisocial behavior primarily within individuals.[2] However, since the early twentieth century, another stream of thought has run alongside the previous paradigm: the situationist perspective, endorsed by sociology and social psychology. This perspective takes a more liberal view of the problem, placing much greater emphasis on the power of immediate situations to affect the expression of a person's behavior.

As is the case with most ongoing debates, there are good reasons for the vehemence and staying power of both sides: The two perspectives have persuasive arguments and can marshal evidence to support their claims. The dispositional view is the product of thousands of years of human observation, introspection, and experience; while some of its older claims have fallen by the wayside since the Enlightenment (e.g., the presumption of unseen, external, demonic forces influencing human character and behavior), it still has much wisdom to offer in terms of understanding and appreciating foundational problems inherent in being a member of the species. On the other hand, the situationist perspective has on its side a significant body of scientific evidence to show that situational power can often trump individual power in certain contexts. Rather than pitting these two perspectives against one another, it makes much more sense to use them as complements or correctives as we attempt to accurately understand objectification and the evil it can inspire. I'm reminded of an aphorism I learned as an undergraduate psychology student: *Complex behavior is always over-determined*. This statement has reference to the human tendency to provide simplistic answers to complicated questions. We often assume one-to-one causal relationships between phenomena that appear to be related, especially with respect to human behavior. However, to make such assumptions regarding complex behaviors—such as depression, sexuality, or one's political persuasion—is typically to engage in gross over-simplification. Perhaps there is no human behavior more complex than the expression of evil in all its varieties. Given this, I've tried to beware of the temptation to give objectification too much credit as *the* cause of evil; rather, I assert that objectification is a *substantial contributing factor*. Toward this end, it seems more than reasonable to assume that the binocular view of the combined dispositional/situational perspective is more accurate than the monocular view that either perspective would provide alone.

2. Ever striving to imbue their professions with the clout of legitimate science, psychology and psychiatry have eschewed value-laden terms, such as good and evil, in favor of the value-free vocabulary of science, which prefers labels such as "well-being" and "pathology."

[Alexander Mitscherlitch] said that most Germans of his generation—the Nazi generation—could not psychologically confront the evil they had been part of, that the human psyche is incapable of inwardly experiencing its own involvement in evil of that magnitude. [. . .]Alexander accurately anticipated my experience with Nazi doctors. It turned out that not one of them was able to say to me that he had been part of something evil that he deeply regretted.

Robert Jay Lifton (2011, p. 244)

Of course, there are many ways of defining or understanding evil. Some are quite lengthy and complex, while others are quite simple.[3] Some scholars assert that an all-encompassing definition of evil must be inadequate because of the problem's complexity, and thus should be avoided (Neiman, 2004). Notwithstanding, since I will refer to evil many times in this book, it seems appropriate that I clarify what I mean by it. While an admittedly imperfect definition, for the purposes of this book, evil is defined as *willful action taken against life and liveliness that is unnecessary for the purposes of self-preservation, when that action taken (i.e., means) is out of proportion with the goal of the greater good (i.e., ends) as determined by the standards of rational, moral society.*[4] By this definition, a wolf's stalking and killing of a sheep (even many sheep without eating them all, as some wolves have been known to do) would not qualify as evil, because the wolf would be acting out of its instinct for self-preservation or its instinct to kill when prey are abundantly available, even when not motivated by hunger, known as "surplus killing."

By contrast, this definition would define the Nazi regime as evil. Though they believed that the end-goal of a racially pure Reich (and larger world) justified the extermination of its Jewish population, along with other marginalized groups, the Allied nations did not concur that the ends justified the means; indeed, they would have argued—despite, in some instances, their own anti-Semitic tendencies—that the end itself was patently evil. On the other hand, the potential evil of dropping two nuclear weapons over Japan, which resulted in a staggering loss of life and contamination of the local environment

---

3. One example of a drawn-out definition of evil can be seen in the *Catholic Encyclopedia*, available at: http://www.newadvent.org/cathen/05649a.htm. By contrast, the sociologist Irving Sarnoff's simple definition of evil is encapsulated in the aphorism, "Evil is knowing better, but doing worse" (Zimbardo, 2008, p. 5).

4. Note that my definition is behavior based. I don't make any definitive statement about the realm of feeling or thought, despite the fact that thoughts and feelings are typically precursors of action. Of course, simply having an "evil" thought or feeling does not necessarily lead to evil behavior. Indeed, how many times have we each experienced such thoughts and feelings, but have worked to restrain ourselves against acting accordingly? Therefore, I do not see these experiences as necessarily constituting evil in and of themselves.

for many years, is a much more complicated case. Some scholars (none of them Japanese) assert that the use of nuclear weapons against Japan was a necessary evil in order to expedite the end of World War II without requiring the invasion of the Japanese mainland by Allied forces, a move that experts estimate would have cost the lives of at least one million Allied soldiers, not to mention many millions of additional Japanese civilians, given the Japanese emperor's pledge to fight to the last man. However, other experts, including former US president Herbert Hoover, have maintained that the already fierce conventional fire-bombing campaign, together with the sea blockade, the collapse of Germany, the potential redeployment of over one million Allied forces into the Pacific theater, and the massive Soviet attack on Japanese forces in Eastern Asia in August 1945, would also have led to a Japanese surrender, so the atomic bombings were militarily unnecessary (Wilson, 2007; Hasegawa, 2006; Dupuy & Dupuy, 1994). The question of whether or not the means of nuclear weapons and the horrors they unleashed on the ground were justified by the ends of bringing the war in the Pacific to a swift conclusion will likely never be completely resolved. Clearly, evil can be something of an elusive concept, admitting shades of gray, and subject to bias. This is one reason that it is wise to include the judgments of "moral, rational society" when attempting to make such determinations, assuming that multiple, thoughtful points of view converging on the same conclusion will help to minimize the possibility of bias. But as this example shows, consensus can be difficult to achieve.

CHAPTER 2

Objectification

"A Slippery, Multiple Concept"

It has often been observed that for every one of us, reality is split into two parts: Here
am I; and there is everything else, the world, including you. . . . How we enter [the field of
knowledge of the other] is indeed one of the most interesting, and also most vital questions that can be posed.

E. E. Schumacher *(1977, p. 62)*

When I decided to write at length about the problem of objectification,
I assumed that given the word's occasional usage in the popular culture (especially in connection with many of the ills of modern society), there
would have been many ahead of me who would have paved the way with a clear
definition of the phenomenon and a well-thought-out theory explaining the
nuances of its manifestations and effects. But I found that this was not exactly
the case. I was surprised to discover that while the term is indeed utilized by
both academics and the general public with some regularity, there's an overall
lack of precision or sophistication regarding its actual meaning.

Not surprisingly, the branch of scholarship that speaks of objectification
most frequently is feminist studies. The general thrust of the argument has
been that patriarchy renders women as things, thus depriving them of the
attributes of personhood. Classic examples of the objectification of women—
such as rape, physical abuse, the exploitation of their bodies for profit, and
unequal pay for equal work—typify ways in which women have been viewed
as inferior to men, providing compelling examples of objectification and the
need for greater gender equality.

Much of the traditional feminist perspective on objectification owes a
substantial debt to the thoughts of the Prussian Enlightenment philosopher
Immanuel Kant, who spoke at some length about this problem in the context
of his larger theorizing about morals. According to Kant, the most essential

quality of human beings is their rational agency: the capacity to reason and the ability to make rational choices in the pursuit of one's desired ends. Kant believed that a being with rational agency is capable of making decisions about values (i.e., what is good) and finding ways to realize and promote those values. Rational agency is the central feature distinguishing human beings from animals and inanimate objects. Because human beings are unique in this sense, they have, unlike animals and objects, *dignity*—inner or intrinsic worth rather than relative worth (Kant, 1998 [1785]). Likewise, many contemporary feminists describe objectification as the process of lowering or degrading a human being to the level of an object by not acknowledging his or her inherent dignity. Kant believed that the essence of morality in human beings was the ongoing, respectful acknowledgement of the humanity of others. He thus argued that in order to be moral, human beings must " . . . act in such a way that you treat humanity, whether in your own person or in the person of any other, never *merely* as a means to an end, but always at the same time as an end" (Kant, 1993 [1785]).[1] It is meaningful to note the word *merely*, in Kant's formulation, for it acknowledges the innumerable unproblematic ways in which people sometimes treat each other as means. As Martin Buber scholar and translator Walter Kaufmann observes (Buber, 1970),

> I ask for your help, I ask for information, I may buy from you or buy what you have made, and you sometimes dispel my loneliness. Nor do I count the ways in which [y]ou treat me as a means. You ask my help, you ask me questions, you may buy what I have written, and at times I ease your loneliness. Even when you treat me only as a means because you want some information, I may feel delighted that I have the answer and can help. . . . But man's attitudes are manifold. . . . (pp. 16–17)

Kaufmann's examples are quite commonplace in human experience. They suggest that human beings cannot help but treat one another as means toward desired ends on a routine basis, but this need not be necessarily problematic; it's when others are treated *merely* as means toward a desired end at their own expense or against their will that possible ethical problems arise.

Understandably, feminist philosophers have been drawn to Kant's early theorizing on this topic and have made attempts to further round out the meaning of objectification. Andrea Dworkin (2000 [1985]) was one of the first to offer a feminist definition of the term in her attempts to underscore the problem of male domination of females as typified by the pornography industry:

> Objectification occurs when a human being, through social means, is made less than human, turned into a thing or commodity, bought and sold. When

---

1. Emphasis added.

objectification occurs, a person is depersonalized, so that no individuality or integrity is available socially or in what is an extremely circumscribed privacy. Objectification is an injury right at the heart of discrimination: those who can be used as if they are not fully human are no longer fully human in social terms; their humanity is hurt by being diminished. (pp. 30–31)

Dworkin's 1985 analysis appears to portray objectification as representing (1) a dynamic social process playing out in the realm of human relationships; (2) treatment of individuals as fungible commodities, identical with others of the same kind and thus replaceable; and (3) commodification, which deprives individuals of their individuality and their inherent worth, thus effectively rendering them less than fully human in the eyes of the objectifier.

Taken together, Dworkin's assumptions seem to possess a certain amount of face validity in that they capture much of what occurs when human beings intentionally do harm to one another, but when analyzed individually, these arguments reveal some limitations. First, it seems entirely reasonable to assert that objectification is experienced within the context of human relationships. However, must this always be so? Is it possible to objectify oneself in isolation? I and others believe the answer is yes (more will be said of this later). Dworkin emphasizes the problem of viewing others as basically replaceable—not in terms of multiple persons' capacities to fulfill certain roles, jobs, and so forth, but in terms of the inherent value of an individual's life—which is indeed problematic. Such a perspective repudiates the ideas of human uniqueness and the equal inherent worth of all humans. But viewing another person as fungible is only one of many ways (and perhaps not the most egregious) that human beings treat each other as objects. Dworkin also emphasizes objectification as "depersonalization," which she equates to the loss of individuality and integrity. This makes intuitive sense. Integrity suggests the importance of the whole—body and psyche—in order to constitute a complete human being. Refusal to acknowledge the validity or existence of a person's "internality" effectively diminishes his or her integrity as a whole person in the eyes of the objectifier. Individuality—one's inherent uniqueness and agency to act in terms of one's specific preferences—also seems to be an important component of personhood, especially in the Western world. However, must the loss or diminishment of individuality make one less of a person? If so, what are we to make of Eastern contemplative traditions, thousands of years old, with hundreds of millions of adherents, which assert that diminishment of self paradoxically increases one's freedom, autonomy, and authenticity? While largely foreign to the Western mind, it's hard to dismiss the results of "self-negation" when such an approach can lead to a life such as Mohandas K. Gandhi's, Mother Teresa's, Nelson Mandela's, or the Dalai Lama's. Dworkin connects objectification with discrimination. This seems to be a valid assertion if discrimination is understood as the denial of rights and freedoms to a person based on the presence or absence of one or more unalterable physical characteristics, such as skin color. But as Dworkin would certainly agree, discrimination is only one form that objectification can take. Finally, Dworkin equates objectification with dehumanization,[2] much as Linda LeMoncheck (1985) does in her book *Dehumanizing Women: Treating Persons as Sex Objects*, written the same year that Dworkin's article was published. As I will argue later, dehumanization is a type of objectification—the most extreme variety— but not all incidences of objectification are tantamount to dehumanization.

Sandra Bartky (1990), a contemporary of Dworkin's, was another feminist thinker in the Kantian vein who asserts that women in patriarchal societies exist in a sort of *fragmented* state: that is, they are " . . . too closely identified with [their bodies] . . . [Indeed, their] entire being is identified with the body," whereas their minds and personalities are devalued or underemphasized (p. 130). This fragmentation sets the stage for objectification, as the body is thought to represent the whole woman. Bartky also presages later feminist thought by explaining that the objectification process need not require two people (i.e., one who objectifies, and one who is objectified). Rather, women living in patriarchal societies, constantly monitored and watched by men who want them to look sensually pleasing as often as possible, come to be *both* objectifier and objectified. As Bartky (1990) puts it, "Woman lives her body as seen by another, by an anonymous patriarchal Other . . . [She takes] toward her own person the attitude of the man. She will then take erotic satisfaction in her physical self, reveling in her body as a beautiful object to be gazed at and decorated" while largely neglecting her own mind as a source of identity (pp. 70, 131–132). This limited self-image encourages various "disciplinary practices" such as dieting, excessive exercise, plastic surgery, as well as the enactment of specific gestures, postures, and movements, all constituting what Bartky (1990) called "the tyranny of slenderness" (p. 67). Who is responsible for this situation? According to Bartky, "the disciplinary power [inscribing] femininity in the female body is everywhere and it is nowhere; the disciplinarian is everyone and yet no one in particular" (Bartky 1990, p. 74). In other words, the message that women should look more feminine is ubiquitous; men are not the only ones to blame. Peers, romantic partners, parents of both genders, teachers, and the media all collude to encourage the perception that women's constant preoccupation with appearance is something natural and voluntary. Thus, according to Bartky, it is very difficult for women to free themselves from their self-objectification.

---

2. Dehumanization will be discussed in considerable detail in a later section. In brief, dehumanization represents a perpetrator's "psychological gymnastic" of removing all human characteristics from his awareness of the victim in order to facilitate the process of killing the victim without remorse.

Since the 1990s, there have been other meaningful developments in our thinking about objectification, primarily having to do with the substantial negative impact of men's tendencies to objectify women. For example, taking a nod from Bartky, Fredricksen and Roberts (1997) developed "objectification theory" asserting that being female in a culture that sexually objectifies the female body leads girls and women to internalize the observer's perspective as the dominant view of their physical selves. This perspective, referred to as "self objectification," often leads to heightened body awareness and compulsive body monitoring which, in turn, increases feelings of shame, inadequacy, and anxiety; at the same time, such neurotic preoccupation reduces one's overall awareness of and sensitivity to positive emotions, including the experience of "flow" (Csikszentmihalyi, 2008).[3] The repetition of such experiences may help explain the wide variety of mental health risks that disproportionately impact women: anxiety, depression, sexual dysfunction, and eating disorders (Fredricksen & Roberts, 1997). Objectification theory also offers an explanation for why changes in the female body over time also seem to lead to corresponding increases in the likelihood of women experiencing psychiatric disorders. Numerous research studies have validated some of the basic claims of objectification theory (Fredrickson, Roberts, Noll, Quinn, & Twenge, 1998; Tiggemann & Kuring, 2004; Tiggemann & Williams, 2012; Calogero, 2004; Moradi & Huang, 2008; Roberts & Gettman, 2004).

Many others have since voiced similar concerns. In *Sex and Social Justice*, Nussbaum (2000) extends a consideration of objectification to the international level, arguing that self-objectification contributes to the other urgent needs of women who live in hunger and illiteracy, or under unequal legal systems. Calogero, Tantleff-Dunn, and Thompson (2011) echo these sentiments, arguing that self-objectification causes psychological problems for women throughout their life spans. In *The Sexualization of Girls and Girlhood*, Zubringen and Roberts (2012) argue that the problems of self-objectification in women are evolving to the point that escalating numbers of younger females under the influence of Internet-driven media and marketing campaigns—are fashioning themselves after sexualized role models around them. In *Beauty and Misogyny*, Jeffreys (2005) argued that despite contemporary societal advances in equality and respect between the sexes, recent years have seen a dramatic escalation in the lengths to which some women go—including electing to undergo heretofore exotic plastic surgeries, such as labiaplasty—to meet idealized cultural standards of beauty.

One of the most substantive contributions to our current understanding of objectification comes from Martha Nussbaum's (1995) classic paper

3. Flow is the mental state in which a person performing an activity is fully immersed in a feeling of energized focus, full involvement, and enjoyment in the process of the activity. In essence, flow is characterized by complete absorption in what one does. See http://en.wikipedia.org/wiki/Flow_%28psychology%29.

"Objectification," which helps to answer some lingering questions relevant to both sexes. For example, if objectification is a matter of treating a person as an object, how exactly do human beings treat objects, and which of these ways become problematic when applied to human beings? Nussbaum goes on to point out that the scientific and philosophical community had not adequately understood objectification, that it was in fact a "slippery . . . multiple concept" (Nussbaum, 1995, p. 251). In order to illustrate her point, she delineates seven different dimensions of objectification (Nussbaum, 1995, p. 257):

1. Instrumentality: Treating the other person as a [mere] tool of your own purposes.
2. Denial of autonomy: Treating the other person as lacking in autonomy and self-determination.
3. Inertness: Treating the other person as if he or she lacked agency or the capacity to act.
4. Fungibility: Treating the other person as if he or she were fundamentally interchangeable or replaceable with other persons.
5. Violability: Treating the other person as lacking in boundary-integrity, as something permissible to penetrate or smash.
6. Ownership: Treating the other person as something that is owned by another, or as something that can be bought or sold.
7. Denial of subjectivity: Treating the other person as someone whose experience and feelings (if any) need not be taken into account.

Fourteen years later, Rae Langton (2009) expanded upon Nussbaum's theorizing, adding three additional features to her list:

8. Reduction to the body: Treating the other person as identified with their body, or body parts.
9. Reduction to appearance: Treating the other person primarily in terms of how they look, or how they appear to the senses.
10. Silencing: Treating the other person as if they are silent, lacking the capacity to speak. (pp. 228–229)

Each of these is a feature of our treatment of objects, though not all objects are treated in all of these ways. For example, a Gustav Klimt painting is something that is owned, but despite being an object, most people would consider it to be inviolable and wouldn't consider destroying or defacing it due to its monetary value, among other reasons. Most objects are treated as inert or lacking autonomy, though at times we regard them as having a life of their own, such as uncooperative computers, vehicles with sticking gas pedals, and so forth. Nussbaum clarified that treating objects as "things" was not objectification, since objectification entails making into an object, treating as an object, that which is not really an object. Objectification is treating a human being in one or more of these ways (Nussbaum, 1995, p. 257).

Nussbaum goes on to assert that not all incidences of objectification in human relations are undesirable. Indeed, some healthy relationships have aspects of objectification built into them. For example, the relationship between parents and children almost always involves some degree of denial of autonomy and some aspects of ownership. On the other hand, it is generally considered unhealthy for parents to treat their children as lacking in body integrity, as tools for their own purposes, as beings whose feelings need not be taken into account, or as fungible (i.e., replaceable) (Nussbaum, 1995, p. 262). In the romantic realm, Nussbaum makes the point that some level of temporary objectification between romantic partners is common and even desirable at times, so long as the objectification is symmetrical, mutual, and undertaken in a context of mutual respect and equality. For example, one might casually lay around with one's lover on a bed and use his or her stomach as a pillow, with the beloved's consent, and in the context of a relationship in which the beloved is generally treated as being more than a pillow (Nussbaum, 1995, p. 265).

Nussbaum (1995) concludes by asserting that the instrumental treatment of others as a mere tool for one's own purposes (item 1) is almost always morally questionable because it is so closely linked with other types of objectification, specifically denial of autonomy (item 2), boundary violation (item 5), and denial of subjectivity (item 7). The other items on the list may or may not be morally problematic, depending upon the situation. Nussbaum declines to stipulate as to whether each item on her list is sufficient to constitute objectification in itself, or whether a cluster of features needs to be present to comprise the objectification of persons. She summarizes by saying that in her opinion, objectification is a "loose cluster term" for which any one of her items might be sufficient to meet the designation; however, much of the time, multiple features are in play when the term is applied (Nussbaum, 1995, p. 258).

There is considerable wisdom in Nussbaum's analysis. In order to adequately capture the multifaceted, often nuanced nature of evil, it makes sense that we have a term broad and loose enough that it has the flexibility needed to capture the many ways in which human beings view one another as non-subjects, and the harm that can attend such perceptions.

CHAPTER 3

Objectification Revisited

A Spectrum of Misapprehension

Our injuring of others . . . results from our failure to know them; and conversely, our injuring of persons, even persons within arm's reach, itself demonstrates their unknowability. For if they stood visible to us, the infliction of that injury would be impossible.

Elaine Scarry *(1998, p. 44)*

If the [9-11] hijackers had been able to imagine themselves into the thoughts and feelings of the passengers, they would have been unable to proceed. It is hard to be cruel once you permit yourself to enter the mind of your victim. Imagining what it is like to be someone other than yourself is at the core of our humanity. It is the essence of compassion, and it is the beginning of morality.

Ian McEwan *(Sept. 15, 2011)*

Demarcation points along the objectification spectrum mentioned previously—casual indifference, derivatization, and dehumanization—while certainly different in terms of intensity and the potential for contributing to destructive acts of violence, are in fact all related phenomena which stem from the same underlying process: *the misapprehension of what human beings are in their totality*. Objectification represents a perceptual error in which the truth of others is either obscured or not honored. Instead of seeing others as Subjects composed of a unified psyche and soma—worthy of respect, dignity, and reverence—we see them more as physical objects divorced to varying degrees from their interior, spiritual dimension. The results of this process run the gamut from trivial to life-altering.

It is my contention that the best term we have at our disposal for capturing the breadth and depth of evil, while also explaining the central mechanism by which it occurs, is *objectification*. Its "loose, slippery, multiple" nature

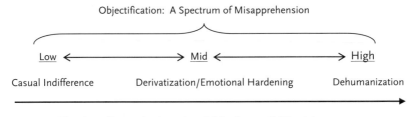

Figure 3.1: Objectification: A Spectrum of Misapprehension

(Nussbaum, 1995) makes it an appropriate umbrella term under which a number of related psychological and behavioral phenomena reside. When thought of in this way, objectification represents a bidirectional continuum of misapprehension in which other human beings are seen as being less than they in fact are. This continuum is bidirectional because individuals (indeed, whole societies) can move up or down the continuum depending upon the degree of misapprehension present in their perspective on the world: The greater their perceptual error, the greater their potential to do violence to others. One could easily argue, for example, that as a collective, Americans in the 1950s (particularly those in the South) had a much more objectified view of individuals of African descent than they now possess; or that Germans had a much more objectified view of Jews during the 1930s and 1940s than they now possess. Figure 3.1 displays the basic elements of this continuum as I propose it.

The tendency to misapprehend the subjectivity of others is itself a symptom of a more fundamental problem of which insightful human beings have long been aware—specifically, the problem of perceiving the self as separate and distinct from the rest of existence. For millennia, Eastern contemplatives have considered this to be a substantial perceptual mistake. His Holiness, the Dalai Lama (2009), summarizes the Eastern perspective when he says,

> What produces suffering? . . . Contaminated actions. What produces contaminated actions? The destructive emotions of lust and hatred. What is their root? Ignorance. *And what is the deepest ignorance? It is mistakenly seeing "I" as inherently existent. When [you] mistakenly consider yourself as existing as a fully independent entity, this engenders an artificial distinction between self and other.* This bifurcation encourages becoming attached to what is on your own side and resistance to what is on the side of others, which opens the door to pride, to inflating your own actual or imagined qualities such as wealth, education, physical appearance, ethnic origin, and fame. (pp. 154, 234, and 157, emphasis added)

In the West, this problem has been approached from a somewhat different angle, and is referred to generically as "the problem of the ego" (much more will be said about the ego in Chapters 9 and 10). The egoic illusion of the separate self fosters a condition of perceived enmity toward the world. It also encourages human beings to perceive a substantial boundary between themselves and everything else. Thus, another way to understand the objectification spectrum is that it makes reference to the degree of "I am not that" which a person experiences, on a spiritual level, not only toward his or her fellow human beings, but toward the rest of existence. The less one perceives a sense of unity, or self in the other, the further along the objectification continuum one is likely to progress, and the greater the possibility of either assenting to the violent treatment of others or engaging in violence personally. Put in more everyday terms, the human capacity to be empathic and compassionate—to "feel with" others as if they were deeply connected to one's own self, as if they were the child of one's own womb[1]—has a number of factors working against it, many of which will be discussed in depth later.

It is also important to point out that the misapprehension of others at the heart of objectification represents, in varying proportions, perceptual immaturity and/or moral failure. For example, self-centeredness is at its peak in childhood. While most young children do have a limited sense of others' inner lives, and thus, some capacity for empathy, these callow sensitivities require years of ongoing mentoring, modeling, and encouragement to refine. Because of this, we don't typically think of young children or adolescents as objectifiers or narcissists, though many may indeed act this way. In these cases, objectifying others—failing to appreciate their inner dimension—reflects emotional immaturity that is developmentally appropriate. However, if a high level of self-centeredness and lack of empathy persists into adulthood, then the problem becomes one of disordered character with moral implications, the most common manifestation of which is narcissistic personality disorder (to be discussed in Chapter 8). Indeed, one of our primary tasks as human beings is to develop the capacity to transcend (albeit temporarily, in most cases) our own self-interest in the service of forwarding the interests of the groups to which we belong, and to more fully appreciate the validity of others' inner experiences. The paradox is that in doing so, we become more fully alive, and more fully human. In essence, we "find ourselves by losing ourselves" (Matt.

1. Thinking of compassion for others in terms of how a mother feels for the child of her womb has ancient roots. Bible scholar Marcus J. Borg points out that the Hebrew word for compassion, which in the singular is identical with the word for "womb," is often used to describe God in the Old Testament. It is translated as "merciful" in the characterization of God as "gracious and merciful," or, as in the King James Version, "the tender mercies of God." It is found in a passage in Jeremiah, which has been translated as follows: "Thus says Yahweh: Is Ephraim [Israel] my dear son, my darling child? For the more I speak of him, the more I remember him; therefore my womb trembles for him. I will truly show motherly compassion upon him." See M. J. Borg, *Meeting Jesus Again for the First Time: The Historical Jesus and the Heart of Contemporary Faith* (San Francisco: Harper Collins, 1994), 48.

16:25), which is in our own ultimate best interests to do. To be an otherwise functional adult but not to have developed this capacity to a reasonable degree represents a moral failure.

Humans objectify others by experiencing them as *it* rather than as *Thou*. This perceptual mistake paves the way for the commission of evil. Conversely, I am in general agreement with Elaine Scarry's (1998) sentiments (quoted at the beginning of this section) when she says that realizing the other's validity as Subject, which is the opposite of objectifying, negates the possibility of committing evil against that person. While this may not completely eradicate the possibility of doing evil to another person, it mitigates the possibility, especially under normal circumstances.[2] It will be helpful to further expand upon each of the components of the objectification spectrum in order to more clearly articulate how each is a type of objectification different in severity from the others.

THE LOW END: CASUAL INDIFFERENCE

One single Anne Frank moves us more than the countless others who suffered just as she did but whose faces have remained in the shadows. Perhaps it is better that way; if we were capable of taking in all the suffering of all those people, we would not be able to live.
Primo Levi *(quoted in Westra et al., 2004)*

In mild forms, objectification is typified by *casual indifference*, which is to perceive little affective connection between oneself and most others (e.g., those outside one's immediate circle of family, friends, colleagues at work, etc.). This is the level of objectification experienced by most people most of the time. It includes the experience of having little or no discernible emotional discomfort at the realization of some distant other's suffering. For example, we hear of an acquaintance who has recently been diagnosed with inoperable cancer and we feel a momentary twinge of concern or perhaps a sense of compassion for the person and his or her family, but it quickly fades as we get back to our busy day, distracted and unaffected, as if that person's anguish, pain, and suffering did not exist.[3] Casual indifference also refers to

2. Elaine Scarry goes further than I am prepared to go when she says that realizing the other's validity as Subject makes the commission of evil against that person impossible. As already mentioned, there are scenarios in which individuals harm others not because they objectify them, but for other reasons. One example includes being pressured by an authority or other situational influence to do so.

3. Ironically, as I was writing this paragraph, I received an e-mail from a colleague who was informing others that a previous colleague—a woman in her late sixties whose position I took upon her retirement—was recently diagnosed with leukemia, was at home by herself with hospice (she never married or had children), and was likely "not

the human tendency to block out, deny, or suppress the reality of the monumental suffering occurring at any given moment on the planet. It could, of course, be argued that this tendency is in many ways adaptive, that it helps us function better in life not to be affected by or preoccupied with the preponderance of suffering occurring at any given moment in the world. True as this may be, our capacity to bracket out the magnitude of the world's suffering while we go on with the mundanities of our daily lives speaks to the tenacity and power that our perceived boundaries of self have to distance us emotionally from the plight of others.

The word *casual* is meant to imply that at the low end of the spectrum, there is no intent to be cruel or to do actual harm to others. Rather, casual indifference's primary manifestation is *non-action*—"sins of omission." For example, readers of this book (I include myself here) are likely to come from what one leading ethicist has designated as the ranks of the "absolutely affluent" (Singer, 1994, p. 221). Such individuals are not necessarily affluent in comparison with all the people they know or those who live in their particular locale, but they are affluent by any reasonable definition of human needs. This means that they have more income than they need to provide all the basic necessities of life for themselves and their families. After purchasing food, shelter, clothing, basic health services, and education, the absolutely affluent are still able to spend money on luxuries. They choose their food more for how it tastes than to stop their hunger; they buy new clothes in order to look good and be more fashionable, not to keep warm; they relocate in order to be in a better neighborhood or to have more living space, not to get out of the weather. At the end of all this, there is still money for discretionary spending. Contrast this with the description of the "absolutely poor" given by Robert McNamara, who served as president of the World Bank from 1968 to 1981.[4] These are those who are poor by any standard. Absolute poverty is "life at the very margin of existence." The absolutely poor are "severely deprived human beings struggling to survive in a set of squalid and degraded circumstances almost beyond the power of our sophisticated imaginations and privileged circumstances to conceive." Absolute poverty is "a condition of life so characterized by malnutrition, illiteracy, disease, squalid surroundings, high infant mortality and low life expectancy as to be beneath any reasonable definition of human decency" (Singer, 1994, pp. 218–219).

going to make it through the weekend." I felt a momentary sense of sadness for her, but quickly lost myself in the project at hand and had only fleeting thoughts of her predicament during the next day or two. She died a week later.

4. Perhaps ironically, in previous years, McNamara was also Secretary of Defense under John F. Kennedy and Lyndon B. Johnson and was in many ways responsible for escalating the war in Vietnam. Late in his life, McNamara openly acknowledged the deeply problematic nature of the war in Vietnam as well as his regret for the role he played in its perpetuation (Morris, 2003).

While there have been recent improvements in the emerging economies of the so-called BRIC countries (Brazil, Russia, India, and China) in terms of living standards, the overall situation for these and many other countries' citizens is still dire. Current estimates by the World Bank are that 1.5 billion people (nearly 15 percent of all human beings on earth) live in conditions of absolute poverty, in which they are able to earn less than $1.25 per day (United Nations General Assembly, October 17, 2011). While the extent and nature of world's level of poverty is beyond most Westerner's ability to conceive, most have a knowledge that there are at least millions of people at any given moment who are suffering greatly because they are in dire need of basic commodities such as food, water, shelter, or medical care due to economic downturn, catastrophic natural disaster, or political unrest. These are individuals who could perhaps have their lives drastically improved, if not saved, with relatively few dollars of aid, and yet we so often do not give.[5] For many of us much of the time, the absolutely poor and the ongoing ordeals their lives represent are not "real" or personal enough to elicit a specific response to help. Although the consequences are severe, this is an example of mild objectification—*casual indifference*—stemming from the misapprehension of the reality and validity of other human lives.

It would seem that the vast majority of human beings do not have the emotional and perceptual wherewithal to value all members of the species equally. Indeed, for most of us, if we are capable of experiencing deep and abiding empathy for others, it is reserved for those few who are nearest in terms of physical proximity, relational intimacy, or biological relation. There are good (i.e., adaptive) reasons for this, as human beings have finite physical, mental, and emotional capacities to care deeply, and thus we're best served—in terms of our survival—by saving our precious emotional resources for those closest to us. However, there is no question that most human beings, especially those of us in wealthier, developed nations, have the capacity to do more good for others than we do, despite the fact that we "know" this.

---

5. There are likely many reasons for this, including cynicism about our money actually getting to those in need, not knowing how else to help, and so forth. While the actual dollar amounts may seem substantial (e.g., the US gives 28.67 billion annually), the scope of the problem is huge, and the amount of charitable aid given per person is in fact quite small ($93.00 per person/per year in the US). Interestingly, the top five countries in terms of charitable donations as a percentage of GDP are small Germanic/Scandinavian countries, which are also the most atheistic on earth: (1) Sweden: 1.12 percent; (2) Norway: 1.06 percent; (3) Luxembourg: 1.01 percent; (4) Denmark: .88 percent; and (5) Netherlands: .82 percent. Perhaps ironically, the bottom five countries tend to have more religious populaces: (19) United States: .20 percent (20) Greece: .19 percent (21) Japan: .18 percent (22) Italy: .16 percent and (23) South Korea: .10 percent. See http://en.wikipedia.org/wiki/List_of_most_charitable_countries.

THE WIDE-RANGING MIDDLE: DERIVATIZATION

Much of the objectification continuum is typified by *derivatization*, a word coined by feminist scholar Ann J. Cahill (2011). In her attempts to solve some of the long-standing problems with objectification's historical Kantian bias about what it means to be a person (i.e., too much reliance on the domain of "the head"—cognition and intellect—and not enough on the sensate realm of the body), Cahill relied on a perspective informed by the theory of "embodied intersubjectivity," which positions both the psyche and the body as central to personhood (2001). This is indeed an important point. For Cahill (2011), a correct perspective on personhood acknowledges that all human experiences occur within the context of embodiment. The desire to invalidate this fact has played a substantial role in "many systems of inequality" throughout history. To appreciate that human subjectivity occurs within the context of the body is to acknowledge that "agency does not consist in overcoming the body, but rather, is constituted by the body and bodily experiences" (pp. 22–23).

Toward this end, Cahill proposed a new concept—*derivatization*—as a way to break free from Kantian understandings of objectification. Regarding derivatization, Cahill explains: "If 'objectify' means 'to turn into an object,' then 'derivatize' means 'to turn into a derivative.'" She continues (2011):

> To derivatize is to portray, render, understand, or approach a being solely or primarily as the reflection, projection, or expression of another being's identity, desires, fears, etc. The derivatized subject becomes reducible in all relevant ways to the derivatizing subject's existence—other elements of her being or subjectivity are disregarded, ignored, or under-valued. Should the derivatized subject dare to demonstrate aspects of her subjectivity that fall outside the derivatizer's being . . . she will be perceived as arrogant, treasonous, and dangerously rebellious. (p. 32)

Cahill (2011) asserts that derivatization can function in a variety of contexts and situations. She provides some examples:

> Many forms of work, most notably the kind found in the service industries, involve various manifestations of derivatization. The hostess at the fine restaurant must smile and make pleasant small talk while escorting the diners to their table. . . . This is not a matter of sheer usefulness . . . but rather, an indulging of the diner's desires. . . . When sports fans demand of their heroes not only excellent athletic performance, but also the fulfillment of certain moral standards in their personal life, they are requiring those heroes to embody and represent the fan's desired ideals (regardless of whether the fans themselves live up to those same ideals). . . . The sexually derivatized subject is not quite a non-person. She may express desires, emotions, and preferences; she may articulate consent or

lack thereof; she may even play a role of alleged dominance in relation to the derivatizer. . . . The ethical problem with such behaviors [is that] feminine subjectivity and sexuality are constructed as wholly derivative of masculine subjectivity and sexuality. The desires, actions, and choices of derivatized women are [. . .] to mirror [. . .] the desires of men. (pp. 33–34)

Cahill's critique of the traditional understanding of objectification was warranted—the body does matter and should be a necessary component in our understanding of what it means to be a person in the full sense of the word. Her contribution of a new term, *derivatization*, adds meaningful complexity and nuance to our understanding of the problem of evil. It is my perspective that as defined above, derivatization is best understood as a subset of objectification and represents its own sub-spectrum of perception and behavior, which can be applied much more broadly than Cahill suggests.[6]

When we speak of derivatization in the way that Cahill describes, we cover a substantial amount of territory. We are talking about a wide range of behavior that can be engaged in nonviolently or violently, to mild, moderate, or severe degrees. At the mild end, one memorable example of derivatization mentioned by Cahill (2011) includes a Miller Lite television ad campaign from 2003 in which two beautiful women begin the typical "tastes great/less filling" argument that is the hallmark of the brand. The disagreement quickly devolves into a physical altercation where the two women, dressed in provocative, light summer attire, grapple with one another and careen into a water fountain where they "fight," tearing off most of each other's clothes. From there, they proceed to stumble into a conveniently located mud pit where they squeal and grunt while exchanging slaps and high kicks. The scene then shifts to two wistful-looking men sitting at a bar, one of whom says to the other, "Now *that* would make a great commercial!" to which his friend replies, "Who wouldn't want to watch that?" The preceding scenes, it turns out, are the fantastical imaginings of the men (imaginings to which two women with disapproving looks on their faces, sitting with them at the bar, are somehow privy). In one earlier, edited out version of the ad, one of the men suggests another ending: " . . . the women pause in their mud-fight, and one of them suggests gleefully, 'let's make out' " (Cahill, 2011, pp. 42–43). The point here is that the women in the ad are portrayed in a highly unrealistic, unethical manner—perpetuating damaging stereotypes, depicting women as being "turned on" by violence—where they are merely derivative of men's (and the beer company's) desires and purposes. The women are depicted and understood only as "women-through-men" can be, and thus are *derivatized* (Cahill, 2011, pp. 44–45).

6. Cahill's use of derivatization is limited primarily to women being mistreated by men in a variety of ways (indeed, she argues that women are far more likely than men to be derivativized).

However, derivatization also has the capacity to capture much more blatant acts of exploitation and violent abuse of the weak by the powerful. For example, the middle of derivatization's spectrum might include the recently popularized pornography genre known as "gonzo," in which many men, sometimes up to 50 or 60 (two or three at a time), engage the same woman sexually (Hedges, 2009). In cases such as this, it is evident how the woman involved has "... become reducible in all relevant ways to the derivatizing person's existence—other elements of her being or subjectivity are disregarded, ignored, or under-valued" (Cahill, 2011, p. 32). From this perspective, Sandra Bartky's late twentieth-century comments regarding "sexual objectification" can be understood as a pre-Cahill description of derivatization, and help underscore the phenomenon's spectrum-like nature:

> A person is sexually objectified [i.e., derivatized] when her sexual parts or sexual functions are separated out from the rest of her personality and reduced to the status of mere instruments or else regarded as if they were capable of representing her. In this definition, then, the prostitute would be a victim of sexual objectification [i.e., derivatization], as would the *Playboy* bunny, the female breeder, and [even] the bathing beauty. (Bartky, 1990, p. 26)

Reducing subjects "down" until they are a mere external shell of themselves, until they represent no more than the embodiment of a derivatizer's desires, wishes, and fears, can go much further than depicting or using women in unrealistic, unethical ways. In its most extreme manifestations, derivatization can include acts of torture or genocidal violence engaged in by perpetrators who somehow maintain a modicum of the victim's humanity in their awareness. One example of such a circumstance would include incidences of abuse and torture engaged in by United States military police personnel stationed at the Baghdad Correctional Facility (i.e., Abu Ghraib military prison) in Iraq. From 2002 to 2004, American military police—men *and* women—engaged in physical, psychological, and sexual abuse of Iraqi detainees. These actions included torture, rape, and eventually homicide. Thousands of "trophy photos" taken by the individuals involved in the abuse documented much of the activity, and leaked photos eventually broke the scandal to the public. One report of many, issued January 12, 2005, detailed testimony suggesting that the following events had taken place at Abu Ghraib: forced nudity, forced masturbation, forced sex acts, and other degrading behaviors between detainees (such as the formation of "nude human pyramids"), and the repeated threat of harm by dogs. Prison personnel also urinated on detainees; inflicted further intentional damage to detainees' previous injuries by jumping on limbs or striking wounded limbs with batons; poured phosphoric acid on detainees; sodomized detainees with batons; and tied ropes to the detainees' necks, legs, or genitals and dragged them across the floor (Zernike, 2005). One detainee described one of many incidences he experienced this way (Higham & Stevens, 2004):

> [The guards asked me] "Do you pray to Allah?" I said yes. They said, "Fuck you. And fuck him." One of them said, "You are not getting out of here health[y], you are getting out of here handicapped." (p. 3)

The guards then asked about the detainee's marital status; when he told them he was married, the guards used this fact to shame him, and then they made lewd comments about his wife. The guards then goaded the prisoner into "praising Jesus"; when he refused to do so because of his belief in Allah, they said they " . . . believed in torture and would torture him" (Higham & Stevens, 2004, p. 3).

From detailed analyses of the circumstances present in the Abu Ghraib prison, it is clear that many factors played a role in the degradation, humiliation, and torture of the prisoners. First, it should be acknowledged that Abu Ghraib was not a death camp but a prison where guards' duties included assuring that inmates' basic needs were met. However, there was a high level of stress intrinsic to working at Abu Ghraib. Long shifts, repeated, randomly occurring mortar attacks, and crumbling prison infrastructure (including poor sanitation, intermittent failures of electricity and running water, and an absence of adequate heating or cooling)—combined with a failure of top-down administrative oversight and structure at the prison to constrain the possibility of abuse—fostered an environment where such abuses became more likely to occur. There was a procedural agenda that dictated the "softening up" of prisoners for interrogation, which led to the de-individuation of prisoners, encouraging prison personnel to engage in creatively sadistic and cruel acts (Zimbardo, 2008). It is difficult to ascertain the extent to which members of the staff were emotionally connected to the humanity of Iraqis before they took their posts at Abu Ghraib. Involvement in the military, especially for those participating in operations on the ground such as the Army, Marines, and Navy SEALS, includes a high degree of ongoing, institutionally sanctioned, dehumanizing portrayals of the enemy in order to encourage soldiers to "do their job" of violently confronting and killing the enemy. It is therefore reasonable to assume that the soldiers imported hardened (though likely not genocidal) perceptions of Iraqis into their work at the prison; the stressful, dilapidated conditions at the prison would only have worked to enhance these tendencies in prison personnel. Soldiers are trained, evaluated, and even promoted based on their capacity to behave ruthlessly toward an "enemy" in various contexts. It should not come as a surprise when these soldiers fail to exhibit decency and restraint when allowed unstructured interaction with this same enemy. Whatever the case, the abuse documented at Abu Ghraib suggests that prisoners became mere extensions of some of the prison personnel's feelings of fear, boredom, impotence, anger, and resentment and were treated accordingly.

Some may question whether or not a human being is capable of torturing or brutally killing another person without having fully dehumanized him or her first. The answer sometimes appears to be yes. As an example, consider a personal report made by Auschwitz commandant Rudolph Höss, who acknowledged that part of his role as camp Kommandant was to ignore or "stamp out all human emotion" while carrying out his duties. He was largely successful at this. He had been exposed to years of propaganda meant to make Jews appear not only less than human, but nonhuman. He had, through his repeated exposure to extreme violence, largely desensitized or emotionally hardened himself to pleas for mercy, screams of pain, and scenes of brutality and suffering, although there were certain prisoners who stood out in his mind, even years later. One of these was a young woman who

> . . . did not have the appearance of being Jewish. . . . In the doorway [to the gas chamber] she stopped and she said, "I knew from the beginning that we were destined to be gassed at Auschwitz. I got through the selection of those who were chosen to work by taking children in my hands. I wanted to experience the process fully and accurately. I hope it will be quick. Farewell!" (Paulsky, 1996, p. 162, as quoted in Lang, 2010, p. 231)

Höss appears to have been genuinely moved and impressed by the example of courage this young woman displayed; he did not see her as a subhuman per se, but at the time, his resolve was to be "like a rock," and she was gassed anyway.

A more current, albeit less egregious, example of this phenomenon could include the US intelligence community's recent practice of waterboarding as an "enhanced interrogation technique" used in attempts to force a detainee to divulge information that he or she is under orders not to disclose. In such scenarios, it is unlikely that government personnel carrying out the procedures have fully dehumanized the detainee in their minds,[7] but it is clear that the detainee's subjectivity has been drastically reduced down to a mere "means to an end"—information—and that his or her basic human rights and desires for dignity have been disregarded, ignored, or deemed irrelevant.

With respect to derivatization, some might assert that a concept with such a broad application loses its power to explain or capture nuances of experience falling under its proposed scope. While the scope of derivatization (itself a sub-spectrum of the larger objectification spectrum) is large, I suggest that such breadth is required in order to acknowledge the vast array of ways in

7. I make the assumption that, unlike those in the military's ground forces, those who did the waterboarding—CIA operatives and private government contractors—were not systematically trained to dehumanize foreign nationals. This, of course, could be wrong.

which human beings can approach, understand, or use others as extensions of their own fears, desires, and wishes, resulting in a reduction in the perceived subjectivity of the other. This basic underlying mechanism is the same, regardless of the severity of the derivatization.

DEHUMANIZATION: OBJECTIFICATION IN THE EXTREME

It was a general rule among Spaniards to be cruel; not just cruel, but extraordinarily cruel so that harsh and bitter treatment would prevent Indians from daring to think of themselves as human beings . . . . So they would cut an Indian's hands and leave them dangling by a shred of skin and they would send them saying, "Go now, spread the news to your chiefs." They would test their swords and their manly strength on captured Indians and place bets on the slicing off of heads or the cutting of bodies in half with one blow. . . .

Las Casas *(quoted in Todorv, 1999, p. 139)*

The above example of extreme violence comes from the early age of Spanish conquest in the Americas. Similar examples could have been pulled from a sea of such incidences from any age in human history, including our own. This type of behavior—brutal, sadistic, calculated, or sometimes whimsical and capricious—can occur for a variety of possible reasons. One of these is that the victim has been reduced to a state of nonhumanity in the eyes of the perpetrator. This phenomenon, called *dehumanization*, has been referred to as "the central construct in our understanding of man's inhumanity to man" (Zimbardo, 2008, p. 307). It has also been understood to be one of the central processes in the transformation of ordinary, normal people into indifferent or even wanton perpetrators of evil (Zimbardo, 2008, p. xii).

As a process, dehumanization involves two central, related components: (1) the denial that an individual or group possesses a "human essence"—that is, to assume that they are not fully human; and (2) the affirmation that the individual or group is *sub*human. In other words, for dehumanization to occur, the dehumanizer must engage in two mental actions: He or she must repudiate a person's humanity *and also* affirm that the person is in fact something less than human. For example, from the "Himmlerian" Nazi perspective, Jews weren't just nonhumans; they were vermin—rats, lice—in human form. Likewise, to the genocidal Hutus in Rwanda, the Tutsis weren't just nonhumans; they were cockroaches (Smith 2011, p. 223).

What capacities of the human mind make it possible for dehumanization to occur? David Livingstone Smith has made a thorough study of the processes of dehumanization in his recent book, *Less Than Human: Why We Demean,*

Enslave, and Exterminate Others. According to Smith, five aspects of human psychology make dehumanization possible (2011, p. 264):

1. The capacity for thinking in "folk-biological" terms, which allows us to intuitively divide up the world into natural kinds which are called "species";
2. The capacity for thinking in "folk-sociological" terms, which allows us to divide up the human world into natural kinds called "races";
3. The capacity for abstract, meta-cognitive, symbolic thought which enables reflection upon the concepts of species and races;
4. The conception that plant, animal, and mineral species have unique "essences" that make them what they are. Essences are distinct from how they may appear (a lump of gold painted silver is still gold), and in the case of organic matter, are transmitted from parents to offspring; and
5. The conception of a hierarchy of natural kinds—some version of the so-called "great chain of being" which ranks what exists in order of consciousness, inner complexity, and so forth.

How is it that dehumanization works? According to Smith, dehumanization is not a biological adaptation; it was not put in place by natural selection and it is not hard-wired into the species. Rather, it's an unconscious strategy for dealing with psychological conflict. More specifically, dehumanization is a response to conflicting motives: It occurs in situations where one group of people wants to harm another group of people, but the first group is constrained by the natural human inhibition against committing murder (Smith, 2011, pp. 264–265). The portrayal of the intended target as both something less than and other than human, when given assent, plays on the sentiments of potential perpetrators. Such images and impressions serve to incite anger, fear, and distrust, gradually shrinking in and rigidifying a person's emotional boundaries of self; that is, his or her perceptions of what counts as "me," and what doesn't, constrict so that certain human beings fall outside the parameter of those who are considered members of the species. The process of dehumanization moves the intended targets both out of the realm of humanity and into the realm of something less than human. It is important to point out that in the mind of the dehumanizer, the transformation of human beings into nonhumans and subhumans is not a result of the dehumanizer having treated other persons violently.[8] Rather, perceiving other people as subhumans can facilitate treating such individuals in brutal, degrading ways. Like objectification, dehumanization represents a psychological process—it

---

8. In other words, dehumanization does not appear to follow a similar psychological path as "cognitive dissonance," in which people attempt to justify behaviors which conflict with their self-image by adopting a new attitude that would make sense of the discrepancy.

occurs in people's minds. It is an attitude, a way of perceiving of other people. Brutal behavior follows dehumanization, not the other way around (Smith, 2011, p. 28).

Fanning the flames of fear by drawing clear distinctions between "us" and "them" has been the role of propaganda over the ages. Incitement (or a call to violence) seems to be a hallmark of genocide; indeed, genocide may not be able to proceed without it. It is important to note that each case of genocide in the modern era has been fueled by a campaign of propaganda orchestrated by a handful of powerful political or social figures. Incitement, however, does not induce people to act against their own beliefs and values; when hate speech motivates people to act violently against another group, it does so because the listener is receptive to such speech (Benesch, 2004).

Never was propaganda used so much as during the twentieth century, given the proliferation of communicative technologies developed during this era. Newspapers, other print media, radio, and television allowed millions to be exposed en masse and on a consistent basis to the portrayal of the intended enemy as less than human in order to down grade public identification with or sympathy for the enemy and to facilitate the use of lethal aggressive action against them. Striking dehumanizing depictions of the opposition have been utilized from time to time in almost all cultures. In 1936, against the backdrop of the rise of the Third Reich in Germany and its tide of propagandistic images of European Jewry, the venerable Aldous Huxley warned against the use of propaganda:

> Most people would hesitate to torture or kill a human being like themselves. But when that human being is spoken of as though he were not a human being, but as the representative of some wicked principle, we lose our scruples. . . . All political and nationalist propaganda aims at only one thing; to persuade one set of people that another set of people are not really human and that it is therefore legitimate to rob, swindle, bully, and even murder them. (Lifton & Humpfrey, 1984, p. 10)

A quick glance at some of the more memorable political posters from the twentieth century provides ample evidence that propaganda from the United States, Great Britain, Germany, the Soviet Union, France, Japan, Korea, China, and elsewhere have regularly depicted "the enemy" as a menacing, less-than-human creature (Keen, 1986). Such messages, combined over time with other types of mass media, work to create the impression that a dehumanized enemy actually depicts reality. Sadly, such simplistic renderings of "the other" are not relics of a bygone, less enlightened era. In 2004, Rush Limbaugh, a syndicated, staunch-conservative radio entertainer with a listenership of well over 10 million Americans daily, made these comments when the shocking revelations of torture and degrading sexual treatment of detainees at the hands of American military police at the Abu Ghraib prison were made public:

> *They* are the ones who are perverted! *They* are ones who are dangerous! *They* are the ones who are subhuman! *They* are the ones who are human debris, *not* the United States of America and *not* our soldiers and *not* our prison guards. (Smith, 2011, p. 22)

Michael Savage, another popular conservative radio talk show host with a listenership of nearly 10 million, responded to the same scandal along similar lines. Rather than calling for reform, he blamed the detainees for their treatment, describing them as "subhuman" and "vermin," even suggesting that "forcible conversion to Christianity was probably the only thing that could turn them into human beings" (Smith, 2011, p. 23). However, examples of dehumanization come from both sides of the political divide. Smith (2011) cites Pulitzer Prize–winning *New York Times* columnist Maureen Dowd's 2003 editorial, which said that Muslim terrorists were "replicating and coming at us like cockroaches," as merely one example. He correctly notes that dehumanization can make for strange bedfellows indeed (p. 23).

If such portrayals are given one's emotional assent, over time one's moral compass—one's sense of right and wrong, decency, respect, and sympathy, what historian Jonathan Glover refers to as "the moral resources" (2001, p. 22)—can become skewed and disoriented. Psychological boundaries of self collapse in on themselves and become rigidified, encouraging the perception that those who fall outside their narrowed parameter are unworthy of consideration or concern. This chilling aspect of dehumanization has been called "moral disengagement" (Bandura, 1986, 1990), where otherwise morally reprehensible behavior is justified.

Most often, dehumanized people are thought of as representing three kinds of creatures: predators, unclean animals, or prey (Smith, 2011, p. 252). Predators have long haunted the human psyche, and for good reason. Beings who fear death above all else, who are capable of self-reflection, and who have the ability to project themselves forward in time can easily envision themselves as prey. They can imagine being deeply gashed, slashed, and then devoured, one chunk of flesh at a time, by a bear, a lion, an alligator, or a shark—or perhaps worse. These thoughts are indeed the stuff that nightmares are made of. David Quammen (2003) observed that " . . . among the earliest forms of self-awareness [in humans] was the awareness of being meat" (p. 3). D. L. Smith points out that "the response to predators is one of terror. The enemy is ferocious, relentless, formidable, and must be killed in self-defense" (Smith, 2011, p. 56). Philosopher Sam Keen's 1986 book *Faces of the Enemy: Reflections of the Hostile Imagination* displays multiple images of relatively contemporary propaganda posters depicting the enemy as a host of different carnivorous beasts, such as giant octopuses, squid, spiders, tigers, bears, and wolves. D. L. Smith chronicles numerous recent headlines from American newspapers that utilize this same tactic, such as, "The viper awaits: Former Arab power is poisonous snake"; "Chained beast—shackled Saddam dragged to court" (2011, p. 24). He notes that whenever words such as *evil, wild,* or *bloodthirsty* are used in political discourse, dehumanization of the other is close at hand (2011, p. 258).

Objectifying others as prey seems another natural way to dehumanize, since human beings have hunted animals as a means of subsistence since before history. The shift toward agrarian modes of food production between 8000 and 7000 B.C.E. led to dramatic changes in how human beings lived, but did not supplant hunting and the eating of meat as a central source of sustenance for human beings. The clear metaphorical connections between warfare and hunting were acknowledged in ancient times and are still utilized today. The taking of "trophy" body parts during war has been a relatively common practice throughout history and continues into the present day. It was believed that the taking of scalps was introduced to the New World by Europeans, but archaeological evidence has shown that Native Americans took scalps and other body parts as trophies long before the arrival of Iberians from Europe (Chacon & Dye, 2007, as quoted in Smith, 2011):

> The removal of heads, scalps, eyes, ears, teeth, cheekbones, mandibles, arms, fingers, legs, feet, and sometimes genitalia for use as trophies by Amerindians was an ancient and widespread practice in the New World. Some groups in Columbia and in the Andes kept the entire skins of their dead enemies. (pp. 259–260).

The final way in which human beings are dehumanized is by seeing them as unclean animals: vermin, such as mice and rats, and disease-carrying organisms, such as cockroaches, lice, flies, or maggots. These tend to elicit an intense combination of disgust and a sense of threat in most people—not a threat of injury like that posed by a snake or a dog, but a fear of contamination with something harmful (Smith, 2011, p. 252). The urge is to eradicate the source of the potential contagion as quickly as possible. Not surprisingly, seeing others as unclean animals is particularly useful in inspiring genocidal ideation. As one example, Heinrich Himmler (second in command under Hitler) issued a speech to the *Schutzstaffel* (the SS) in 1943 at Poznan in which he used this train of thought to inspire officers to follow through with the project of the extermination of Jews in Europe:

> . . . Because at the end of this, we don't want, because we exterminated the bacillus, to become sick and die from the same bacillus. I will never see it happen, that even one bit of putrefaction comes in contact with us, or takes root in us. On the contrary, where it might try to take root, we will burn it out together. But

altogether we can say: We have carried out this most difficult task for the love of our people. And we have taken on no defect within us, in our soul, or in our character. (The Complete Text of the Poznan Speech, 2004)

The theory of dehumanization assumes that typical persons do not have the capability to kill other people *en masse* without first psychologically reducing these people to something less than human in order to transform murder into something much more trivial. The conventional wisdom on genocide has been that the attempt to annihilate an entire collective of people is tied very closely to the doctrine that those being destroyed aren't really human beings. Indeed, it stretches credulity for most people to imagine how a campaign of genocide could be carried out without first dehumanizing the intended victims. Many experts have weighed in on the matter supporting the contention. H. C. Kelman, for example, opined that all sanctioned massacres "presuppose a degree of dehumanization" (1973, p. 49). Daniel Goldhagen said, "[T]he term *dehumanization* is rightly a commonplace of discussions of mass murder. It is used as a master category that describes the attitudes of killers, would-be killers, and larger groups toward intended victims" (2009, p. 319, as quoted in Smith, 2011, pg. 142). Noted social psychologist Albert Bandura said that "it is difficult to mistreat humanized persons without risking self-condemnation" (2003, p. 36). Gregory H. Stanton, founder and president of the human rights organization *Genocide Watch*, agrees that dehumanization is a regular feature of genocides (1998):

One group denies the humanity of the other group. Members of it are equated with animals, vermin, insects, or diseases. Dehumanization overcomes the normal human revulsion against murder. At this stage, hate propaganda . . . is used to vilify the victim group.

Sociologist Daniel Chirot and psychologist Clark McCauley say essentially the same thing:

In most genocidal events the perpetrators devalue the humanity of their victims, often by referring to the victims as animals, diseased, or exceptionally filthy . . . notably pigs, rats, maggots, cockroaches, and other vermin. (2006, p. 80)

Neil J. Kressel (2002) writes that "[n]o mass atrocities in the contemporary world have occurred without some form of dehumanization" (p. 172). There is indeed much historical evidence documenting the use of propagandistic, dehumanizing images and messages for successfully inciting one group of people to act out genocidally against another. The atrocities in Nazi Germany, Bosnia, and Rwanda come to mind as more recent examples. But dehumanization may not tell the whole story here.

DERIVATIZATION REVISITED: OTHER FACTORS CONTRIBUTING TO EXTREME VIOLENCE

Power and Its Psychological Meaning to Perpetrators

In some cases, it seems apparent that perpetrators of extreme violence may not entirely dehumanize their victims into nonhuman or subhuman oblivion before killing them. Therefore, extreme derivatization is a more appropriate explanation of the processes involved. In an important article, genocide researcher Johannes Lang asserts that the assumption of dehumanization in all cases of genocide has short-circuited further analysis which reveals that perpetrators don't always thoroughly dehumanize their victims before torturing and/or killing them, and that the relationship between perpetrator and victim can be more complicated than the theory of dehumanization would suggest. Lang asserts that the psychological meaning of *power* to perpetrators is one important variable explaining extreme forms of violence (2010). He argues that in situations of absolute power, such as a concentration camp, violence soon becomes the coinage of the realm. The more isolated the locale, the more freely a subculture of violence can develop. In the case of the Nazi SS personnel of the concentration camps—especially camps in Poland—these men were far from home and the familiar surroundings of their pre-war lives. This lack of civilian context broke them loose from social mores that might have acted as a restraint. In these isolated locales, SS men felt they were all-powerful. Prisoners might be allowed to remain alive for a time, but guards were free to kill them at will if they chose to do so. Lang sites Wolfgang Sofsky's (1997) acclaimed sociological analysis of concentration camps to underscore the role that power played in the relationship between perpetrator and victim:

> Absolute power is not bent on achieving blind obedience or discipline, but desires to generate a universe of total uncertainty, one in which submissiveness is no shield against even worse outcomes. It forces its victims together into an aggregate, a mass; it stirs up differences and erects a social structure marked by extreme contrasts. . . . It does not wish to limit freedom, but to destroy it. It does not seek to guide action, but to demolish it. It drains human beings, depleting them by labor both useless and senseless. . . . Even killing, that final reference point of all power, is not sufficient. Absolute power transforms the universal structures of human relatedness to the world: space and time, social relations, the connection with work, the relation to the self. It seizes on various elements and methods of traditional forms of power, combining and intensifying them, while casting off their instrumentality. (pp. 17–18)[9]

9. For a critique of Sofsky's argument with regard to the death camps, see O. Bartov, The Penultimate Horror, *The New Republic*, October 13, 1997, 48–53.

Lang asserts the importance of shifting the analysis of such atrocities from the psychological level to the sociological level, in which cruelty takes on a social meaning given that it occurs in a social context. Once violence evolves into a social norm, potential perpetrators then feel pressure to conform and perform. Excessive displays of violence become a way to confirm and strengthen one's commitment to the group while also setting oneself apart. Lang writes, "In a context where violence is the norm, excessive cruelty—which has often been described as the effacement of the victim's human aspects—can also become a way to *personalize oneself*," both by distinguishing oneself in the eyes of one's fellows through creative, utterly destructive acts of violence, and by contrasting the perpetrator's capacities to choose and act versus the victim's utter helplessness and ultimate death (2010, p. 239, emphasis in original). On the surface, what might appear to be dehumanized violence is instead an extreme manifestation of derivatization: Extreme violence is used as a means to exert power over another person *without ending the social relationship*. It is a way to continue dominating the victims before (or instead of) killing them. Excessive cruelty can even serve as a means for perpetrators to escape the boredom that they often experience—a means to escape their "ho-hum," routine violence. Here is one such example that took place at Buchenwald:

> The construction supervisor ordered two Jews whose strength appeared to be waning to lie down in a pit. He then commanded a Pole to fill it in and to bury the two men alive. When the Polish prisoner refused, the supervisor beat him with a shovel handle, ordering him to lie down next to the two Jews in the pit. The two Jews were then commanded to cover the disobedient Pole with earth. When all that could be seen was the Pole's head, the supervisor halted the operation and had the man dug out. The Jews had to lie down once more in the pit, and the Pole was told once again to cover them. This time he obeyed. . . . When the pit was filled in, the supervisor, *laughing*, stamped the ground solid. Five minutes later, he called over two prisoners to dig the Jews out again. One was already dead; the other still showed weak signs of life. Both were transported to the crematorium. (Sofsky, 1997, p. 200)

Lang points out that the supervisor's laughter betrays his enjoyment at the suffering of others, but also his personal amusement at breaking with ordinary routine and creating a novel approach to displaying his absolute power. It is also important to point out that the Pole in the incident was

> . . . instrumentalized, but not dehumanized; he becomes an instrument in the hands of the perpetrator, but an instrument whose humanity—or more precisely, subjectivity—is a centrally important element of its instrumentality. . . .

Cruelty is not constrained by the requirement that the victims be dehumanized (Lang, 2010, p. 241)

The supervisor's sadistic approach to enhancing his sense of personal power at his victims' expense is yet another manifestation of *derivatization in the extreme*. The victims are approached primarily as the projection or expression of the supervisor's desires for entertainment and self-enhancement. The victims are reduced in all ways to the supervisor's existence; other elements of their being or subjectivity are denied.

The Problem of Sexual Violence

History is replete with examples showing that sexual violence goes hand in hand with mass murder, as in Nanking, Rwanda, and Congo. This fact underscores yet again that the relationship between mass murderers and their victims can have more complexity at times than dehumanization alone would suggest. Neil J. Kressel (2002), in his summary of the large body of research on war rape, concludes that three motives seem to animate would-be rapists: (1) to hurt or humiliate the victim, (2) to demonstrate power over the victim, and (3) to satisfy the desire for sex (p. 37). Thinking back on Nussbaum's seven aspects of objectification, it seems reasonable to ask whether or not such rapists—while instrumentalizing victims, denying victims' autonomy, and treating victims as if they were violable—ever fully deny victims' subjectivity, which is a hallmark of dehumanization. Lang makes the point that in the rapist's mind, the desire to humiliate, display power, and have sex all typically require the acknowledgment of a thinking, feeling presence in the victim. While personal identity may not be important for the rapist, subjectivity certainly seems to be. Consider the perspective of one Japanese soldier who engaged in the rape of a Chinese woman during the "rape of Nanking": " . . . [P]erhaps when we were raping her, we thought of her as a woman . . . but when we killed her, we thought of her as a pig" (Chang, 1997, p. 50. as quoted in Lang, 2010, p. 236). In other words, when she was being raped, her aggressors thought of the woman as a human being, but when they killed her, they dehumanized her in order to trivialize the murder's consequences, thus reducing the soldiers' feelings of guilt (if they had any to begin with). Clearly, human beings don't necessarily require that their "partner" be human in order to engage in sex (indeed, the legacy of human beings engaging in sexual acts with animals likely pre-dates recorded history), but rape is facilitated when victims are perceived by perpetrators to possess human elements (Lang, 2010, p. 236). Thus, rape is most appropriately understood as a byproduct of derivatization rather than dehumanization.

Emotional Hardening Leading to Extreme Violence

Finally, Lang (2010) makes the point that a humble, basic psychological process can play a monumental role in the perpetuation of extreme violence: *habituation*, leading to desensitization and emotional hardening. To support his case, he makes reference to the Gypsy camp at Auschwitz-Birkenau. Gypsies as a group, while persecuted, had largely been spared the propaganda campaign of dehumanization hurled at Jews and Slavs. Those housed in this particular camp were allowed to keep their civilian clothes and appearance. Most spoke German and interacted openly and frequently over time with the guards. At the request of the Nazis, some of the children there had put on a performance of *Snow White and the Seven Dwarves*, which was attended and applauded by many SS officers. Nonetheless, in August 1944, almost 3,000 persons from this section of the camp, including many of the children, were killed in the gas chambers. A surviving member of the Sonderkommando (a mostly Jewish collective forced to operate the crematoria) described what happened when these prisoners were finally killed:

> Today a peculiar atmosphere reigned in the changing room. The gypsies who were to be gassed had known some of the SS men present for some time, and they tried to get into conversation with them as they usually did. In the course of time they had come to be on almost familiar terms with the SS. This was probably because most of them spoke German, and perhaps also because the SS men had had no plausible reason to hate them. Unlike the Jews, Bolsheviks, Slavs, and other "sub-humans," the gypsies had never had many pronouncements of a compromising nature made against them by the official Nazi propaganda. . . . One could see that most of the SS men had a bad conscience. They hadn't shown any scruples about annihilating Jews, the killing of whom was now a daily routine for all of them, yet they clearly found it unpleasant and distressing to help exterminate people with whom they had been on quite good terms up to now. But in this dismal place there was no room for sentiment. (Muller, 1999, pp. 150–151)

Here, the mechanisms of dehumanization are mentioned in terms of how the SS had been indoctrinated to view Jews and others as "subhumans," but the perpetrators show obvious discomfort at taking such an active role in killing those whom they perceive to be human beings—inferior humans, but human beings nonetheless. The incident shows that dehumanization can be undermined by factors such as physical appearance and language, but that dehumanization is not altogether necessary for the commission of atrocious acts, for the guards still ended up killing the Gypsies—they simply "pushed sentiment out of their awareness." When such sentiment is present at the outset, it is the capacity to suppress such feelings, "the ability to adapt and harden," that can enable genocidal violence (Lang, 2010, p. 231). The SS were selected in large part based on their commitment to Nazi ideology and their devotion to Hitler. Chosen to implement the "Final Solution," they were then trained to be callous, merciless, and fanatically loyal. Joining the SS meant that one's civilian life was largely left behind in order to carry out assignments that meant the torture and death of millions of people, including people whom SS members had not fully dehumanized. According to Rudolph Höss, the top commander at Auschwitz, "only iron determination could carry out Hitler's orders and this could only be achieved by stifling all emotion," by " . . . being like a rock." For these individuals, for whom killing became a daily routine, the well-documented, ubiquitous processes of habituation leading to desensitization[10] played a major role in the undertaking of such actions. Innate feelings of shock, disgust, and horror can be attenuated through "routinization"— persistent exposure leading to the perception of ordinariness—without necessarily leading to a total cognitive shift in the perpetrator's outlook on the victims. Not that such attenuation is without consequences, nor is it necessarily easy to maintain. Höss acknowledged that for many of those carrying out the exterminations at Auschwitz, anxiety and melancholy were common and they often sought him out, seeking reassurances about what they were doing (Pasculy, 1996, p. 161). Józef Paczyński, a non-Jewish prisoner-barber at Auschwitz, described what it was like to shave the guards who worked the crematoria:

> After every selection and gassing they would come to the barbershop, after the deed, and they seemed abnormal people. I could smell the stench from them. And I could see in their faces that they were conscious of what they did, but no one said a word. (Goldberg, 2005)

For the illusion of dehumanization to be effective in the mind of the perpetrator, it must, at least to some degree, reflect the perpetrator's actual experience of reality on the ground. Indeed, dehumanization was built right into the structure of the camps. They were specifically designed not to encourage, prolong, or enhance life, but rather to foster illness, fatigue, hopelessness, decline, and death. Franz Stengl, the head commander of the infamous camps of Sobibor and Treblinka, remarked that the system itself—the nakedness, the whips, the horror of the cattle pens—degraded the victims to the point where, on the brink of being put to death and in a state of terror and confusion, they thoughtlessly obeyed instructions. Their very compliance inspired feelings of disgust and contempt in those who carried out the genodical policies (Sereny, 1974, p. 202, as cited in Lang, 2010, p. 232). This type of resolve in the guards

---

10. In other words, repeated exposure to a stimulus, leading to a gradual lessening of the perceived intensity of that stimulus.

suggests a psychological reality that is perhaps even more troubling than the theory of dehumanization itself: that it is possible for genocidal atrocities to take place *despite* the perpetrator maintaining some realization of the victim's humanity. It is difficult to know which is worse in an ethical sense—death-dealing facilitated by the psychological illusion of dehumanization, or death-dealing facilitated by the degradation of one's innate moral resources while nonetheless maintaining some realization of the victim's humanity. For the victim, it makes no difference, as the end result is the same. Whatever the case may be, Lang offers a chilling, bottom-line summary of such processes when he claims that " . . . the limits of the human potential for destruction have yet to be established" (Lang, 2010, p. 241).

PART TWO

The Human Situation

Limitations and Possibilities

CHAPTER 4

Three Observations from Antiquity

Philosophia Perennis

Mundus vult decipi: the world wants to be deceived. The truth is too complex and frightening; the taste for truth is an acquired taste that few acquire.

Walter Kaufmann *(as quoted in Buber, 1970, p. 9)*

We don't see things the way things are; we see things the way we are.

Talmudic saying

When attempting to understand objectification and its various manifestations, it makes sense that we look to what is most fundamental about us as a species in order to gain some perspective. Contemplatives over the past several millennia have accumulated much wisdom regarding the human experience, the depths of the human interior, and our capacities for both loving-kindness and abject cruelty. In order to respond in a more informed way to the question, "What causes human beings to objectify each other?," it will be helpful to look closely at some of these insights. It is common to assume that contemporary human beings have greater intelligence, understanding, and insight than their forebearers. While it is true that in comparison to their ancient counterparts, modern societies have made remarkable advances in the realms of human rights, communication, transportation, governance, and healthcare (to name but a few), it also seems to be true that human society has not made similar advances in terms of overall happiness or well-being, and in fact, we may be worse off in some important ways than societies existing centuries or millennia ago (Taylor, 2005).[1]

---

1. See especially Chapter 6: "The New Psyche." It must also be acknowledged that despite not being happier overall, few if any people living today would choose to trade places with their human counterparts living centuries or even a few decades ago.

While our understanding of the physical world and its various features has increased dramatically since the beginning of the previous millennium (thanks entirely to the development and use of the scientific method), western thought seems to have advanced little from earlier eras in our understanding of the basic problems of what it means to be human. As Alfred North Whitehead (1979) famously suggested, "The safest general characterization of the European philosophical tradition is that it consists of a series of footnotes to Plato" (p. 39). In other words, according to Whitehead, our current wisdom has not evolved substantially from the wisdom declared by the ancients, of which Plato is exemplar. And yet, at the same time, we have forgotten some of the deeper wisdom of our progenitors. In order to better understand the human tendency to objectify, we will be well served to remind ourselves of some of these nuggets of wisdom while also attending to the insights of some outstanding contemporary thinkers. In so doing, we will be broadening our exploration of the underpinnings of objectification in order to better understand this tendency, and how such inclinations can be minimized, if not transcended altogether.

In recent years, the eminent philosopher Jacob Needleman (2007a) asserted that when the world's great wisdom traditions are analyzed and sifted for big ideas common to all, three primary themes emerge. Not surprisingly, Plato's simple allegory of the cave encapsulates much of this ancient wisdom:

1. Human beings live in a world of illusions and appearances;
2. human beings' ordinary sense of self-identity, what is referred to as "personality," is not their true, fundamental identity; and
3. an over-arching Reality—what has been referred to as "the Universal Ground of all Being" (Huxley, 1970, p. 21; Tillich, 1964, p. 15; 1951, p. 236)—exists which gives order to the cosmos and connects all that exists together into one great whole (Needleman, 2007a, pp. 46–48).

Upon reflection, adherents of the world's great spiritual teachings and philosophies will find that while their doctrines or assertions may differ dramatically with respect to specifics, their general worldviews have grounding in the three basic, ancient ideas described by Needleman. The three monotheistic traditions—Judaism, Christianity, and Islam—endorse these concepts, as does the polytheism of Hinduism. The non-theism of Buddhism advances the same assumptions, as do other, less prevalent religious and philosophical systems of thought, such as Taoism, Jainism, and Sikhism. Prominent ancient Greek philosophers and the great Stoic philosophers of Rome promulgated similar ideas. Even contemporary "new atheists," such as Sam Harris (2011; 2005), Richard Dawkins (2011, 2010, 2008), Christopher Hitchens (2007), and Daniel Dennett (2007, 2004) either endorse versions of these three concepts or make room for them in their larger systems of thought.[2] As rare as a synoptic perspective is in the world's collection of religion and philosophy, there is an astonishing degree of agreement upon these claims, so much so that Needleman called them ". . . the one central doctrine of all the wisdom of humankind, the idea around which all the great spiritual teachings revolve, as planets revolve around the sun" (2007a, p. 48). Other renowned thinkers, such as Liebniz, Steuco, Guénon, Jaspers, and Huxley, have alluded to these ideas under the term *Philosophia Perennis*, or "the Perennial Philosophy," suggesting that such concepts represent key recurring philosophical insights independent of era or epoch.

It seems readily apparent that conditions one (i.e., human beings live in a world of illusions and appearances) and two (i.e., human beings' ordinary sense of self-identity, what is referred to as "personality," is not their true, fundamental identity) are closely related: Both assertions have to do with human beings not perceiving reality correctly, or perhaps more to the point of our discussion on objectification, not apprehending reality correctly. In other words, like those to whom Plato referred in his allegory, we do not grasp the true nature of our own or others' being, nor do we appreciate the true nature of our relationship to others and the cosmos in which we exist.

Given that these two conditions are valid, it is easy to understand how human beings could be largely oblivious to, or grossly misunderstanding of, condition number three—the Universal Ground of all Being. I have preferred this term (most often associated with the renowned twentieth-century theologian Paul Tillich) to the much more commonly used "God" because it is less theologically loaded, and more readily applicable to a variety of spiritual and religious conceptions, both theistic and nontheistic, from the East and West. From Tillich's perspective, God is beyond being itself, and is manifested in the underlying structure of beings. God is not a supernatural entity among other entities. Instead, God is the ground upon which all beings exist. We cannot perceive God as an object that is related to a subject because God precedes the subject-object dichotomy (Tillich, 1964, p. 15). Nonbelievers will reject these assertions because they are statements of faith. However, Tillich's underlying premise—that the self can be transcended, providing one with a profound sense of living connection to the universe as a whole—will likely find

2. Through my own analyses of their writings and lectures, it appears that each of these impressive, penetrating thinkers would endorse parallel versions of Needleman's three assertions. For example, they would likely agree that (1) human beings have a tendency toward irrational thought, often interpreting their experiences in a way that furthers their neuroses; (2) that accurate knowledge of the self is hard won and represents highly unconventional wisdom about the nature of consciousness, which most people never acquire; and (3) that an over-arching process (i.e., natural selection) guides the direction of life on earth, uniting all that exists in a complex web of interrelationship.

resonance. From this perspective, it makes sense to think in terms of an ultimate generative background upon which all of existence rests. In the context of Needleman's three conditions, lack of self-awareness seems to go hand in hand with lack of "cosmic awareness," or unawareness that one is part of this Ground (indeed, cosmic awareness may be a precondition for self-awareness). This was Needleman's (2007a) own realization when he mused upon the three conditions:

> I suddenly understood that the ancient idea that we live in a world of appearances veiling the real world was only half of an idea. And as such, it was impossible to make sense of it. . . . And what was the other half of the idea—which fit into the first half with the precision of a Swiss jigsaw puzzle? Simply this: Like the great surrounding world, one's own self was also a tissue of appearances, beneath which existed the real Self. And it was only through contact with this real Self behind the appearances of one's own socially conditioned surface personality that the real world outside oneself could be experienced and known! Only the real internal Self hidden within could know the real external universal world hidden behind the appearances. . . . It is this real Self which has the intellectual intuitive power to verify the idea of the world behind the appearances. It is the real Self which has the power to see this real external world and to understand it and eventually, to merge with it. The surface self can only know the surface world. (pp. 49–50, emphasis in the original)

Extending this insight, the Perennial Philosophy asserts that the only way to come into awareness and harmony with this Ground is to make progress toward dispelling our ignorance of self and others. Said Huxley (1970):

> The divine Ground of all existence is a spiritual Absolute, ineffable in terms of discursive thought, but (in certain circumstances) susceptible of being directly experienced and realized by the human being. This Absolute is the God-without-form of Hindu and Christian mystical phraseology. The last end of man, the ultimate reason for human existence, is unitive knowledge of the divine Ground, the knowledge that can come only to those who are prepared to "die to self" and so make room, as it were, for God. Out of any given generation of men and women, very few will achieve the final end of human existence; but the opportunity for coming to unitive knowledge will, in one way or another, continually be offered until all sentient beings realize Who in fact they are. (p. 21)

One need not invest too much energy trying to imagine how the consequences of Needlemans's three conditions play out in human life. A quick glance at the day's news headlines will suffice, or perhaps a reminder that approximately 200 million individuals lost their lives during the twentieth century due to politically motivated conflict (Bassiouni, 1997; Brzezinski,

1995). Needleman's three conditions represent three types of ignorance—ignorance of self, world, and the Ground of all being—all of which are part of what contemplatives have called *parikalpita* (Sanskrit for "the imagined), "the illusion of independent arising" (His Holiness, the Dalai Lama, 2009, pp. 4–5) or "discriminative perception" (Thich Nhat Hanh, 1998, p. 134). Each of these terms refer to the illusory perception of the self as a separate, distinct entity. This same idea, universally understood as a problematic state of consciousness, has been spoken of but labeled differently by the world's various religious systems of thought. All of these perspectives share the assertion that human consciousness, in its typical form, obscures the deeper realities and leads to conflict. One byproduct of this obnibulated consciousness is anxious self-preoccupation, because the separated self is a concerned self. Another troublesome by-product of the perception of separateness is enmity, a seldom-used word outside religious circles, which refers to the state of being in opposition or at odds with others. If our needs, desires, and wants are incessant and everyone else is experiencing the same pressures, then all of us are competing for scarce resources, be it food, water, or love and affection. Sibling rivalries are one depiction of this state of being—the archetypal story of enmity in the biblical tradition being Cain killing his older brother, Abel, out of envy. Life in a prison setting is a more contemporary, stark example, where many inmates live out their daily lives in a context rife with enmity. One recent, deeply disturbing example from a state prison reads as follows (Rogers, 2011):

> Video footage captured another inmate holding [inmate 2, a thirty-two year-old man] down while [inmate 1, a twenty-six year-old man] stabbed him 67 times with a shank. [Inmate 2] was serving a sentence for robbery and theft. [Inmate 1], a white supremacist, yelled, "White power!" while wiping the blood of [inmate 2], an African-American, from his hands as other inmates cheered.

The report goes on to specify that inmate 1 stabbed inmate 2 nine times in the eyes, supposedly to ensure that inmate 2 suffered the most excruciating pain possible. It was also alleged that inmate 1 had yelled that he had "nothing to lose" by acting viciously in prison because he was already serving two life sentences (Rogers, 2011).

Heightened self-concern stemming from feelings of separation, alienation, and estrangement enhances our tendencies to objectify others, which makes conflict more likely. To be fair, we should acknowledge that human beings also have strong social tendencies that motivate us to form groups, to cooperate, and to compromise in order to better ensure our survival. We receive most of our sustenance from our relations with others. As a species, we are indeed proficient at working together to meet each other's basic needs. Coupling our innate social tendencies with our remarkable intelligence, we can accomplish great feats of governance, engineering, advances in technology, and health-care. We can work together to solve complex problems, such as global hunger and global warming. But stirring just below the surface remains the constant hum of self-concern and perceived separateness. For many of us, it doesn't require much perturbation at the surface for our undercurrent of unenlight-enment to be tapped. Most of us are only a few carelessly chosen coarse words away from relational estrangement; and while most human beings will never intentionally kill another person, those individuals who do murder someone else are most likely to kill someone they know well. While the majority of children will never experience physical or sexual abuse, most of those who do will be abused by their primary caregivers. During most 24-hour periods com-prising the days of our history as a species, there has been—somewhere—open, hostile conflict between individuals or groups culminating in death. The Perennial Philosophy asserts that human conflict is fueled by the perception of a separate, boundaried self. These perceptions comprise the status quo of human experience; they constitute the conventional wisdom of our species that describes "the facts" of our existence. However, the Perennial Philosophy asserts that nothing could be further from the truth.

CHAPTER 5

Unity Consciousness

Reality at the Deepest Level

To see a world in a grain of sand
And a heaven in a wild flower,
Hold infinity in the palm of your hand
And eternity in an hour.

William Blake (Auguries of Innocense)

If we had a keen vision and feeling of all ordinary human life, it would be like hearing the grass grow and the squirrel's heart beat, and we should die of that roar which lies on the other side of silence. As it is, the best of us walk about well wadded with stupidity.

George Eliot (Middlemarch)

The highest wisdom of the ancients intuited a vast, obfuscating tissue enveloping the human experience. This suggests that they must have had occasion to penetrate this thin veneer into other ways of seeing, knowing, and relating to life which exposed the problem of everyday perception. If human beings living millennia ago were able to transcend typical modes of perceiving, moving into a more substantial, truthful mode of discerning that transcended time and place, then such experiences ought to be available to contemporary humans as well. Such is indeed alleged to be the case. Nearly 100 years ago, the Canadian psychiatrist Richard Maurice Bucke called such a condition of awareness "cosmic consciousness" (1901); 50 years later, Abraham Maslow referred to these states as "peak experiences" (1970). Over the last 1,500 years, the Sufi mystics of Islam have called the experience "supreme identity"; and the renowned contemporary American philosopher of consciousness Ken Wilber calls this state "unity consciousness," which is the term I will use here (2001, p. 3). All of these superlatives make reference to the same reality: that despite appearances, all things, and all of us, are like waves on the surface of a lake, photons in a ray of sunlight, or the notes of a chord of music. The deepest truth of our existence is that we are One. Thus, if the great contemplatives are correct, the sense of separateness that we all experience—the perception that "you" and "I" are individuals with a spark of life separate from the rest of the universe—is not ultimately true. The self is a mirage, a fabrication of everyday consciousness; but from the ultimate perspective, everything is One.

Upon hearing this, some are likely to feel incredulous, or perhaps under-whelmed, confused, or disappointed. This idea seems so at odds with con-ventional wisdom and with our own life experience—that we are in fact separate, distinct, and all too often in opposition with other forms of life in terms of our thoughts, feelings, and interests. But the assertion of a com-plex web of unity undergirding all things attested to by the proponents of the Perennial Philosophy is not a mere "deepity" (Dennett, 2009),[1] not a whimsical, idealistic fantasy, totally divorced from reality. Recently, while lis-tening to National Public Radio, I heard a memorable segment entitled "My Grandson, the Rock" (Krulwich, 2010). While it was not intended to provide a corollary in support of unity consciousness or the oneness of all existence, it was nevertheless intriguing in this respect. In it, Dr. Robert Hazen[2] dis-cussed how inorganic and organic matter are quite interdependent and, in fact, "need" each other. Dr. Hazen noted that shortly after the Big Bang 13 billion years ago, there were perhaps only 12 distinct minerals in existence—carbon, nitrogen, silicon, and iron, along with eight others. Gravity began to pull these elements together into asteroids and small planets, then into larger planets, then into planets with plate tectonics which moved surface rocks into the interior, melting and freezing them. Water then appeared and billions of years later, rocks had water molecules in them. At this point—10 billion years later—the number of minerals had gone from 12 to approxi-mately 1,500. Then, about 3.5 billion years ago, life mysteriously began. "Life is a great sculptor," Dr. Hazen observed. Pond scum, one of the earliest forms of life on the planet, emitted oxygen into the air, leading to the creation of rust in the earth's iron, which combined with organic chemicals to help create creatures with hard shells and bones. Those creatures died and became rocks (for example, the White Cliffs of Dover are merely heaps of dead plankton).

1. A term coined by the philosopher Daniel Dennett's daughter which he used at the 2009 American Atheists Institution conference. Deepity ". . . refers to a statement that is apparently profound, but actually asserts a triviality on one level and something meaningless on another. [Deepity] has (at least) two meanings; one that is true but trivial, and another that sounds profound, but is essentially false or meaningless and would be 'earth-shattering' if true" (see http://rationalwiki.org/wiki/Deepity).
2. Dr. Hazen is a research scientist at the Carnegie Institution of Washington's Geophysical Laboratory; he is also the acting Clarence Robinson Professor of Earth Sciences at George Mason University.

Life also created plants that had roots which could slowly break down rocks; worms ingested rocks and broke them down into soil. All of this "life" activity brought the total number of types of rocks to 4,500. Living things need rocks to live. For example, humans need to ingest minerals; iron deficiency leads to anemia, iodine deficiency leads to goiter, and calcium deficiency leads to osteoporosis. According to Dr. Hazen,

> Life has tripled the rock population on earth. Rocks make life, but life makes rocks. We humans live [and . . .] die and become ashes and go back into the ground and become minerals again until those same minerals get re-organized into plants which get eaten by animals which then get eaten by humans. (Krulwich, 2010)

And the process occurs over and over again, so long as the earth spins.

According to the great contemplatives, there is not only a literal physical and chemical connection between living and nonliving things, but also a nontangible, spiritual one. The collective work of the human developmentalists over the past century has converged with the disclosures of the world's great contemplative traditions from millennia ago: Both agree that human spiritual evolution moves in one direction and in fairly predictable stages—from egocentric (self-centered) to ethnocentric (my people/clan-centered) to world-centric (global-centered) (Wilber, 2001a). In other words, identity shifts from being defined by personal concern, to concern for similar others, and finally, to concern for and realization of one's connection with all people, indeed all of existence. Late in his life, Albert Einstein had this same insight. In a personal letter to a friend he put it this way:

> A human being is part of a whole, called by us the Universe, a part limited in time and space. He experiences himself, his thoughts and feelings, as something separated from the rest as a kind of optical delusion of his consciousness. This delusion is a kind of prison for us, restricting us to our personal desires and to affection for a few persons nearest us. Our task must be to free ourselves from this prison by widening our circles of compassion to embrace all living creatures and the whole of nature in its beauty. Nobody is able to achieve this completely, but the striving for such achievement is in itself a part of the liberation and a foundation for inner security. (Eves, 1977, p. 60)

Human history holds many examples of individuals experiencing just such a liberation from the illusion of separateness and self-centeredness that is the norm for our species. R. M. Bucke focused much of his later life on the study of "cosmic consciousness"—having experienced such himself. In the late nineteenth century, he identified numerous documented cases from history of individuals who had experienced such illuminations. A few firsthand accounts from his compendium will help to illustrate what the experience of unity consciousness is like:

> All at once, without warning of any kind, I found myself wrapped in a flame-colored cloud. For an instant I thought of fire, an immense conflagration somewhere close by in the city; the next, I knew that the fire was within myself. Directly afterward there came upon me a sense of exultation, of immense joyousness accompanied or immediately followed by an intellectual illumination impossible to describe. Among other things, I did not merely come to believe, but I saw that the universe is not composed of dead matter, but is, on the contrary, a living Presence; I became conscious in myself of eternal life. It was not a conviction that I would have eternal life, but a consciousness that I possessed eternal life then; I saw that all men are immortal; that the cosmic order is such that without any peradventure all things work together for the good of each and all; that the foundation principle of the world, of all the worlds, is what we call love, and that the happiness of each and all is in the long run absolutely certain. The vision lasted a few seconds and was gone; but the memory of it and the sense of the reality of what it taught has remained during the quarter of a century which has since elapsed. (Bucke, 1901, p. 34)

Experiences such as this should not be mistaken for the delusions of a man or woman suffering from a psychosis, for such illuminations lack the derangement, disorganization, and other sequelae so typical of schizophrenic or other delusional experiences. Why do such experiences occur? In some cases, such as the one above, it seems there is "preparation" laid through a breadth of life experiences and the possession of an uncluttered, yet inquiring, open mind; in other cases, it seems more a random "act of grace." William James, one of the greatest scholars America has ever produced, was of the opinion that our typical state of consciousness is only one of many that are available, almost as if our usual mode of perceiving were an island—surrounded unaware—by a vast sea of higher, more expansive consciousness, the waves of which constantly break against the protective barrier reef of daily consciousness surrounding the shore. Occasionally and inexplicably, however, a wave gets past the barrier (Wilber, 2001, p. 2). Here is another such experience recorded by Thomas Traherne, seventeenth-century poet and philosopher:

> The dust and stones of the street were as precious as gold. The gates were at first the end of the world, the green trees when I saw them first through one of the gates transported and ravished me; their sweetness and unusual beauty made my heart to leap, and almost mad with ecstasy, they were such strange and wonderful things. Boys and girls tumbling in the streets, and playing, were moving jewels. I knew not that they were born or should die. But all things abided eternally as they were in their proper places. Eternity was manifest in the light

of the day, and something infinite behind everything appeared. (Traherne, 1992, p. 226)

Almost without exception, such experiences suffuse the life of the experiencer with a profundity, depth, and significance never before realized. Indeed, according to R. M. Bucke (1901),

> The prime characteristic of [such an experience] is a consciousness of the cosmos . . . the life and order of the universe . . . . There occurs an intellectual enlightenment which alone would place the individual on a new plane of existence—would make him almost a member of a new species. (p. 2)

The great scholar of comparative religion Rudolph Otto (1869–1937), referred to such experiences, and the human emotional response to such, as "mysterium tremendum" (Otto, 1958). Otto asserted that such an experience is composed of a variety of elements—awe-fullness, overpoweringness, urgency, and fascination—which can be experienced as a "gentle, sweeping tide," or as a "sudden eruption up from the depths of the soul [. . .] leading to the strangest excitements, to intoxicated frenzy, to transport, and to ecstasy" (pp. 12–13).

Abraham Maslow, who spoke at length regarding such experiences, called the new way of thinking and feeling about life resulting from such illuminations *B-values* and *B-cognitions* (i.e., "Being-values" and "Being-cognitions"). In analyzing the change in thoughts and values of those who have had such illuminations, Maslow saw that peak experiences cause a person's life-orientation to center upon *being* rather than *doing*: the fact that oneself, other individuals, other forms of life, and other features of the world merely exist makes them ends in and of themselves, rather than means for one's own purposes (Maslow, 1970, p. 91). Some examples from William James and R. M. Bucke follow:

> . . . The moments of which I speak did not hold the consciousness of a personality, but something in myself made me feel myself a part of something bigger than I. . . . I felt myself one with the trees, the grass, the birds, insects, everything in Nature. I exulted in the mere fact of existence, of being a part of it all—the drizzling rain, the shadows of the clouds, the tree trunks, and so on. In the years following, such moments continued to come. . . . (James, 1958 [1902], p. 303)
>
> Now came a period of rapture, so intense that the universe stood still, as if amazed at the unutterable majesty of the spectacle! Only one in all the infinite universe! The All-loving, the Perfect One! The Perfect Wisdom, truth, love and purity! And with the rapture came the insight. In that same wonderful moment of what might be called supernal bliss, came illumination. I saw with intense inward vision the atoms or molecules, of which seemingly the universe is composed—I know not whether material or spiritual—rearranging themselves, as

the cosmos (in its continuous, everlasting life) passes from order to order. What joy when I saw there was no break in the chain—not a link left out—everything in its place and time. Worlds, systems, all blended in one harmonious whole. Universal life, synonymous with universal love! (Bucke, 1901, p. 326)

Such self-transcending experiences are manifest across the wide spectrum of humanity. When they occur, the experiencer often goes on to make ancillary claims about the nature of the universe that are unique to their particular culture and, therefore, at odds with other cultures' "revealed" ontological proclamations (to be reviewed in depth in Chapter 15). Nonetheless, there is very good evidence to infer that human beings have experienced dramatic instances of self-transcendence for millennia. According to the insights of the world's great contemplatives, unity consciousness is not the result of a thought experiment; it is not the result of a hallucinogenic experience;[3] it is not the result of striving to be a better person—more pleasant, more positive, more optimistic, more tolerant, or more patient. Good as these efforts can be, they tend to come from intentional striving, leaving the person largely unchanged as they act from the same limited perception of self. Rather, unity consciousness represents a dramatic shift in one's experience of themselves and the rest of the world such that they are opened up as a "new being," experiencing all about them with a new level of awareness. The central shift that occurs as a result of such experiences is in what it means to be a "self." Such individuals come to perceive that they are in fact one with the world; that their sense of identity expands far beyond the narrow confines of the self and merges with the rest of existence. Perhaps it goes without saying that for any given individual, the chances of such a remarkable illumination occurring will be remote. However, intimations of unity consciousness—those precious moments when we feel a greater sense of appreciation or connection with the rest of existence, or when we engage mindfully with the present moment of experience—are much more common. Indeed, any action on our part—however small—that works to diminish our own self-centeredness works to counteract our tendencies to draw our circles of those who count as neighbor too parochially. Intimations of unity consciousness help us to transcend our tendencies to objectify others; they move us in the direction of greater enlightenment. However, there is much about us—both within and without—that works against this type of growth, and it is to these problems that we now turn.

3. While it is true that many experiments with hallucinogenics during the early 1960's, such as those conducted by Richard Alpert, Timothy Leary, and Stanislav Grof, proved that such experiences could be approached with the use of hallucinogenics such as LSD, these chemically induced experiences did not seem to provide the same sort of "lasting effects toward the positive" that non-hallucinogenically induced states of transcendence do. See Schwartz (1995), especially chapter one: "Redefining Reality: Ram Dass, Psychedelics, and the Journey to the East."

PART THREE

What We Are

Dispositional Factors Contributing to Objectification

CHAPTER 6

The Paradoxical Nature of Language and Other Boundaries

Homo Loquax, the talking animal, is still as naively delighted by his chief accomplishment, still as helplessly the victim of his own words, as he was when the Tower of Babel was being built.

Aldous Huxley *(1970, p. 129)*

After the damage assessment study, our weapons systems revisited the site to further suppress enemy assets; we achieved effective attrition, but unfortunately, there was collateral damage due to incontinent ordnance.

an example of Pentagonese

THE PROBLEM OF LANGUAGE

As Huxley (1970) reminds us, the subject matter of the Perennial Philosophy is the nature of eternal, spiritual Reality as disclosed by unity consciousness, but the language in which it is concealed was developed by human beings for the purposes of dealing with phenomena in time. This leads to all sorts of paradoxes, nonsequiturs, and contradictions when human beings attempt to speak of what is ultimately ineffable. Joseph Campbell (1991) recognized this fact when he remarked to his interviewer, Bill Moyers, in their popular late 1980s *Power of Myth* PBS interviews, that the very best things—the highest things—that human beings are capable of experiencing can't be put into words or even thought, because they transcend thought. The second best things tend to be misunderstood because they come from the thoughts that refer to that which can't be captured by words, and the third best things are what we can actually talk about (Campbell, 1991, pp. 57–58). Words and their corollary, written language, are perhaps the greatest tools that humanity has ever known. After all, without language and the written word, we would be severely hampered in our capacities to know ourselves or our world. We would not be able to conceptualize, identify, categorize, problem-solve, plan for the future, communicate, create rules and laws for governing behavior, pass on information or knowledge, or benefit from the experiences of those who have gone before. Indeed, without language and writing, what separates us from other animals—namely, culture and its many refinements—would cease to exist. The paradox is that our use of language also contributes substantially to suffering and is a stumbling block to enlightenment.

The Language of War

Because words are symbols, they distance us from the immediacy of our own experience by allowing us to substitute one thing for another. Words take us into the realm of the symbolic and the abstract, and therefore contribute to the process of objectifying existence. Though words have been devised in every language to describe the good, the true, and the beautiful, certain kinds of words—labels—have also been used by every society in times of war to facilitate the killing process. Such "social engineering" is not the result of intentional research; it is not the work of scientists trying to grease the skids of violence by giving us a method by which we can overcome our aversion to killing members of our own species. Rather, the use of dehumanizing labels comes down to us as a sort of folk wisdom from the ancients. The practice has been used effectively for centuries, indeed millennia, to facilitate violent conflict.

In America's wars, dehumanizing labels have been so ubiquitously used in the culture that most contemporary citizens of the United States still know them well. In the US Civil War, Southerners were called "rebels/rebs," while Northerners were called "yankees/yanks." In World War I, Germans were "huns." Twenty years later, during World War II, Germans were again "huns" as well as "jerries" and "krauts," while the Japanese were called "japs," "slants," "tojos," "slopes," or "nips." In Korea, the term "reds" was used to refer to North Koreans, along with the infamous "gook" label. In the Vietnam War, the North Vietnamese, initially referred to as the Viet Cong, were later referred to as the "VC" or "Victor Charlie" (from the NATO phonetic alphabet), and finally, to just "Charlie." They were also widely referred to as "gooks." Current conflicts with Arab and Muslim combatants have seen the proliferation of the labels "towel head" and "sand nigger." There are very specific reasons for the use of such demeaning labels. First, they work to enhance in-group solidarity. Being a member of a cherished, righteous collective requires that outsiders be specifically identified and derogated. Second, such derogatory labels do the work of labels in general: They're a sort of shorthand to simplify the world by stereotyping all specified members of a group into one mass. Nuances of character, personality, or other aspects that would help differentiate individuals or otherwise contribute to the realized humanity of others are minimized. As is so often the case with labels, once the derogated group has been marked with a tag, the perception is that they have been understood in their totality—no need to look, listen, or investigate further. Finally, the use of labels distances perpetrators from the reality of their actions. Labeled fatalities don't necessarily conjure up details of the often slow, bloody, agonizing process of dying in war; labeled fatalities don't quite have the same salience as those who have names, families, vocations, hopes, dreams, and so forth.

The use of euphemisms—delicate, nuanced, inoffensive terms or phrases used in place of those that have unpleasant associations—also comes down to us from antiquity. Euphemisms historically were substitute phrases used in place of a variety of words or phrases that were deemed taboo within a particular culture, such as terms involving religion, sexuality, or death. The word comes from the Greek word *euphemia*, which refers specifically to a word or phrase used in place of religious terminology that should not be spoken aloud. While euphemisms are prevalent in many realms of human life, war is especially rife with such "double speak." D. L. Smith (2007) notes that in Vietnam, for example, dropping bombs was "delivering ordnance," and defoliant chemicals that laid bare the landscape and poisoned those who came into contact with them were simply "weed killers." Today, we don't kill people, but we "neutralize targets" or we "take them out." Killing our own soldiers by mistake is "friendly fire," while accidentally killing civilians is known as "collateral damage" or "regrettable byproducts." Bombings that are contained to one central location, decimating all those present, are known as "clean surgical strikes." A rebellion is an "insurgency," and kidnapping enemies in order to have them tortured in another country where torture isn't prohibited is called "extreme rendition." Torture itself is no longer torture but "enhanced interrogation," and assassination is "wet work." Land mines are "area denial munitions." Shooting a person with numerous bullets is called "lighting him up." When a sniper shoots a person, it's known as "smoke-checking a target." Indeed, people are never referred to, if at all possible; rather, they are designated as "targets" (Smith, 2007, p. 109). All of this works to keep the realities of warfare at a safe emotional distance, both for those who actually do the fighting, and for those who anxiously await news at home. It acts as a sort of mass delusion, allowing us to define ourselves as compassionate, moral, pious people while we support policies and perspectives that lead to destruction and death. I'm reminded of a few highly conservative Christian religious denominations in the United States that ironically rank as the most "hawkish" of all social groups in terms of support for foreign wars of intervention, while also considering themselves to be the most authentically Christian (Jones, 2007). It is also common for these denominations to incorporate as part of their elaborate system of purity codes the non-viewing of R-rated films, which means that their members, if they adhere strictly to such codes, will never see vivid cinematic depictions of the realities of the policies they endorse. War is certainly R-rated (if not NC-17).

How Language Contributes to Suffering

Long ago, the Buddha intuited that language could play a detrimental role in human spiritual progress. His philosophy identifies five categories or states of being: *appearance, name, discrimination, right knowledge,* and *suchness*. The first three are considered impediments to enlightenment, whereas the remaining two are aspects of it. *Appearances* can be discriminated by the sense organs—those things that can be touched, seen, heard, smelled, and so forth. These are then set into place or reified in the mind through the process of *naming*—much as the Book of Genesis depicts Adam doing with all the animals and even his wife, Eve, in the Garden of Eden—so that a word, such as "woman," becomes synonymous with the object. According to the Buddha's perspective, language acts as a distancer and is a main contributor to the sense of separation that most human beings feel from each other and the world around them. Language is also thought to foster the illusion of self-sufficiency and mastery, a sense that a thing is genuinely understood because it is represented by a label. This foreshortening or minimizing of existence by the use of labels contributes to the "fallen passions" of greed, envy, and the lust for power, because in the mind of the labeler, a woman, for example, is now magically understood in her totality, though in reality, she is drastically underappreciated. The label, while allowing the user to quickly identify, categorize, and *discriminate* between perceived objects, also covers up the unfathomable depth that these entities possess, and when depth is lost, perceived separation increases and objectification becomes more likely. What is gained in cleverness and efficiency comes at the cost of deeper wisdom, and from the fallen passions mentioned above springs the continuing repetition of separated existence under the influence of wanting and attachment. Thich Nhat Hanh (2007) put it this way.

> A name can be very dangerous. To touch the nature of reality while inquiring into the word, we need to see that it is only a word and not be deceived by it. Names and words have a strong tendency to bring up feelings, emotions, and ideas of discrimination. With this awareness we will know how not to be caught in the word and in the name. (p. 57)

By this same philosophy, only through a creative act of the will, assisted by "Buddha-grace," can there be a way out of the problem (Goddard, 1994):

> When appearances and names are put away and all discrimination ceases, that which remains is the true and essential nature of things and, as nothing can be

predicated as to the nature of essence, it is called the "Suchness" of Reality. This universal, undifferentiated, inscrutable, "Suchness" is the only Reality but it is variously characterized as Truth, Mind-essence, Transcendental Intelligence, Noble Wisdom, etc. (pp. 80–81)

Continuing with Buddhist philosophy, *right knowledge* consists of understanding how *appearances, names,* and *discrimination* provide certain practical benefits, but also deceive and warp perception at a deeper level. *Suchness*—the true, unfathomable depth of being that encompasses all of existence—is the state of perceiving which exists when we transcend the level of names and labels and understand that the ultimate Ground of all things can only be pointed toward, but can never be adequately described or captured by verbal formulae (Huxley, 1970, p. 135).

More recent, empirically validated perspectives have supported the ancient claim that language contributes to suffering. "Relational Frame Theory" (RFT) and its psychotherapeutic ancillary, "Acceptance and Commitment Therapy" (ACT), a current and highly influential paradigm of psychotherapy, assert that human behavior is governed largely through networks of mutual relations in the mind called "relational frames." Such relations form the core of human language and cognition, allowing us to learn without requiring direct experience. For example, a dog won't touch an electrified fence twice, but it needs to do so at least once in order to pair the shock with the grid. A human child, on the other hand, can learn through her own and her parent's verbal abilities never to touch the fence even once. ACT points out that in the outside world, this can be an immeasurably helpful tool, but in terms of the inner lives of human beings, verbal rules can detrimentally impact life in many ways (Hayes & Smith, 2005). Because humans think relationally, they are able to arbitrarily relate objects, thoughts, feelings, and actions to other objects, thoughts, feelings, and actions. In truth, there is practically nothing that human beings can't relate to something else in any number of ways (e.g., viewing one thing as the same as, better than, different from, more valuable than something else). This ability to think relationally has permitted humans to engage one another and the world in remarkable ways, but it also creates new ways to suffer.

In our minds, words are synonymous with the things to which they refer. This is because words are symbols, and symbols are literally things that "throw" (*bol* in Greek) the "same" (*sym*) thing back at us. When we think, we arbitrarily relate or connect mental events together. The words (symbols) that we think enter into a vast relational net of meaning that the mind generates over the course of a lifetime. These relational frames, or sets of learned relations, can include myriads of possible relationships between mental events, such as *temporal/causal frames* (e.g., before/after, if/then, cause of), *comparative/evaluative frames* (e.g., better than, bigger than, faster than, more valuable than, etc.), and *spatial frames* (e.g., near/far), just to name a few. Frames such as these can be applied in many ways to arrive at a vast array of outcomes. This is what ACT clinicians refer to when they speak of "the human mind" (Hayes & Smith, 2005, p. 18). For a concrete example, try the following exercise from an ACT self-help workbook (Hayes & Smith, 2005):

Write down a concrete noun here (any type of animal or object will do):_____ Now write another noun here:_____
Now, answer this question: How is the first noun **like** the second one? Next question: How is the first noun **better** than the second one? Final question: How is the first noun **the parent of** the second one? Although the answer to this last question may not be readily apparent, stay with it, and it will come. (p. 19)

This exercise shows that human beings can relate anything to anything else in any possible way, and then find the relation between the two things quite plausible (this is the same process referred to earlier in the discussion of identifying ourselves with our thoughts and feelings). *Cognitive fusion* is the technical term for the tendency we have to get caught up or trapped by the content of what we are thinking.[1] Furthermore, we are incredibly capable of deriving arbitrary relations between variables, because the mind justifies these relations by features it distills from the related facts, despite the fact that such relations cannot be true in all cases. In other words, referring back to the exercise above, it cannot be true that anything (such as an airplane) actually can be "the parent of" anything else (such as a dog), but the mind can always find a justification for that relation or any other it can conceive of (Hayes & Smith, 2005, p. 19).[2]

This ability to arbitrarily derive relations between seemingly disparate things makes human beings quite adept at creative problem-solving. For example, if you were presented with a novel "McGyver-esque" problem, such as a Phillips-head screw inserted deeply into a board, and you wanted to get it out, but all you had to work with was a toothbrush and a cigarette lighter, you could probably figure out how to do so. Sooner or later, you would realize that toothbrushes are made of plastic and that plastic melts, and that if you made the handle of the toothbrush soft with heat from the cigarette lighter flame, you could then press the softened end of the toothbrush against the head of the screw, making an impression of its Phillip's-head shape in the toothbrush's soft plastic. Once you did that, you could then remove the melted end from the screw and wait until the plastic hardened enough to use it again later as a custom-fit screwdriver. If the plastic was hard enough, and if you could

1. *Thinking* refers to any mental content that is symbolic or relational in an arbitrarily applicable sense, such as words, thoughts, gestures, images, and emotions (Louma, Hayes, & Walser, 2007, p. 13).
2. In this instance, an airplane could be the parent of a dog in the sense that airplanes often bring or "deliver" puppies to their new owners. In my family, we've had two puppies flown in from dog breeders out of state.

get enough torque on the toothbrush, you could then (theoretically, at least) remove the screw from the board (Hayes & Smith, 2005).

Such an example of "verbal problem-solving" displays the capacity we have to think in terms of specificity (names/labels), temporality (time orientation), contingency (if/then), and evaluation of outcomes, which allows us to imagine the future, make plans, and compare outcomes—in essence, to engage in science. Given our relative lack of size, speed, strength, agility, armor, or native weaponry, these capacities have made all the difference for our species. However, these same mental capacities also cause problems. Having specific names for people, events, and objects allows for better recall and the ability to quickly relate such things to each other creatively. This is why a seemingly pleasant occurrence, such as the comforting aroma of a turkey roasting in the oven, can lead to emotional pain (e.g., recalling a family argument during a past Thanksgiving dinner). Because of the human capacity to think temporally, we can predict that bad things will happen in the future, which can lead to anxiety or depression. For example, we can be afraid of acquiring an illness we have never had, or that a relationship, presently satisfying and enjoyable, will inevitably end badly. We might also worry about our impending death, despite reassurances from a life insurance actuary that death, barring any abnormally risky behavior, most likely won't occur for decades to come. The ability to think comparatively leads to our tendencies to stack ourselves up against perceived ideals, inevitably finding inadequacies in ourselves in the process (e.g., as in someone with an eating disorder), despite the fact that we have all we need and much of what we want in life.

Another reason that language enhances the capacity for suffering is that we erroneously apply the same problem-solving approach we use in the external world to problems in our inner lives (Luoma, Hayes, & Walser, 2007). The way we habitually talk to ourselves, including our personal style of verbal problem-solving, can set our responses into rigid patterns. For example, if the kitchen stove is dirty from use, we can simply go at it with scouring pads and spray cleansers until it's clean. The reasoning seems to be, "If you don't like something in your life, figure out how to change it or get rid of it, make a plan, then follow the plan." However, this approach doesn't work well when it comes to getting rid of emotional pain. For instance, the attempt to get rid of or suppress certain thoughts may work in the short term, but not in the long term. We can distract ourselves for a time, but the more we actively attempt to suppress certain thoughts, the more we have to think about something else. Yet, this something else can act as a reminder of what we're trying to forget. The same is true for emotions. If we try not to feel an unpleasant emotion, such as anxiety, we have to think about what we are trying to avoid or forget, which tends to evoke the very thing we are trying to avoid. All such approaches to fixing suffering by "getting rid of it" contribute to what is known as *experiential avoidance*, which is the attempt to control or alter the form, frequency, or situational sensitivity of internal experiences, even when doing so causes harm to the self (Hayes, Wilson, Gifford, & Follette, 1996). Examples could include avoiding work, class, get-togethers, or other outings because of social anxiety, or avoiding outdoor hobbies because one is too depressed to leave the house or even get out of bed. The irony is that such avoidance, done in the name of controlling unpleasant internal experience, actually ends up taking us out of living the kind of life we actually want and value, which is perhaps the greatest form of suffering.

Each of humankind's unique attributes—such as the capacity to love, to create, to experience self-esteem—contains the possibility of its opposite negative—to hate, to destroy, to experience self-loathing (Gerrig & Zimbardo, 1989). Not surprisingly then, language represents a substantial paradox: It is perhaps the crowning achievement of our species, but it often acts as an impediment to enlightenment. Because of language's dual nature, we are well served to be mindful of both its benefits and limitations. As Huxley reminds us, words are not synonymous with facts, and even less so are they "primordial fact" (1970, p. 128). If we take words too seriously, if we believe that labels are synonymous with reality, we become enveloped in *maya*, in *manas*, Hindu and Buddhist terms for the illusion of worldly appearances, which distances us from reality at its deepest level. But if we don't take words seriously enough, we don't come to realize that there is a more enlightened way of living to be sought in the first place.

If enlightened individuals didn't attempt to communicate their wisdom to the world, there would be much less chance of progress for anyone. Yet, because the human condition is what it is—we have only our minds and our use of language to work with—the dispensation of wisdom is fraught with potential problems. The history of the world's great systems of thought are unanimous on this point. Using Jesus' imagery (found in three of the four Gospels and also in the non-canonical Gospel of Thomas), the enlightened dispense the seeds of wisdom; a few hear and become enlightened because they are like fertile soil—they receive the seed and it becomes a lovely plant bearing lasting, good fruit. Others receive only a partial salvation because they respond with only partial reciprocity. They are like soil that is already encumbered with brush and weeds, so the seed has difficulty taking root and the resulting sprout has a short life span. Finally, there are those who actually do damage to themselves and others because they respond with total inappropriateness by either ignoring the word altogether, or more often, taking the words themselves too literally, treating them as though they were synonymous with the truth to which they refer (Huxley, 1970). As Maslow (1970) noted,

> What happens to many people, especially the ignorant, the uneducated, the naive, is that they simply concretize all of the symbols, all of the words, all of the

statues, all of the ceremonies, and by a process of functional autonomy make them, rather than the original revelation, into the sacred things and sacred activities. [. . .] In idolatry the essential original meaning gets so lost in concretizations that these finally become hostile to the original mystical experiences, to mystics, and to the prophets in general, that is, to the very people we might call from our present point of view the truly religious people. Most religions have wound up denying and being antagonistic to the very ground upon which they were originally based. (pp. 24–25)

Language plays a substantial role in sustaining neurosis through our personal investment in the stories of our lives, in the complex web of associations or frames of meaning comprising our felt sense of who we are, and in our understanding of the world around us. Since we can relate anything we experience to anything else in novel ways, we can derive suffering out of the most seemingly idyllic, innocuous of occurrences (such as an ocean-side sunset) because it can remind us of the past as much as it can be a pathway into the present moment. An entirely literal approach to language also encourages an over-reaching of the problem-solving mode of thinking as a way to solve emotional pain. As a result, we attempt to avoid unpleasant feeling states, become tangled up in our thinking, and lose contact with the present moment, which leads to living a life of restrictive avoidance. In short, an overextension of language leads to inflexibility and rigidity in life (Louma et al., 2007, p. 11). The consequences for both the individual and society can be significant.

THE PROBLEM OF BOUNDARIES

He is to be recognized as eternally free
Who neither loathes nor craves
For he that is freed from pairs,
Is easily freed from conflict.

Bhagavad Gita (15:5)

Given the seemingly other-worldly descriptions of unity consciousness mentioned in Chapter 5, it will perhaps be meaningful to assert the simple fact that at the super-atomic level—the level at which we live our lives and interact with the world around us—human beings have a distinct location as physical entities where boundaries place very real restraints upon our movement and experiences. The human mind is also subject to various types of limiting boundaries, such as intellectual capacity, processing speed, neuronal maturity, and flexibility/inflexibility of thought, just to name a few. Boundaries such as these place restraints upon the quality of thoughts we can think, and our capacities for discerning reality in a more nuanced way. Unlike the body, however, the mind also operates at the level of symbols, where mental boundaries can be erected or transcended many times over a lifetime, regardless of the body's capacities. Sigmund Freud was one of the first to realize that an overabundance of certain types of mental boundaries—tantamount to quarantine compartments or "storm cellars" within the mind—create restricted access to one's own experience and thus have a stultifying effect upon personal growth. On the other hand, doing the hard work of learning to transverse such boundaries allows for greater awareness of self and an enlarged capacity to realize one's connectedness with the world. The mind, therefore, has a plasticity and fluidity that transcends the physical confines of the body. We can think of numerous individuals who, despite great geographical, cultural, or physical limitations (such as the famous theoretical physicist, Stephen Hawking) have minds that are capable of contemplating and illuminating what is unfathomable for most people.[3] However, we can also think of many individuals who, despite considerable health, prosperity, and the many other advantages modernity has to offer, nonetheless fail to evidence much inner, spiritual growth as human beings. Indeed, Pulitzer Prize–winning journalist and author Christopher Hedges argues that the United States, despite being "the richest nation on earth," appears to have a populace gradually withering in its ability to read, speak, think critically, and discern transcendent values (Hedges, 2009).

There are other important points to consider about the nature of boundaries. First, human existence seems impossible without the perception of boundaries. Indeed, reality, as humans experience it, seems to be composed of pairs of opposites, which are boundaries of perception that we create around conditions. Think of any condition—mental, spiritual, physical, spatial, sexual, political, and so on, and you will soon realize that our awareness of the condition is composed of corresponding opposing poles. For example, the *mental* category is composed of opposites like smart versus stupid, awake versus asleep, conscious versus unconscious. The *spiritual* category is composed of opposing poles such as intangible versus tangible, soul versus body, good versus evil, god versus devil. The *physical* category is composed of the boundaries of hard versus soft, alive versus dead, healthy versus sick, and strong versus weak. The *spatial* category is composed of the contrasts of up versus down, in versus out, and near versus far. The *sexual* category is composed of male versus female, heterosexual versus homosexual; and the *political* category is composed of the contrasts of conservative versus liberal, communist/

3. Despite being severely crippled by a motor neuron disease, Steven Hawking is an Honorary Fellow of the Royal Society of the Arts, a lifetime member of the Pontifical Academy of Sciences, and was awarded the US Presidential Medal of Freedom in 2009. He has written a number of books on cosmology that have been best sellers in the United States and Europe.

socialist versus capitalist. This same perceptual tendency exists in the realms of aesthetics, economics, social values, epistemology, ontology, and so forth. Such should not be surprising, because each of these perceived contrasts is a human creation in which the basic tendency is to understand reality in terms of a juxtaposition of extremes. Why is this so?

Ken Wilber, in his highly insightful book *No Boundary: Eastern and Western Approaches Toward Spiritual Growth* (2001), points out that a primal human tendency was written into one of the great foundational narratives of the human condition, the Book of Genesis, where the mythical first man, Adam, takes time out of his very (un)busy day in paradise to name every living creature. The important point was not so much the specific names he came up with, but rather, the sorting out process that Adam went through. He made distinctions based on each creature's appearance, sounds, means of locomotion, preferred places of residence, and so forth. In other words, Adam made divisions and created dividing lines through creation where there were none previously (Wilber, 2001, p. 26; Genesis 2:19–20).

Second, Wilber explains that opposites, such as those mentioned above, do not exist in nature. In other words, there are no good ducklings, bad ducklings, pretty ducklings, or even ugly ducklings; there are just ducklings. While it is true that some things we call "opposites" exist in nature, such as big whales and small whales, or ripe or unripe bananas, this is not a problem for nature; it brings forth all kinds and varieties, and these species live out their existence, either passing on their genes or not, but whether or not they do does not imply any sort of value judgment on the part of nature (Wilber, 2001, p. 17). Nature, as anyone who has ever been caught unprepared by weather or somehow stranded in the wild or at sea knows, is an amoral, impersonal force. As Thoreau reportedly said, "nature never apologizes" because it does not adhere to a system of values, nor does it operate according to the principle of opposites, as human beings do (Wilber, 2001, pp. 16–17). There is, of course, life and death in nature, as well as pain and pleasure, scarcity and plenty, and suffering and well-being. All species have the innate drive toward survival, but the animal world does not have the same sort of chronic anxiety regarding the possibility of pain and death that human beings do.

Third, making decisions is tantamount to drawing boundaries through the course of our lives, for each time we choose one possibility of action over another, we are expressing a preference for one outcome over another. Moreover, as Robert Frost (2012 [1915], p. 9) intimated in his most famous poem, we are actually "slaying" the alternative not chosen.[4] Whether we consciously realize it or not, our daily lives consist of making a myriad of micro-choices—when to wake up, what to wear, what to eat for breakfast, what

4. Note how the word *de-cide* contains the same suffix as words such as suicide, homicide, and infanticide, which reveals a psychological truth about decision-making.

Figure 6.1: An Example of Boundary Creation

to say (if anything) to family members who are also present in the kitchen, when to leave the house, what route to take, how to behave on the road, where to park the car, and so forth, to say nothing of the larger decisions we make regarding right and wrong, pleasure and pain, what to focus on and what to ignore, what is fair and just, whether to fight or not, *ad infinitum*. Human life is composed of decision-making, which is another way of creating boundaries.

Fourth, to reiterate the point made above about Adam, the process of drawing boundaries—sorting things out, making distinctions—creates opposites where there were none previously. Take, for example, Figure 6.1. We will recognize this figure as a star, but it is also a simple boundary on a blank space which did not exist until I told my computer to create it. Where there was only unified "white" space before, there is now a boundary that contains space *inside* the star, which is now differentiated from the space *outside* the star. In short, drawing boundaries manufactures opposites (in this case, inside versus outside; Wilber, 2001, p. 19).

Finally, just as drawing boundaries creates opposites where there were none before, the creation of opposites leads to the potential for tension and conflict where there was none previously. In other words, as every military strategist knows, boundary lines become battle lines. Examples of this dynamic are almost too many to number. One recent conflict resulting from new boundaries is the 2011 law passed in France forbidding the wearing of the burqa— a head to toe covering worn by Muslim women when outside the home—in any public space within its national boundaries. The burqa ban was part of a larger ruling (the "Act prohibiting concealment of the face in public space"), which forbids the wearing of any face-covering headgear (e.g., helmets with faceguards, masks, balaclava, etc.) in public spaces. Rising anti-Islamic sentiment in France, coupled with incidences of criminals donning burqas to conceal both their identities and their weapons, helped to bring about the new ban. The law stipulated that any woman caught wearing a burqa in public could be fined $200; however, a man who was convicted of forcing a woman to wear a burqa in public could be fined up to $43,000 (Newcomb, 2011). Soon after the law went into effect, conflict often erupted when police attempted to enforce the ban. In one example, a policeman was strangled by a man when he attempted to cite the man's wife for wearing a burqa in public. This incident touched off three straight days of riots in Trappes, a suburb of Paris, resulting in torched cars and bus shelters, and a police station being attacked (Trouble in Trappes, 2013). Over 5 million Muslims currently reside in France; however, only 2,000 are thought to be observant enough to cover their faces with a veil when in public (Erlanger, 2010). Nonetheless, given the emotional investment that both secular French society and its devout Muslim community have in this issue,[5] tensions are not likely to diminish anytime soon.

OBJECTIFICATION AND THE BOUNDARIED SELF

Unity consciousness is the underlying nature, condition, and capacity of human beings. However, we progressively limit ourselves and our world by creating and embracing boundaries (Wilber, 2001). It is true that boundaries are necessary and beneficial to us in a variety of ways. For example, identifying, categorizing, naming, and classifying observable phenomena into distinct groups based on perceived similarities and differences forms the very basis of the scientific method, an approach that has allowed us to enhance our lives and our understanding of the world to an astonishing degree. Boundaries are also an important component of healthy emotional functioning. Part of what is implied by the label "emotional well-being" is the possession of intact emotional boundaries where one is able to reliably distinguish between one's own and another's emotional processes. Emotional well-being also makes reference to the capacity to transcend one's emotional boundaries—when appropriate—in order to create and maintain lasting, satisfying intimate bonds with others, whereas dropping one's boundaries of self too quickly or too completely in the attempt to neurotically "merge" with others leads to conflict and suffering. Boundaries, therefore, represent a paradox: Without them, our capacity to know the world is severely limited; without them, we cannot evolve into emotionally stable, functional, healthy adults. However, the incapacity to transcend boundaries appropriately keeps us too rigidly locked in the perception of ourselves as separate and distinct entities, which also has a profound detrimental impact upon our ability to know ourselves and the world around us. Our capacity to objectify others is a symptom of our boundaries. Indeed,

5. President Nicholas Sarkozy said the burqa is not a religious symbol, but rather, "a sign of enslavement [and] will not be welcome in the French Republic" (Newcomb, 2011), whereas Ahmed, a Muslim woman, said, "[Wearing the burqa] is my choice. Nobody can force me to take it off. I would not take it off even if you paid me to do it. And the fact of the matter is that there's never—I have never met a single Muslim woman in all of my travels around the world—that is being forced to wear it" (CNN, 2011, April 12). "I will not obey [the new law]," said Wahiba, a Muslim woman from a town north of Paris. "I will only respect laws of the French Republic which are not in contradiction with me, my religion and my faith" (Navasivayam, 2011, April 11).

objectification is the result of an overly boundaried self. Objectification is not possible under conditions of no boundaries—unity consciousness—where we perceive no spiritual separation between ourselves and others. Rather, objectification only becomes possible when we are able to say with regard to other individuals and other forms of life, "I am not that; that has nothing to do with me." Making such distinctions allows us to treat that which is not perceived as part of ourselves as an *it*, as an object, the interior experience of which does not register as worthy of consideration. This "spirit of objectification" can even take place in our interactions with inert, inorganic objects, such as a parcel of land or a lake, were we to fail to consider the object's place or role in the natural order before deciding how or whether to act upon it. Of course, some objects, such as a stone, will merit little or no consideration, whereas others, such as an 800-year-old Redwood tree, should merit considerable attention. Some of how we proceed will be based on the amount of interiority we assume is present in "the other." This is why we are correct to be more concerned with the experience of a gorilla than we are with a grasshopper, for example. But interiority is not the only criterion worthy of consideration. The ocean, for example, has no discernible consciousness or interiority that we are aware of, and yet, it represents an extraordinarily vast ecosystem of life upon which the planet's well-being depends. Our capacities to experience self-in-other in a condition of no boundary (unity consciousness) allows us to honor all of existence as manifestations of the Great Whole, while at the same time making pragmatic distinctions of intrinsic worth, "realizing that it is better to kick a rock than an ape, much better to eat a carrot than a cow, much better to subsist on grains than on mammals" (Wilber, 1996, p. 36).

As one's boundaries of self are constricted and rigidified, non-identification with the other becomes the status quo, making objectification more likely. Conversely, as one's self-boundaries are expanded and increasingly flexible, the ability to feel connected to or identified with the other becomes more possible, making objectification less likely. Given that unity consciousness is quite rare among human beings, it seems reasonable to conclude that most of us have a sense of self that is boundaried to some degree, and we are therefore prone toward some degree of objectification.

BOUNDARIES AND THE SELF

Above, I made the assertion that objectification is a byproduct of a boundaried self, a by-product of the declaration, "I am not that." A moment's reflection will lead to the realization that simply referring to oneself as "I" is to create a boundary between oneself and everything else. Therefore, referring to oneself as "I" is the primary or foundational boundary that makes all other boundaries possible.

Our best science tells us that human infants, so far as we can tell, and so long as they are parented reasonably well, can perceive no real division or separation between themselves and the world around them: If they feel hungry, they cry and are soon fed; if they are wet, they cry and soon get changed into dry clothing; if they feel other types of distress, they cry and are soon picked up and soothed. In the mind of the infant, she is all that exists; she is synonymous with her caregivers—not as the result of a long process of maturation and self-transcendence ending in enlightenment (i.e., unity consciousness), but because she is immature or "primitive" in that she has not yet developed the mental capacity to perceive of differences at all.

However, at some point, typically within the first two years, the child comes to realize—due to increasing cognitive complexity, and to not having her immediate desires and needs met in every instance—that she is, in fact, not synonymous with her caregivers, but physically distinct from them. The establishment of "object permanence" is an important part of this process. Although there is some controversy over just how early very young children begin to develop this capacity, there is agreement that during the first few months of life, infants do not understand that objects out of sight do not in fact disappear. For example, a toy car moving along a track which then disappears behind a screen would be perceived by an observing young infant as an object that has ceased to exist. However, as cognitive capacities and life experience increase, infants come to realize that the car continues to exist despite it having disappeared behind a screen.

This type of awareness is an essential part in beginning the process of differentiation that has as one of its results the awareness of "I" or a consciousness of self. These perceptions are further nurtured and encouraged by caregivers and others who interact with the young child as an entity separate and distinct from themselves, striving, among other things, to teach the child appropriate boundaries of self (e.g., "This is Jimmy's cup, not yours. You shouldn't take Jimmy's cup. How do you think that made Jimmy feel when you took his cup?"). When the child becomes old enough to conceptualize, even in a rudimentary way, her sense of self, she is, in essence, drawing further mental boundaries through the totality of her experiences. When she responds to the question, "Who are you?" she describes herself as what's on the inside of the line she has drawn. For example, she knows she is a human and not a dog, and she knows this because of the line she has drawn between humans and animals; she also knows she is a girl and not a boy, has blonde hair and not brown hair, so she includes these aspects within her self-boundary, and so forth. As she continues to grow and mature, her boundary lines, and thus her self-definition, will likely grow in complexity; she may come to see herself in relational terms, political terms, scientific terms, theological terms, philosophical terms, and so forth, but for the rest of her life, whenever she responds to the question, "Who are you?" she makes reference to the figurative boundary she has drawn that demarcates what is inside as "me" and what is outside as "not me" (Wilber, 2001, p. 4).

Throughout life, this boundary of self can and does fluctuate depending upon where a person draws the line. In other words, boundary lines are not carved in stone; they are fluid and fluctuating. For some individuals, the self-boundary can be quite constricted and rigid. Others, in the midst of a so-called "identity crisis," lose their bearings regarding their sense of self and struggle to find new comfortable parameters of self-definition. And yet for enlightened others, as we have seen above, the self-boundary can be re-mapped so extensively that there is, in effect, no boundary at all. In the case of unity consciousness, the person comes to be identified with the "one harmonious whole," which places no limiting factor on the self (Wilber, 2001, p. 5). Most individuals, however, seem to lie somewhere between the two extremes. While there are as many unique ways to draw self-boundaries as there are people who draw them, there do seem to be some commonalities, which can be grouped into recognizable categories as depicted in Figure 6.2. Again, Wilber is highly informative in this realm (1996, 1998, 2001).

Wilber (2001) makes the crucial point that the different "doctors of the soul" who appear to be clamoring for the allegiance of the suffering masses are best understood not as spokespersons proclaiming a particular brand of

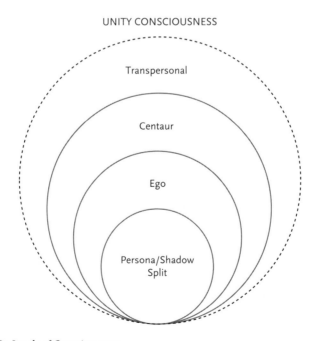

Figure 6.2: Levels of Consciousness
Source: Adapted and used by permission from K. Wilber, *No Boundary: Eastern and Western Approaches to Spiritual Growth* (Boston: Shambhala Publications, 2001), p. 9.

therapy as the ultimate answer for all (despite the fact that some of them seem to feel this way about their therapeutic approach), but rather, as a remedy for suffering occurring at a *particular level* of the "consciousness spectrum" (pp. 11–12). Typically, this involves helping a person transcend their current perspective. When this happens, the person has effectively "re-mapped [her] soul" to enlarge its territory (p. 13). Because objectification arises from a misappropriation of boundaries that place limits on ourselves and exclude the "other" from our consideration of what really matters, it will be important to understand the different self-boundaries available. It is to these that we now turn.

CHAPTER 7

Boundaries of Self

The emergence of suffering is not so much good as it's a good sign, an indication that one is starting to realize that life lived outside unity consciousness is ultimately painful, distressing, and sorrowful. . . . Suffering, then, is the initial movement of the recognition of false boundaries.

Ken Wilber (2001, p. 76)

THE SKIN BARRIER

Wilber (2001) begins by acknowledging the most basic and least complex of self-boundaries, the skin barrier. This seems to be accepted as a nearly universal line demarcating the self from the not-self. Everything beneath the level of the skin is considered "me," while everything outside this barrier is thought of as "not me." Anything lying outside this limit, such as a house or a job, can be thought of as "mine," that is, as something possessed, but it is not thought of as "me" in the same way as that which lies within the skin. As the barrier that protects the inner organism from the external environment and forms the external contours constituting the unique physical appearance of each human being, the skin boundary seems the most natural of boundaries to reference when understanding boundaries of self. Though this skin boundary may seem the most natural boundary, it is not the most primitive or the most restrictive of the self-boundaries.

LEVEL 1: THE PERSONA

Wilber (2001) points out that most people, when asked, will say that their sense of themselves is not necessarily synonymous with their body or the skin that covers it. In fact, most people feel that they *have* a body, not that they *are* a body. Their sense of self seems to be located within a very specific, bounded region of the body—namely, somewhere inside the head where the mind and personality are felt to reside. Wilber points out that, biologically, there is not the least warrant for this split or dissociation between the mind and the body; in other words, "brain-meat is still just meat." But psychologically, this is how it seems. The head—a discrete location within the head to be precise—is in charge, and the body is perceived to come along as it's told by the head's control center. Wilber mentions the thirteenth-century Catholic monk Saint Francis's reference to his body as "poor brother ass" as speaking a truth about how Western men and women have come to view their bodies—as an appendage of their heads, often in conflict with their heads. Developmental psychologists tell us that the mind/ body split is not present at birth, nor is it present in very young children—they have not the slightest qualms with their bodies nor their body's products, as every parent knows. However, as children begin to draw up boundaries of self/ not self, they have to sort out how to view their bodies: Is the body a friend, given the very real sources of fascination and pleasure it provides? Or is the body primarily a problem, given the fact that it gets sick, injured, pimpled, odorous, has appetites, and that its byproducts are usually the first source of conflict with parents? Typically, by the time we reach adulthood, we have centered our sense of self not with our body, not with our organism as a whole, not even with our mind as a whole, *but only with a portion of our mind*.

For a variety of reasons, we can be threatened by some of our own thoughts and tendencies to the extent that we refuse to admit them into our self-boundary. Such impulses could include anger, resentment, erotic impulses, assertiveness, aggressive impulses, doubt, creativity, enthusiasm, and even joy. Because of our extreme negative appraisal of such material, we repress, split off, or project such tendencies onto others in order to disavow them or to deny their existence. Carl Jung made reference to the symbolic realm of the mind where such thoughts and impulses are banished as *the shadow*; the narrowed self-image that we allow into awareness and self-image he called *the persona* (Greek for "actor"). Because we resist the shadow, we erect a figurative boundary in the midst of our psyche in an attempt to banish the threatening material from our conscious awareness. However, such banishment is more like forcing the impulses into the closet and then trying to forget about them. Such actions do not destroy or eliminate the impulses; they still exist, but are only disavowed. We have narrowed our boundaries to include only those parts of ourselves that are consistent with our preferred self-image, while the rest of our thoughts and feelings are pushed out of awareness. We then live our lives as emotionally impoverished, limited persons.

Healing the Persona/Shadow Split

Wilber asserts that most people find themselves "trapped in the persona" (Wilber, 2001, p. 80). Because of the lack of integration existing within the our psyche and the internal conflicts that this engenders, the persona level of self-boundary is where we find the most common types of emotional suffering experienced by human beings (e.g., depression, anxiety, phobias, eating disorders, obsessions and compulsions, and so forth). Sometimes, however, suffering at the persona level can be extreme. Take, for example, a young woman (let's call her Sally) I once worked with. In large part because of sexual abuse suffered at the hands of her stepfather as a young child, Sally spent much of her free time by herself in a state of semi-starvation, often cutting and burning herself repeatedly. This pitiable young woman was so alienated from central aspects of her own being—mind and body—that she derived a sort of detached pleasure from seeing her own blood and creating blisters on her own flesh, almost as if her body and certain of her thoughts and feelings were not part of her self-system, but a "bad," foreign entity, unworthy of compassion or consideration. There were surely other reasons for her habit of self-injury, but a central cause was the high degree of alienation she experienced from her own body and emotions. In essence, our work together consisted of my attempts to help her gradually transverse the rigid boundaries she had erected around parts of herself—memories, thoughts, and especially feelings—that she viewed as unacceptable. As she gradually came to assimilate these previously denied parts of her experience into her self-image, remarkably, her symptoms and urges toward self-destruction gradually subsided, despite numerous setbacks and attempts on her part to sabotage our work together.

It is no coincidence that Freud experienced his unique insights into the shadow and persona during the Victorian era; a time period that coupled an outward appearance of dignity and restraint with a prevalent (albeit underground) hedonistic aspect. In truth, the Victorian era epitomized the persona *en masse*. Therefore, the aim of the various techniques of psychoanalysis that Freud invented was to mend the chasm between the conscious (persona) and unconscious (shadow) aspects of the psyche so that the person would be in touch with *all* of his or her mind. While psychoanalysis has largely fallen out of vogue, its basic aims still undergird therapies aimed at suffering occurring on the persona level: acknowledging unacceptable "shadow tendencies"—experienced as emotional symptoms or projections onto others—as part of the deeper self needing integration. This is accomplished in the context of a therapeutic relationship of warmth, respect, and acceptance in which the therapist helps the client view his or her symptoms as signals of unresolved inner conflict. The client's resistance to shadow material often takes the form of slips of the tongue, "going blank," feeling embarrassed, or expressing hostility toward the therapist or other people. This is tactfully explored and interpreted by the therapist. With ongoing acceptance and support, the client can gradually come to acknowledge and accept disowned parts of herself, owning and integrating them in healthy, non-destructive ways. Pieces of wisdom coming from therapies oriented toward helping sufferers transcend the limiting boundaries of the persona might include some of the following:

- That which we resist persists.
- If you're unwilling to experience a negative emotion, you will; if you're willing to have the emotion, you likely won't.
- Acceptance of the seemingly unacceptable leads to transformation.
- To diminish anxiety in the long run, do the opposite of what it is telling you to do now.
- Fighting or resisting anxiety worsens it; accepting anxiety—"floating" through anxiety—causes it to fade sooner.
- That which we loathe or hate in others is typically that which we can't accept in ourselves.
- Depressive symptoms can be an adaptive response of the psyche to unresolved emotional conflict.

The goal is to help the client move past the persona/shadow split and into a strong and healthy ego, which is an accurate and acceptable self-image where all thoughts and feelings are deemed "tolerable, even if not actionable" (Wilber, 2001, p. 12).

LEVEL 2: THE EGO

If the persona level can be likened to living in a cramped apartment, moving into the level of the ego is like upgrading to a roomier and well-appointed home (Wilber, 2001, p. 94). For many orthodox psychologists who practice one of the many versions of cognitive/behavioral therapy (CBT), a strong, healthy, "accurate" ego, freed from the confines of the persona's limiting boundaries, is considered to be a person's real self. This is as good as it gets.

The ideal of the ego level is to think rationally about life's many adversities; doing so helps keep our negative emotions at a manageable, healthy level. The ancient Roman philosopher Epictetus's maxim, "People are not upset by things, but rather, by the view they take of things," undergirds the entirety of the ego level's wisdom. From this perspective, the capacity to think rationally and logically is considered to be the best solution to emotional and relational problems because changing one's thoughts often leads to a change in the way one feels and behaves. Therefore, enhancing the client's ability to think rationally under all situations is the ultimate goal of cognitive/behavioral therapy (CBT). Empirical research has shown that there is truth in this assumption: Many neurotic problems, such as depression and a variety of anxiety disorders, can be helped by the conscious attempt to bring rational thought to bear on one's perceived problems in living (Butler, Chapman, Forman, & Beck, 2006). Rational thought can be a great boon to one's life. Many problems are avoided by thinking rationally about circumstances and their implications, just as many problems are solved through the use of logical thought. Indeed, it seems that much of the world's conflict and suffering could be diminished if the parties involved simply increased their capacity and willingness to think rationally about their problems. In addition to Epictetus's maxim mentioned above, other pieces of CBT wisdom can help alleviate suffering when understood and internalized deeply:

- All human beings are flawed, imperfect, and fallible; therefore, it is irrational to believe that we or other people should always be competent and not make mistakes.
- All human beings are self-interested and free to act as they choose; therefore, it is irrational to believe that people must do what we want them to.
- Conditions in the world (i.e., the weather, the price of gas at the pump, traffic on the freeway, etc.) are not subject to our ability to control them; therefore, it is irrational to say that they must be to our liking in order for us to have equanimity.
- There are very few genuine "musts" in life (e.g., you must breathe if you want to live; you must die at some point). In truth, most desirable outcomes are actually *preferences* rather than *musts*; therefore, it is irrational to think in terms of musts rather than preferences.
- Ultimate human worth comes not from one's performance in various life realms, but from being a member of the species. Therefore, all human beings have equal worth, and ultimate human worth cannot be added to or diminished from.

Despite this collection of wisdom, significant problems may still arise at this level. As boundaries remain present at all non-unity levels of the consciousness spectrum, so too are they present at the ego level. Here, we befriend or identify ourselves with our unboundaried mind (speaking figuratively, of course), but not with our organism as a whole. In other words, we identify ourselves with a more or less accurate mental self-image, along with the intellectual and emotional processes associated with that self-image, but our self-boundary ends here. The remainder of our organism is not included—"I am my head, but I own my body" (Wilber, 2001, p. 95). Identified with our ego, we are largely disconnected from our deeper feelings and impressions, as they seem to arise from our viscera, "from the gut." Many emotions, urges, and feelings that arise in the body are threatening or socially taboo, and therefore are difficult to accept.

What the shadow was at the persona level, the rest of the body is at the ego level—a disowned aspect of the self. Yet, these discarded elements often return in the form of projections, which can torment the individual in indirect and often symbolic ways. Imagine, for example, a pious, soft-spoken religious man who, as part of his identity, sees himself as a good golfer. He's also personally invested in the idea that he doesn't need to impress others. One afternoon, he's on the golf course with some of his work colleagues for the first time; he's typically a competent golfer, but today, in front his colleagues, he misses short putts, skulls chip shots, and hits errant drives. His egoic need to be a good golfer (and to impress others, despite his unwillingness to acknowledge this to himself) has likely impeded his performance. Consequently, he's more anxious than usual, his face is flushed, he sweats profusely, his muscles are tight, and he's not very communicative. He suppresses his awareness of the stress reaction of his body and what this could teach him, as these are not in keeping his perceived ability as a golfer. As in the case of issues at the persona level, this suppression pushes the reality of his problem—that he cares too much about playing well in front of others—out of consciousness, but doesn't solve it, and he continues to operate in a state of dysfunction, creating discord between his body, his mental state, and reality. This denial keeps him from acknowledging his egoic desires and adjusting his perceptions accordingly, an adjustment that might decrease his anxiety and allow him to enjoy the game. All of his defensiveness keeps him from turning golf into a "spiritual practice" in which his primary goal is to accept in a rational way whatever his golf game dishes out, all while attempting to play each shot as well as he can.

It should also be pointed out that proponents of the Perennial Philosophy (i.e., unity consciousness) assert that the "egoic self," despite its capacities for reason and logic, has other defining aspects: wanting, attachment, and self-preoccupation, to name a few. Because of this, the ego is thought to be the well-spring of human conflict and suffering. Contemplatives over the millennia have also considered the ego to be synonymous with the incessant, often random, unproductive thought content typical of most people's wakeful experience. Such thoughts, they allege, are largely centered on worrying about the future or regretting the past; they do not represent a focus of attention on the present moment of experience. The ego is highly oriented toward this "existence in time," or a focus on past and future as separate from the present. Because of this, the ego exists in a state of perpetual flight from death, preventing a person from residing in the present moment (more will be said of this in Chapter 11).

Perhaps it is also no coincidence that Fritz Perls and Abraham Maslow came to prominence when they did—during the late 1950s and 1960s. The sixties, were, of course, a time of throwing off the restraints, pretensions, and allegiances of previous generations. Questioning authority and reconnecting to the body's capacities became hallmarks of the era. Both Maslow and Perls championed philosophic and therapeutic approaches to help mend the rift between the mind and body. The "human potential" movement, as it was called, emphasized gaining access to the full range of human capacities—mental, physical, emotional, and spiritual—in order to reach one's ultimate potential. Wilber uses the symbol of the centaur from Greek mythology to represent the goal of integrating the mental with the physical. The centaur—half human and half horse—represents a harmonious union between the mind and body: not a person riding on and in control of her horse, but a person who is one with her horse; "not a psyche separated from and in control of soma, but a self-controlling, self-governing, psychosomatic unity" (Wilber, 2001, p. 72).

Because the person at the ego level is identified with his or her mind, and the mind's primary capacity is to generate thoughts, the primary resistance at the ego level is to *resist the present moment of experience in favor of thought*. In other words, the ego's resistance is to true present-centered awareness for any length of time (Wilber, 2001; Tolle, 2004, 2008). Therefore, "centauric" therapies (i.e., humanistic, existential, and Gestalt) focus on grounding the person in his immediate experience, the immediate present in all its forms, and the body-mind awareness, which discloses the present moment. Thus, the person involved in such therapies is asked to recognize and suspend her "mind chatter" and focus awareness on the immediate here-and-now. The therapist helps by watching for any flight from present awareness into the realm of detached intellectual analysis or avoidance. Over time, the person comes to understand how she evades the centaur by escaping into the ego, and she sees the main effect that this has on her life—detracting from the present, the only place where life actually happens. The integration of mind, body, and emotions allows the person to achieve a higher degree of self-unity and a greater connection to her life experience. This puts her on the path toward becoming her highest potential self.

LEVEL 3: CENTAURIC AWARENESS

At the level of the centaur, the person has successfully integrated mind and body. She has made peace with her body in all its facets: its appearance, its processes, and the wisdom of its signals and messages. She has connected her mind and soma, a seamless blend where "me" is seen as a unity of one's physical and mental self. She no longer divides herself into spirit/mind (good) and body (bad). In addition, attending to the body's immediate experience has taught her how to cultivate mindfulness, which is simply another way of saying that she has learned how to be more fully present, aware, and accepting of the current moment of experience, whatever that experience may be (e.g., washing dishes, driving to work, playing golf poorly, jogging in the park, sitting with family around the dinner table, attending an insurance seminar, lying sick in bed, etc.). She has also come to understand the truth of two pieces of related, paradoxical wisdom, which assert:

- The best way to create suffering is to refuse to accept reality because you're out of alignment with "what is" (Tolle, 2008; Brach, 2003).
- The only way to change oneself and the world is to bring full acceptance to both oneself and the world as it is (Schuler, 1985; Rogers, 1961).

She does not resist "what is," but accepts present circumstances and experiences (without necessarily preferring them), which puts her in a psychological position of resonant alignment with reality. She has come to understand that this position allows her to be more peaceful and calm and to act in ways most appropriate to actual circumstances.

However, this centauric focus on the present moment, remarkable as it is, has its limitations: It is a focus on a moment that is perceived as always passing away into the past while expecting a future which always has yet to be. In other words, centauric awareness is present awareness—meaningful present awareness—but it is not awareness of *the now* as an eternally existing present. The concept of an "always existing present moment" may be difficult for many Westerners to comprehend and may smack of New Age deepity, but this need not be. Wilber (2001) uses the Latin term *nunc fluens* to designate the type of awareness of the present that is fragmented by seeing a past behind it, and a future before it. This is contrasted with the *nunc stans*, the highest type of present awareness (i.e., unity consciousness), which experiences the past as memory occurring in present experience, and the future as a sense of expectation, also in the present moment. In this way, *nunc stans* is an experience of life that is perpetually present-focused and present-experienced (Wilber, 2001, p. 63). Also, centauric awareness is limited by its identification with the mind/body fusion. Unity consciousness, on the other hand, shows that human existence is a seamless blend with the rest of existence, that the inner-self, body-self, and outer environment are manifestations of the same universal entity. Centauric awareness is limited because it perceives a disconnection with what lies outside the individual's mind and body.

In order to move beyond the familiar and common-sense boundaries of the physical and mental self, further shifts of perspective are necessary. Experiences which demonstrate that identity can transcend the boundaries of self, species, even life itself are required for further spiritual evolution. Most modern human beings, at least those in the West, are often disconnected from the realms of the transcendent due to a loss of previous religious moorings. They are likely to consider such ideas or experiences as being tantamount to a loss of sanity. They will be incredulous at the notion that they possess the capacity, buried deeply within themselves, to transcend their own individuality and to connect to a world beyond conventional space and time (Wilber,

2001). Yet, the disclosures of the world's great contemplatives have been attempting to communicate these realities to us for thousands of years.

LEVEL 4: THE TRANSPERSONAL

What Freud was to the persona, and Maslow and Perls were to the ego, Carl Jung was to the centaur. Jung was the first major Western psychologist to not only systematically document his insights and observations into the realms of selfhood that transcend the individual's mind/body fusion, but he also devised an approach to psychotherapy aimed at enhancing individuals' ability to access such vast, subtle territory in order to further expand their dormant potential.

Jung, who started his illustrious career as Freud's most promising disciple, soon parted ways with his mentor. Though a gifted analyst, Jung was most deeply fascinated not by the problem of specific neuroses per se, but rather, by the wisdom revealed by the world's great mythologies, legends, and systems of religious thought from antiquity and by how the lives of modern human beings could come into alignment with the deeper sources of wisdom disclosed by these traditions. In the midst of his studies of gods, goddesses, totems, animisms, symbols, images, mythological tales, motifs, and sacrificial and sacramental rites from cultures the world over, he discovered that some of his patients, without prior exposure to such esoteric material, nonetheless exhibited in their dreams and daydreams an astonishing "awareness" of some of the symbols and motifs he had uncovered in his studies. Because these individuals had no prior awareness of such material from the content of their lives, Jung postulated that such information must represent a vast storehouse of subtly felt but deeply imbedded human truth passed on over the millennia, perhaps spiritually, perhaps within the very neurons of the brain itself, from ancestors to progeny. The symbolic forms themselves—such as the earth mother, the trickster, the shadow, the persona, the mandala, the hero, and others—he called *archetypes* or "universal forms," representing the collective experience or wisdom of the species. The vast reservoir of these impressions he called the *collective unconscious.* Jung saw these processes as representing innate human programming for transcendence. He came to believe that attending to these subtle impressions within could lead one into new realms of self-awareness, whereas ignoring, suppressing, or denying the existence of these processes would lead to personal stultification and collective pathology. Here is a classic description of just such a process at work in the life of one of Jung's (1960) female patients:

> My example concerns a young woman patient who, in spite of efforts made on
> both sides, proved to be psychologically inaccessible. [. . .]After several fruitless

attempts to sweeten her rationalism[. . .] I had to confine myself to the hope that something unexpected and irrational would turn up, something that would burst the intellectual retort into which she had sealed herself. [. . .] I was sitting opposite of her one day, with my back to the window, listening to her flow of rhetoric. She had an impressive dream the night before, in which someone had given her a golden scarab—a costly piece of jewelry. While she was still telling me this dream, I heard something behind me gently tapping on the window. I turned round and saw that it was a fairly large flying insect that was knocking against the window. . . . This seemed to me very strange. I opened the window immediately and caught the insect in the air as it flew in. It was a scarabaeid beetle, or Rose-Chafer, whose golden green color most nearly resembles that of a golden scarab. I handed the beetle to my patient with the words "Here is your scarab." This broke the ice of her intellectual resistance. The treatment could now be continued with satisfactory results [. . .] Any essential change of attitude [in the patient] signifies a psychic renewal which is usually accompanied by symbols of rebirth in the patient's dreams and fantasies. The scarab is a classic example of a rebirth symbol. [. . .] The psychologist is continually coming up against cases where the emergence of symbolic parallels cannot be explained without the hypothesis of the collective unconscious. (pp. 23–24, 109)

Jung went on to acknowledge that he realized that such experiences would not convince anyone who was determined to see chance as the operative principle at work in such situations to change his or her mind. But for Jung, such archetypally pregnant "meaningful coincidences [often] present themselves in practical life" (Jung, 1960, p. 23).

A variety of approaches can allow us to access the transpersonal realm of consciousness. Some involve the more classically Jungian approach of analyzing the archetypal images and themes present in our dreams and daydreams. Other, more "Eastern" strategies, such as mindfulness meditation, while not specifically related to Jung's concepts of archetypes or the collective unconscious, are aimed at helping us make the realization that we are "more" than our thoughts and feelings. Indeed, we are "the conscious awareness in the background" behind the incessant chatter of thoughts and feelings, an ". . . unmoved witness of all [our] thoughts, emotions, feelings, and desires" (Wilber, 2001, p. 115). Making frequent contact with this background consciousness and perceiving reality from its perspective allows us to be at one with life. Wisdom from the transpersonal perspective might sound like this:

- Our sense of self is determined by where we are focusing our conscious awareness.
- We have thoughts and feelings, but our true self is not synonymous with them. We can observe and intuit our thoughts and feelings, and what can be observed or intuited cannot be the true Knower.

- Accessing the present moment of experience in an attitude of complete acceptance—in other words, becoming truly mindful—brings liberation from neurotic suffering and is the doorway to enlightenment.

This dis-identification with our thoughts and feelings provides liberation from the suffering they so often engender. From the perspective of the "witness," we begin to view our thoughts and feelings much as we would view an object, such as a desk, a briefcase, or a tree—that is, with relative calm and objectivity. Paradoxically, on the other hand, because of their divestment from their own egoic processes, individuals at the transpersonal level also begin to experience all objects from the environment as if they were part of their own selves. These experiences are intimations of unity consciousness. In Figure 6.2 in Chapter 6, this is represented by the "broken" circle, which suggests periodic openness to intuitions which confirm that the world really is one's own self/body and is to be treated as such. When understood from such a perspective, it becomes clearer how the world's great saints and mystics, such as the Buddha, Jesus, or Mahatma Gandhi, were able to garner such radical compassion and identification with all of existence.

The primary goal of transpersonally oriented therapies is to assist human beings in acknowledging, befriending, and "utilizing these powerful forces instead of being moved by them unconsciously, against their will" (Wilber, 2001, p. 113). Individuals are encouraged to intuit the universal stirrings within, to see themselves not from a limited, boundaried, idiosyncratic perspective, but from the vantage point of the entire species throughout history. Transpersonal therapies are also aimed at helping individuals become more consciously aware of the limitations they too often place on themselves through identification with their own mind and body. Transpersonal therapies encourage individuals to recognize that whatever adversities are being perceived at present, a deeper, wiser Self transcends current problems and makes available a broader, more liberated perspective from which to act. Nonetheless, the transpersonal level of consciousness still has in place one final boundary: the "background witness" as an entity separate from all that is witnessed. Transpersonal awareness realizes the mirage of identifying oneself with anything other than consciousness itself. But in unity consciousness, all boundaries collapse and there is no perceived separation between the witnesser and what is witnessed. The final boundary, then, for the transpersonal stage of consciousness, is the realization of unity consciousness itself.

At every level of the consciousness spectrum (other than unity consciousness), boundaries exist either within the self or between the self and the environment. Wherever a boundary is drawn, the potential for conflict arises and objectification of "the other" becomes more likely. Upward movement through the spectrum—for example, from persona to ego, from ego to centaur, from centaur to transpersonal—entails the transcending of boundaries, which is simply another way of saying that some disowned aspect of the self has been reclaimed. Psychotherapy is only one method that can be helpful in assisting some individuals with dissolving their stultifying boundaries, but it alone cannot provide the radical transformation necessary for the dissolution of the final boundary. That—as the Perennial Philosophy asserts—is the ultimate problem of enlightenment, requiring transcendence of the egoic self. Or, as Aldous Huxley (1970) put it, in language borrowed from the biblical tradition, "becoming loving, pure in heart, and poor in spirit" (p. x).[1] This final frontier entails, in all but a few cases, the work of a lifetime, or—from the perspective of Eastern wisdom traditions, as if to emphasize just how monumental the task is—many lifetimes.

I use the word *work* in this context, but this is misleading, for while enlightenment can be desired and striven for, these processes can also block or impede the goal. Indeed, having enlightenment as an end goal can be problematic because it suggests one's misalignment or unacceptance of "what is" in the present moment, which is a substantial impediment to growth. The problem of selflessness is one that cannot be approached directly; it represents a paradox that can be successfully approached only as one becomes increasingly attuned to and accepting of the present moment. In this state, one drops the distractions, ambitions, anxious strivings, worries, regrets, and resentments that represent the status quo of self-preservation and self-promotion. As this occurs, paradoxically, one becomes more authentically oneself. In other words, one becomes more Self and less self as one forgets the self's personal agendas and becomes one with the present moment. This process seems to include substantial portions of what might best be termed "grace," or unmerited assistance coming from a Source that transcends the self. The world's great wisdom literature shows that there are multiple starting points and many paths leading to the proverbial Rome of boundary dissolution and selflessness. While relatively few in number, men and women have been transversing the consciousness spectrum for millennia—long before the invention of psychotherapy; and the select few who have attained the highest levels of enlightenment, such as the Buddha or Jesus,[2] have gone on to forever change the course of human history.

1. The language used here by Huxley is clearly biblical in nature, but such concepts are universal throughout the world's great wisdom traditions.
2. In this example, I do not compare Jesus and Buddha in terms of the specific claims the two faiths make regarding their respective figures (i.e., Buddha was born human and attained enlightenment, whereas Jesus was born part human and part divine, becoming God), but rather, with respect to the degree to which both figures are representative of the very best that human beings can strive for.

Above, I made what appears to be a glaring contradiction: On one hand, I stated that transcending boundaries is simply another way of saying that a person has reclaimed some disowned aspect of the self, and in so doing, progresses up the spectrum to higher levels of consciousness. On the other hand, I have asserted that from the perspective of the Perennial Philosophy, becoming enlightened is synonymous with the negation of the self: "becoming truly loving, pure in heart, and poor in spirit." Naturally, this suggests (again) a paradox in which the self, as it becomes more whole, unified, and thus "large," also moves toward the possibility of merger with the Ground of all being. Such a merger results in the self's parameters becoming so expansive that they are, in effect, obliterated as the self "becomes one" with others, even one with the rest of existence. One no longer sees a separation between oneself and the dirt beneath one's feet, or oneself and the ocean, or oneself and a tree; there is only one. While the realization of unity consciousness is indeed rare, intimations of it are much less so. "Successive approximations" of unity consciousness comprise the background informing much of the world's great poetic literature, its mystical-religious literature, and even some of its philosophical literature. One such example is contained in Martin Buber's 1913 book, *Daniel*, which recounts a small but profound experience he had one day while out walking:

> On a gloomy morning, I walked upon the highway, saw a piece of mica lying there, picked it up, and looked at it for a long time; the day was no longer gloomy, so much light was caught by the stone. And suddenly, as I raised my eyes from it, I realised that while I looked I had not been conscious of "object" and "subject"; in my looking, the mica and "I" had been one; in my looking, I had tasted unity. I looked at it again, but unity did not return. Then something flamed up inside me as if I were about to create. I closed my eyes, I gathered my strength, I bound myself with my object, I raised the piece of Mica into the realm of that which has being. And there, Lukas, I first felt: I, there I first was I. He that had looked had not yet been I; only this, this being-in-association bore the name like a crown. Now I feel about this former unity as a marble image might feel about the block from which it has been carved: it was the undifferentiated, while I was the unification. As yet, I did not understand myself. (pp. 140–141)

Buber's brief experience with the mica is an example of the ancient Upanishadic principle, *Tat tvam asi*, or "Thou art that," which asserts that the human Self is a part of the ultimate reality that is the Ground and Origin of all existence. This realization, a result of the deepest perceiving possible (i.e., unity consciousness), appears to come most often to those who have fulfilled the necessary conditions of such knowledge that Huxley mentioned above. Moreover, Huxley asserts:

> [. . .]Direct knowledge of the Ground cannot be had except by union, and union can be achieved only by the annihilation of the self-regarding ego, which is the barrier separating the "thou" from the "That." (1970, pp. x, 1–2, 35)

The highest level of spiritual evolution for any human being is to discover this fact for him- or herself. From this supreme vantage point, one comes to know that not only is one *one* with this Ground, but one is one with all other expressions or manifestations of this Ground. The martyred Iranian Sufi master, Al-Hallaj (ca. 858–922 C.E.), who had tasted of unity consciousness, put it this way:

I saw my Lord with the eye of the Heart
I said: Who are you? He answered: You
You are He Who fills all place
But place does not know where You are
In my subsistence is my annihilation
In my annihilation, I remain You. (Katz, 1978, p. 92)

This was not a case of Al-Hallaj claiming to be God (which was the primary allegation made against him and the reason for his brutal martyrdom), but rather, that he was a manifestation of the divine, and was therefore of divine essence.

Since all human beings share this same essence, all human beings are in this sense equal and represent manifestations of ultimate reality, whether they realize it or not. This perspective is taught in the Christian Gospels when Jesus, in his explication of the parable of the sheep and the goats, says, ". . . Inasmuch as ye have done it unto one of the least of these, my brethren, ye have done it unto me" (KJV; Matt. 25:40). To the extent that all of existence is a manifestation of this same Ground, then everything else has its place in the order of things and has its level of sacredness. This perspective stands in stark contrast to the separated, objectifying self's proclamation, "I am not that," which is a necessary precursor to violence against what one is not.

Some have made the observation that more humans than ever before are moving their way back toward the mouth of Plato's cave—moving in the direction of enlightenment (Taylor, 2005; Keck, 2000). Such comments may seem outlandish, especially when viewed against the backdrop of the seemingly unstemmable tide of human-generated suffering occurring on any given day. However, the gradually increasing awareness and implementation of representative government, broader human rights, animal rights, and concern for the environment, as well as the impulses to act in order to combat the effects of hunger, poverty, disease, famine, and natural disaster in the world's poorer regions, are just a few pieces of evidence that this shift in consciousness is in fact occurring on a larger scale than ever before (Pinker 2011). As more individuals transcend their limiting boundaries of self, it's as if a psychic template is laid down, which impacts others around them and the generations that follow them. Certainly, such influence results, in part, from the behavioral example set by such individuals. But other less obvious factors are likely at play, too. One can imagine that to be in the presence of a Martin Luther King, Jr., a Gandhi, a Buddha, or a Mother Teresa was to find oneself in a psychological and spiritual "zone of liberation" (Fowler, 1981, p. 200) hard to describe. Unfortunately, it also seems to be true of unenlightened individuals—a Mao, a Stalin, a Hitler, a Pol Pot, a bin Laden—their charisma tends to beget further unenlightenment in its various forms. Of course, one need not be famous (or infamous) in order for one's degree of self-liberation or self-centeredness to have an impact on others and generations which follow. The ancient concept of "the iniquity of the fathers being answered upon the heads of the children unto the third and fourth generation" (see, e.g., Exodus 20:5, Deut. 5:9 for just a few biblical examples) seems to speak to such a multi-generational influence, whatever the mechanism. Communities, institutions, and families possess their own "spirit," their own levels of enlightenment or lack thereof, which have undeniable and powerful effects on their constituent members; but enlightenment itself seems to be a personal, individualized process, one that takes place not at the level of the group, nor even between two members of the same community of believers, nor between adherents of a particular creed or code of conduct, but between each person and the Ground of all being. As a once popular song so bluntly put it, ". . . men go crazy in congregations; they only get better one by one" (Sting, 1991). The Dalai Lama has said essentially the same thing: "Although attempting to bring about world peace through the internal transformation of individuals is difficult, it is the only way" (Thich Nhat Hanh, 1991, p. vii).

In the last section of the book, we will be exploring some potential paths out of Plato's cave mentioned previously. These represent humankind's best attempts to solve the problem of objectification. However, it will be worthwhile to first explore more fully some of the all too human stumbling blocks that contribute to our objectification of others.

CHAPTER 8

Narcissism

If you took a blind and deaf organism and gave it self-consciousness and a name, if you made it stand out in nature and know consciously that it was unique, then you would have narcissism.

Ernest Becker *(1974, pp. 2–3)*

When considered superficially, Needleman's first observation (i.e., human beings live in a world of illusions and appearances) is likely to strike most of us as odd. We can acknowledge that we take many things for granted—family, friends, possessions, opportunities, physical and emotional health, and so forth—but we will typically resist the notion that our lives have an illusory quality: "What is it about my life that is an illusion?" we will ask. "Are not my computer, my cell phone, my car, my house, and my spouse and family real?" The sense objects that we encounter daily are, of course, real, though more recent advances in science reveal that their deeper reality is much different from our experience of them (i.e., solid objects are, at subatomic level, mostly open space). But this misses the point. Rather than making specific reference to subatomic particles, the great contemplatives of the past were referring to the typical human being's experience of life as composed primarily of perceptions stemming from a self-centered frame of reference—literally, with the self experienced as the most precious, relevant entity in existence and all else being seen as separate, secondary, and ultimately expendable. Inquiry conducted by developmental psychologists over the past century has echoed these insights from the past: Simply by virtue of being alive, human beings have a profound tendency toward self-preoccupation. This phenomenon has, since the late nineteenth century, gone by the label *narcissism*, a word borrowed from Greek mythology's tale of Narcissus. Several versions of this myth exist from antiquity, but the primary gist of these stories is that a beautiful male youth is condemned by the gods to fall in love with his own reflection in a pool after spurning a would-be lover. As a result, he sits and stares at himself for eternity.

The myth's implications for our tendencies to objectify are obvious: If we view ourselves as vastly more important than others, then it will be hard for them to register as more than superficial blips on our psyche's radar screen.

THREE PERSPECTIVES ON NARCISSISM

Narcissism can be defined in a variety of ways, depending upon the scope of analysis. At the macro level, and most relevant to our purposes here, narcissism can be understood as a reflection of the species-wide tendency toward self-preoccupation and self-concern. The underpinnings of this drive are rooted in the biological pressure toward self-perpetuation and survival. All organisms have a life instinct—a drive to live and go on living. Human beings have as much of that instinct as any other species. But narcissism represents more than just the instinctual desire to survive. I note, for example, that I don't consider my two small dogs to be narcissists, despite the fact that they compete shamelessly against one another for the attention of my wife and me, knocking and pawing each other out of the way in order to be attended to at the other's expense. On the other hand, if our young adult sons exhibited similar behaviors, as their parents, we'd be deeply concerned. Dogs and other animals, while conscious and possessing distinct personality quirks, do not possess a self that can be projected forward in time—they cannot contemplate the inevitability of their physical demise. They act out of instinct, not out of concern for the self's preservation and enhancement in the future, which means they cannot be selfish. Human beings, on the other hand, have the capacity for self-consciousness which makes possible the often problematic conditions of self-inflation, self-promotion, and self-concern—in a word, narcissism. Self-consciousness is necessary for narcissism to exist.

Much more will be said of the problem of death awareness in Chapter 12. Suffice to say that we each hold a few precious individuals dear in our hearts, individuals for whom we claim we would be willing to die. But outside a very limited circle, most of us view our own lives as being more precious and relevant than the lives of others. Combine our innate drive for self-perpetuation with our boundaried sense of self, and our vulnerability to objectifying others makes perfect sense. The sagacious Ernest Becker, who had a knack for seeing through pretense, put it this way:

> We are all hopelessly absorbed with ourselves. If we care about anyone it is usually ourselves first of all. [. . .] It is one of the meaner aspects of narcissism that we feel that practically everyone is expendable except ourselves. [. . .] This narcissism is what keeps men marching into point-blank fire in wars: at heart, one doesn't feel that he will die, he only feels sorry for the man next to him. [. . .] None of these observations implies human guile. On the contrary, man does

not seem able to "help" his selfishness; it seems to come from his animal nature. (1974, pp. 2–3).

At a more practical level of analysis, narcissism can be viewed as a trait that exists on a continuum, like most other human traits. Relatively benign forms of narcissism can be observed in "well-adjusted" men and women whose daily lives are composed of a mixture of selfish aims interspersed with meaningful service to others (though perhaps not surprisingly, men tend to score higher on measures of narcissism than do women [Carroll, 1987]). More malignant varieties of narcissism are exhibited by those who aggressively and repeatedly promote their own interests in ways that detrimentally impact the lives of others. Indeed, such individuals show a marked inability to connect to the inner experience of others, because other people rarely register as more than pawns to be used toward their own ends. The ability to be moved by the suffering of others decreases as physical or emotional distance increases. One example of this would be the calm, collected pilot who "just follows orders" and drops tons of high explosives on an unseen civilian population thousands of feet below. Indeed, narcissism appears to be a built-in emotional distancer to which all human beings are subject, though narcissistic tendencies are thought to vary from person to person as a measurable personality variable (Raskin and Howard, 1988).[1] While there is some controversy, most mental health experts seem to be in agreement that a mild degree of narcissism is healthy as a sort of self-defense against life's adversities, such as criticism, loss of status, and disappointments of various types.

At the micro/individual level of analysis, narcissism is understood as a maladaptive personality condition: a state with deleterious impacts on the lives of the subject and those around her. At present, so-called "narcissistic personality disorder" (NPD) is not considered to be a mental illness per se (which would presume a causal defect in the brain's normal chemical functioning). Rather, NPD is thought to be a characterological defect that may have both hereditary and environmental determinants (Lively, Jang, Jackson, & Vernon, 1993). The list of traits associated with the disorder is long, and reads like a caricature of a bad Roman emperor. Those who meet diagnostic criteria for NPD exhibit the following behavior and attitudes (American Psychiatric Association, 2013):

- A high degree of grandiosity;
- Fantasies of unlimited power;
- Preoccupation with success, brilliance, beauty, and ideal love;

---

1. The Narcissistic Personality Inventory (NPI) is perhaps the most widely used measure of narcissism presently in use. It is relatively quick and easy to self-administer. To assess your own level of narcissism, take the NPI located in the Appendix at the back of the book.

- Perceptions of specialness or uniqueness;
- A need to associate with high-status people or institutions;
- A sense of entitlement;
- Unreasonable expectations of especially favorable treatment;
- Interpersonal exploitativeness;
- Lack of empathy;
- Envy of others or assuming others are envious of oneself;
- Arrogant, haughty attitudes. (p. 327)

Narcissistic personality disorder is thought to be present in approximately 6 percent of the population, and to decrease in severity with age (Mays, 2010). Narcissistic traits are commonly (i.e., normally) observed in adolescents, but they typically diminish significantly by adulthood and continue to lessen as the person ages. There are likely a number of factors responsible for this diminution. The inevitability of aging is perhaps the single greatest factor that decreases an individual's tendencies toward narcissism—nothing takes a person down a few pegs like realizing the obvious toll time has taken on his or her body and mind. Other substantial factors can include the impact of having children, the gradual accumulation of life-adversities and setbacks, and in males, the general decrease in testosterone concomitant with age.

THREE TYPES OF NARCISSISM

Experts believe that there are three variants of narcissistic personalities (Mays, 2010). *High-functioning* narcissists tend to be exhibitionistic and display a substantial degree of self-importance, but they are also quite energetic, articulate, outgoing, and achievement-oriented. Some politicians, Hollywood celebrities, sports stars, and other well-compensated, socially prominent individuals seem to match this description. On the other hand, *vulnerable/compensating* narcissists, despite their show of self-confidence and bravado, have fragile self-esteem requiring constant over-compensation. In my therapeutic practice, most of the relatively few clients I've seen with diagnosable NPD have represented this subtype. In such cases, there has often been a history of severe parental neglect and emotional abuse in the form of significant criticism, belittlement, or abandonment. This type of narcissism is therefore "come by honestly," acting primarily as a cover or compensation for the person's deep sense of inferiority and insecurity. Finally, the *malignant* narcissist displays intense grandiosity, and believes that he embodies perfection. These individuals tend to feel privileged, to exploit others, and to crave power.

Regardless of subtype, all narcissists share a desire to be adored—to be given attention for being unique and special. As a result, these individuals can be very difficult to treat in psychotherapy because they rarely (if ever) engage in self-scrutiny or seek out psychiatric help on their own. They tend not to see themselves as having problems; if they do, they view the cause of these problems as other people. For example, a narcissistic man might come to therapy for the first time and say, "Doctor, you've got to help me do something about my (expletive) wife—she's driving me (expletive) nuts. . . ." If the therapist were to hastily suggest to this man that he had some substantial personal problems himself in need of intervention, the client would see the therapist as yet another person who "just doesn't get it," and likely would abandon treatment.

A former client of mine offers a remarkable example of both vulnerable and malignant narcissism, as well as the difficulties of working with such individuals in psychotherapy.[2] This client was an intelligent, charismatic, attractive young woman in her mid-twenties who came from a deeply troubled background that included severe parental neglect and abuse.[3] She was a highly opinionated, married woman with a three-year-old daughter. Despite her chaotic and highly dysfunctional past, my client seemed to have accomplished much— including marriage to a rather passive young man—and somehow knew a great deal about almost any topic you could imagine—politics, philosophy, biology, current events, airplane piloting, guitar playing, operatic performance, poetry, sky diving, scuba diving, fishing, home repair, golf at some of the country's most exclusive courses, and the nuances of travel on both US coasts and many points between. Indeed, just in terms of her general fund of knowledge, she was unlike any young person I had met before, reminding me of a (somewhat tongue-in-cheek) twist on a recent television advertising campaign for the Dos Equis brand of beer, narrated wryly by PBS *Frontline's* Will Lyman—"Meet [Jane] Goldsmith: the most interesting [woman] in the world. . . ."

Her reasons for coming to therapy had largely to do with her frustrations with authority figures. They had an agenda for her which she resented: "Play by the same rules as everyone else." To her, this was all too often experienced as an insult to her sensibilities. She had managed to develop something of a small following. She and some like-minded individuals were planning a confrontation with city council and police regarding a number of grievances regarding "unreasonable" restrictions on parking and other perceived hassles. Her life seemed to revolve around such causes.

My task early on was to simply attempt to build a rapport with her so that I would have a chance of being more helpful to her later on. I listened

---

2. Out of respect for my client's privacy I have followed the American Psychological Association's guidelines (American Psychological Association, 2009) to protect confidentiality. Also, it will become clear through this example that narcissists are rarely "pure" in terms of their subtype.

3. Narcissistic personality disorder, with a general population prevalence of 6.2 percent, is almost twice as common in males (7.7 percent) as it is in females (4.8 percent) (Stinson et al., 2008).

attentively as she elaborated at length on her diverse topics of interest. I attempted to establish common ground with her wherever I could. The fact that we shared some common interests and experiences helped me gain credibility with her. Within the first few months of our work together, she went so far as to proclaim that she knew that she and I were "destined" to work together because of these commonalities. True, as her therapist, I was an authority figure, but I seemed to be one of the few authority figures who could understand or appreciate her.

Rather than focusing on her difficult, traumatic past and its impact on her life, she instead wanted feedback from me regarding her causes: What did I think? Did I agree with her, or did I side with others? More to the point, she seemed to want me to appreciate just what a remarkable individual she was. More than once, she repeated a cliché that was something of a personal mantra for her: "There are three kinds of people in the world: those who make things happen, those who watch things happen, and those who wonder what happened. I want to be solidly identified with category one." At the end of one particular session, I recall her exclaiming a *non sequitur* with an air of confidence, "By the way—I've recently decided that I no longer believe in hell, and that whenever someone doesn't like me, or has an issue with me, well that's their problem." My attempts to process these pregnant comments in the next session or two didn't produce much fruit.

In a session a few weeks later, she complained about being more distractible, being more irritable with her husband, and experiencing feelings of rage just under the surface, which could potentially erupt into a string of profanity or a screaming fit if somebody did or said something she didn't like (this had happened before). All of this was occurring during a week when she was particularly involved in forwarding her causes. I encouraged her to take a moment and reflect on whether there might be a connection between these things. Without much hesitation, she went on to speak intensely about her desires to be seen as an "absolute authority" whose meticulous background research and infallible logic would leave her opponents literally awestruck, dumb-founded, and unable to respond because of the forcefulness of her arguments. The stress she was under was a small price to pay for her development as an expert. I decided that it might finally be appropriate to tactfully confront her. It appeared that her investment in her causes was damaging her relationships (especially with her husband and her daughter), and that this investment was manifested by her deep need to be right, and for others to be wrong. Toward this end, I told her that her personal theme of "I'm fine, but the world is screwed" was a significant problem in her life. Given the religious component to her sense of self, I attempted to add additional incentive for self-reflection by suggesting that "such a deep personal investment in being right and others being wrong was the antithesis of what it meant to be an enlightened person." Of course, she found the idea of enlightenment quite appealing for reasons that were less than ideal. We spoke frankly about these things for a time as she asked for clarifications, definitions of terms, and so forth. I felt some sense of relief inside that she seemed to be tolerating fairly well my blunt appraisal of her current mode of living versus the ideals that her religiosity suggested. It seemed that some of the first cracks in her self-aggrandizing narcissistic perspective were beginning to appear, and she seemed to be tolerating this well. I was pleased with the way I had handled her thus far; perhaps she wasn't going to be so difficult after all.

Some weeks later, my client disclosed, in a rather frank manner, a new facet of her life to me. I knew that she was married with a young daughter, and that she rarely spoke of her husband (who seemed much more invested in the care of their daughter than she was) in anything but detached, dismissive tones, almost as if he were an afterthought. My client made it clear she was "not in love" with her husband, and that she was with him primarily because he allowed her to do whatever she wanted. She disclosed that she had long held fantasies of engaging in sex with her husband and another man together, and that this too was a central reason that she was with him—he would likely go along with this when the opportunity finally arose. I asked regarding her husband's take on these plans; she stated that he was "not really that into it," but would end up reluctantly acquiescing because he wanted to stay with her. She went on to relate how she had recently made friends with a young man in one of her classes. He knew that she was married (she always wore a wedding ring), but nonetheless, the two of them got together one afternoon to drink, then went to her house, where they had sex that evening and throughout the night while her husband and daughter "slept" in adjoining rooms. The next day, a couple who were friends of hers from out of town happened to drop by. For the remainder of the weekend, the daughter stayed at a friend's house so that all five of the adults (her husband included) could have sex with each other. My client went into considerable detail as she described the sequence of events. Many thoughts ran through my mind as I listened to her: What was her purpose in being so frank and graphic about her sex life? Was she trying to shock me? Seduce me? Impress me? Was she even telling me the truth? We had little time to process what she had shared before the session ended, so the next week, we focused specifically on these events after she related that there had been more such experiences in the interim. I asked her what her motives had been for sharing this information with me in such detail. Her reply was that she "no longer seemed to know which way was up," that she wasn't sure what she really believed anymore. I felt that both of these reactions were potential leads into promising therapeutic territory. After further process-ing her reactions, feelings, and the possible implications for a session or two, I decided to share with her my reactions and perspective: Such a mode of living was not in her own best interests, nor her husband's, nor her daughters, nor was it conducive to happiness and well-being in the long term. Her reply was chilling despite being classically narcissistic: "Whoever said I want me or my daughter or my husband to be happy? I want my daughter to be powerful. . . ."

Though my client represents a more blatant example, her case shows how narcissism can contribute substantially to our tendencies to disregard and objectify others. Her husband, her daughter, her multiple sex partners, and various others in her life registered as little more than mere means to achieve her desired ends—power, prestige, and social prominence—and they were treated accordingly. Indeed, during our work together, I was often reminded of the heavily narcissistic lead character, Frank Underwood, from the Netflix series *House of Cards*.

And yet, despite their relative rarity in the population, individuals with NPD embody tendencies that all human beings share to varying extents: a sense of entitlement, difficulty with empathy, and the desire to be adored as unique and special. The primary difference is that narcissists have an inflated sense of these things, and are more up front about their sense of entitlement or their perceived specialness, whereas most other human beings do a better job of either keeping such beliefs in check, or at least keeping them to themselves. Despite these efforts, most people go on to repeat the Greek tragedy of Narcissus to some extent throughout their lives. Even admirable human impulses toward bettering ourselves, "expanding our horizons," or making positive differences in the lives of others can also be understood as manifestations of our narcissistic tendencies. Such impulses and the endeavors they engender, such as having a large family, amassing large quantities of money or other valuable goods, creating works of art, establishing philanthropic foundations, writing a book, running for public office, and so forth, are often praiseworthy, admirable acts, but they also represent our need to affirm ourselves as squarely at the center of existence, to feel heroic, to deny the finitude of our lives, and to feel the satisfaction of having our egos stroked, which is the subject to which we now turn.

CHAPTER 9

The Ego (Part One)

Its Nature and Manifestations

Watch me! Watch me! I got it. . . Watch me! I got it, Heyyyy!!! I got somethin' that makes me wanna shout. . . I got somethin' tells me what it's all about. . . I got soul! And I'm super bad!

James Brown *(1970)*

From the depths of your being you need to view self-centeredness as faulty.

His Holiness the Dalai Lama *(2009, p. 291)*

Referring again to Needleman's three observations from antiquity in Chapter 4, condition two is also likely to strike many readers as counter-intuitive: *Our ordinary sense of self-identity, what we call our personality, is not our true, fundamental identity.* Most people might respond to such an assertion with, "How could I not know myself? If I am not who I think I am, then who could I possibly be?" Ancient contemplatives understood that the sense of self most readily available to human awareness represented only a superficial identity dominated by self-centeredness and influences stemming from one's immediate social environment. Since the late eighteenth century, this readily accessible layer of self has been referred to by the Latin word *ego*, which simply means "I." The ego cannot be observed directly within the brain by means of a PET (positron emission tomography) or fMRI (functional magnetic resonance imaging) scan. Rather, the ego is an abstraction used to refer to certain qualities or attributes of human thought, feeling, and behavior; it is a theoretical construct that helps us describe certain tendencies that all human beings share to varying degrees.

As it is presently used by academics and specialists, the ego is identified in two different ways. Psychologists most often refer to the ego as a sort of self-organizing principle in the psyche. It is thought to be that part of consciousness that pulls together the different elements of the self in order to create some semblance of wholeness or integration. Understandably, without this, human beings would not be able to function in any consistent, coherent, equanimous sort of way. The ego as *organizer*, then, is thought to be a necessary and beneficial adaptation of the human mind that brings about self-integration necessary for personality to exist. On the other hand, from the perspective of philosophies of enlightenment and many theologies, the ego is understood as that part of a human being's recurring thought and conditioned mental-emotional patterns which is invested with a sense of "I, me, mine," separate and distinct from all other things. Here, the emphasis is not on an organizing principle as such, but rather, on a psychic mechanism that has the *protection and enhancement of the self* as its primary function.

Contemplatives have long considered this self-enhancing mechanism of the psyche to be the seat of wanting, attachment, and self-preoccupation. As such, they considered it to be the wellspring of human conflict and suffering, and the primary stumbling block to enlightenment. I speak at some length about the ego, in this chapter and the next, because it is crucial to understanding the problem of objectification. Metaphorically speaking, the ego can be understood as the fetters—the chains on the wrists and ankles, the restraints on moving one's head from side to side—that bind and restrict those inhabiting Plato's cave. The ego is perhaps *the* primary obstacle limiting the perspective that we have of ourselves, others, and the world around us. We are much more likely to objectify others when we are in the ego's grip. Were it not for the fetters of the ego, the cave's inhabitants would no longer be prisoners; they would be freer to perceive the reality of their situation, and would likely beat a hasty exit. The venerable Huston Smith, who, along with Joseph Campbell, is perhaps the greatest student of the world's religions of the last century, spoke often of the ego, especially as it's been understood within the great religions. Regarding the ego, he explained:

[The ego] consists of all those inclinations which tend to continue or increase [perceptions of] separateness—the separate existence of the object of desire. . . . Life being one, all that tends to separate one aspect from another must cause suffering. Our duty to our fellows is to understand them as extensions, as other aspects, of ourselves—fellow facets of the same Reality. This is some distance from the way people normally understand their neighbors[. . .]. Here, said the Buddha, is where the trouble lies; this is why we suffer. Instead of linking our faith and love and destiny to the whole, we persist in strapping these to the puny burros of our separate selves, which are certain to stumble and give out eventually. Coddling our individual identities, we lock ourselves inside "our skin-encapsulated egos" [. . .] and seek fulfillment through their intensification and expanse[. . .]. Can we not see that "tis the self by which we suffer?" Far from being the door to abundant life, the ego is a strangulated hernia. (1991, p. 103)

Figure 9.1: Ego/Narcissism Relationship

In this one paragraph, Smith reiterates numerous points made thus far: the reality of life's unity is opposed by the ego; its fruits of perceived separateness and self-centeredness work to enhance the enmity we feel toward others and increase our tendencies toward objectification.

For the sake of clarity, it may be helpful to differentiate the ego from narcissism, since in some minds they may be synonymous terms. Both are, of course, theoretical constructs used to describe aspects of human thought and behavior, and the two concepts are indeed related. It seems to make the most theoretical sense to say that the ego is the larger host entity of which narcissism is a subset, as represented by Figure 9.1.

Narcissism is understood as being synonymous with the desire for self-preservation, self-promotion, and the perception of one's uniqueness, specialness, supremacy, and separateness. The ego, too, can be understood in these ways, but it is more than this. Later in this chapter, we will see that the ego comprises unique tendencies such as the identification of self with objects, thoughts, feelings, ideas, roles, and tendencies toward wanting and attachment. Narcissistic personality disorder (NPD) can be considered as a disorder of inflated ego, but it does not have as part of its current diagnostic criteria over-identification with things, too strong a tendency to equate one's identity with one's thoughts and feelings, or too strong a desire for specific objects. Rather, NPD has to do with an abnormally inflated sense of self-importance, specialness, and entitlement, as well as tendencies to be exploitative of others and an inability to experience empathy. All human beings experience these traits to some degree, but NPD is the description used when a person evidences an over-abundance of such problematic traits.

It is arguable that most psychological problems—not just NPD, but other conditions, such as anxiety, depression, eating disorders, obsessive-compulsive disorder, phobias, and so forth—are disorders of ego. The conventional psychological wisdom is to think of these disorders as problems of too little ego; thus, the solution is to buttress or enhance the sufferer's sense of self. Perhaps an equally valid way of understanding these problems and providing help is to acknowledge that yes, the person lacks confidence in herself, which is a problem, but her deeper problem is not that her ego is too small, but rather, it is still too large; she over-identifies her own miserable thoughts and feelings as being synonymous with who she is (more will be said of this later in this chapter). Such individuals are also often preoccupied with comparing themselves to others. Their concern is that they somehow don't measure up—that they are "less than" others when they want to feel "as good as" others, if not "better than" others. These are all ego concerns.[1] This is in no way to suggest that all manifestations of such conditions reflect only problems of ego. There are physiological, environmental, and hereditary components of many psychological conditions that are important to acknowledge and treat effectively in order for relief to occur. But it is to say that the ego, the sense of "I," can be a problematic factor in most psychological conditions, not just in narcissistic personality disorder.

THE DEVELOPMENT OF THE EGO

Earlier, I discussed how young children come to perceive themselves as separate, distinct entities. This process, which typically gains momentum within the first two years, results from a child's developing the cognitive capacity to realize that objects have permanence even when the objects are no longer visible, and that she herself is not synonymous with her caregivers. The fact that she has already been given a unique name contributes to this process, as she comes to equate her name with herself. Soon, the child associates the word "I" with her concept of "me," and the mental concept of "mine" follows shortly thereafter. This development is significant because it represents the beginning of the young child's ego becoming identified with external objects—"stuff." This can be verified directly in a variety of ways. For example, when a child's toy breaks or is taken away, distress results. The child's emotional reaction occurs not because of any intrinsic value the toy has. As all parents know too well, children very quickly lose interest in specific toys; they are also easily and rapidly replaced by others. Rather, emotional distress results because the toy has become invested with a sense of "mine," which is connected with a sense of "me." The loss of the toy, therefore, is equated with a corresponding loss of self, which distresses the child.

Concomitant with the child's ongoing physical growth is the development of the child's mental and emotional sense of "I," which expands as it

---

1. Thich Nhat Hanh (1998), following this line of thought, suggests there are three kinds of egoic pride: (1) Thinking I am better than others; (2) thinking I am worse than others, and; (3) thinking I am just as good as others (p. 189). Each mindset is faulty because one's central concern is with ranking one's ego rather than dis-identifying with it.

incorporates other aspects of experience. The young child's ego now begins to include thoughts and feelings as part of its sense of "I-ness": thoughts and feelings about his or her body, gender, friends, family, and possessions. As the young person continues to develop, more complicated perceptions and emotions about nationality, race, and religion may be added. Opinions, preferences, roles, and an accumulated selective memory of events thought of as "the story of my life" help to further round out the adolescent's egoic sense of self. All of these aspects of identity have in common the fact that they are mere thoughts and feelings, held together because they are all invested with a sense of self (Tolle, 2008).

By the time of young adulthood, most people have become "fused" or completely identified not only with this host of objects and perceptions of self, but with their mind's stream of consciousness, most of which, if they could have it somehow written down for them verbatim, would sound quite fragmented, tangential, repetitive, monotonous, even bizarre. Notwithstanding, this stream of mind, this incessant "voice" in the head, so often sets the tone for most individuals' sense of themselves at any given time: "Am I in a good mood or bad? Am I relaxed or tense? Am I contented or dissatisfied? Am I intrigued or bored? Do I like myself or not? Is this a good day or bad?"—the stream of consciousness provides the answer. Unfortunately, most don't realize that this steady flow of often random, reiterative, pointless thought and attending emotion is simply another manifestation of the ego. Instead of readily identifying with its content and experiencing life *from* the standpoint of the particular flow of thoughts and feelings occurring at any given moment, it is possible for a person to develop the capacity to acknowledge his or her thoughts and feelings, but to do so from a more distant, detached, "diffused" perspective: being the awareness *behind* the thought or feeling rather than *being* the thought or feeling. Some individuals who have experienced this shift in perspective—from being the content of their minds to being the awareness in the background, which is aware of having thoughts and feelings—never forget the first time they realized that their mind had this capacity; others have experienced this shift many times in subtle ways and have felt for inexplicable reasons, an infusion of calm or inner peace.

EXPOSING THE EGO: NEEDLEMAN'S SIMPLE EXPERIMENT

Helping students to appreciate the significance of this latent capacity of mind has been an important part of Jacob Needleman's teaching. Through his readings of ancient philosophers (principally Marcus Aurelius), he developed a seemingly simple method for encouraging this shift in perspective away from egoic identification with the stream of conscious thought and feelings toward an experience of consciousness "behind" the ego. At the end of a particular class one day, Needleman gave this challenge to his students:

> In addition to your reading assignment, I would like to invite you to try something during the next few days. . . . The exercise is this: Over the next few days. . . try to experiment with a new kind of relationship with the things that annoy you—starting, if you like, when you leave the classroom in a few minutes. The exercise is simply to step back in yourself and observe your state of being annoyed or being irritated. Don't try to do anything about it. Don't try to get rid of it or justify it or judge it to be good or bad. Just observe it and whatever you can see that is connected with it. Step back from it without trying to change it or escape from it. Do you understand? . . . Just observe that you are being annoyed by saying silently within yourself, "Oh, here I am—I am annoyed." Just step back from it within yourself. Every day, every hour, every minute, things annoy us, irritate us, so there's no lack of occasions to practice this "philosophical" exercise. (Needleman, 2007a, p. 122)

Needleman reports that at the next class gathering, when he followed up by asking if anyone had actually tried the experiment, almost all of the students, despite saying previously that they would try the experiment, said they had simply forgotten to do it. For Needleman, such forgetting represents one of the fundamental problems in human being's failures to carry out good intentions. So often, we simply do not remember or hold on to our deeper, subtler impressions in the midst of our harried, distracted lives, and so we do not do what we know to be "good" unless impacted by a crisis into a deeper state of awareness. This tendency to forget, however, is not the main point of the exercise. Needleman goes on to contrast the experiences of the two students who actually remembered to do the experiment but came to different conclusions as a result. The first student, an older, retired medical doctor who was auditing the class, understood the experiment as an exercise in attempting to change his feelings of irritation and frustration once he became aware of them; he was successful in this endeavor, and so was quite satisfied with himself, "falling," as Needleman observed, "into an even deeper circle of hell as a result"—the hell of self-absorption (2007a). But the other student, a rather quiet, demure young woman, had a very different experience. When realizing her own annoyance over her dry cleaning not being ready when promised, she suddenly remembered the assignment, and so made the attempt to simply "observe" herself being annoyed by saying to herself, "Oh—here I am, I am annoyed." In the midst of this, she reported what was for her a most unique experience:

> Suddenly, it was almost as if I became two people: one who was quite irritated and frustrated with the clerk, and one who was simply observing myself in the

midst of a situation, in a much more neutral, detached fashion. (Needleman, 2007, p. 129)

What impressed Needleman most, however, was her conclusion, "*I didn't know my mind could do that!*" He finishes by saying:

> Could it be true that the power of the mind to step back from itself, the power of the attention of the mind to watch one's own thoughts and feelings, to separate from one-self in this simple, fundamental way; could it be that not everyone knows about this—simply by virtue of being a living, breathing human being? Or, could it be true that we've raised a whole generation of men and women who don't know about this? (2007, p. 129)

In its essence, Needleman's simple experiment is designed to unmask the ego through a person's experiencing what contemplatives have called "Presence," "Being," or "the awareness in the background"—a deeper sense of self that has the capacity to "step back" and observe the egoic clamor of the mind without necessarily being hijacked by it. Since learning about Needleman's experiment, I have tried it many times myself and with my own therapy clients who complain of chronically distressing emotions. As in Needleman's example, most of the time, nothing substantial or lasting results. However, there have been a few individuals for whom the experiment yielded what seemed like an epiphany to them—they could actually practice, in an intentional way, a type of detachment from their own egoic thoughts and feelings for the purpose of not engaging in what is so often counterproductive, negative, or destructive reactivity. One readily available method for doing this is to simply take two or three deep "mindful breaths" to help us become more conscious of the experience of breathing. This brings our mental focus much more fully into the present moment where we become more aware of the aliveness—what Buddhists call the *suchness*[2]—of all things.

THE COMPOSITION OF THE EGO

Ego Content

The problem of the ego has been a perennial focus for enlightenment philosophers and theologians over the millennia. In recent years, there has been a new surge of attention given to the ego and its relation to the problems in living encountered by individuals, groups, and societies. Eckhart Tolle (2003, 2004, 2008, 2009) is one of many contemporary thinkers who have had much

---

2. Suchness, also known as *tathatā*, is a central concept in Buddhism and makes reference to understanding the true nature of reality in any given moment.

to say regarding the mechanisms of the ego and its various manifestations. According to Tolle, the ego is composed of two primary elements: *content* and *structure*. Ego content is the material that the ego fixates on. In the case of the child and her toy mentioned earlier, the toy represents content, which is interchangeable with any other object so long as the child identifies with it. Content is idiosyncratic, meaning that the particular material that a person identifies with will depend on his or her unique experiences, environment, and culture. For example, some of my ego's favorite content includes Rickenbacker electric guitars and vintage Italian motor scooters. I can trace the genesis of these specific preferences to fond memories of my much older sibling's love of the Beatles and my hearing their catchy, memorable music at a very young age. The fact that both John Lennon and George Harrison played Rickenbacker guitars during the Beatles' earlier years and that hordes of Vespa and Lambretta scooter-riding "mods" in England also loved the Beatles made it a cinch that I would self-identify as a mod when such became fashionable during my high school days in the early 1980s, and that I would carry a fondness for these particular affectations into my middle age. Tolle extends the idea of ego content further by asserting that the ego fixates on other forms of various types, not just external objects. For example, forms also include thoughts and feelings.[3] When thoughts and their attendant feelings so absorb our attention that we are completely lost in or "fused" with them, then we are entirely identified with form, and thus, in the grip of the ego. The ego can be thought of as a collection of recurring thought forms and their attendant, conditioned emotional patterns, which are invested with a sense of self. Ego is present when the authentic, deeper sense of self (referred to as "Presense" or "Being" behind the thoughts and feelings) is buried beneath forms with which the person has fused, thus experiencing them as being the essence of his or her identity. This is what it means to be "unconscious," to "forget Being," to engage in the "primary error," to be deceived by the illusion of separateness, which leads to objectification (Tolle, 2008, p 54).

Ego Structure

While the ego's content and forms are idiosyncratic, ego *structure* is quite consistent across the human species. Structure represents the specific processes, tendencies, or mechanics of the ego. It is important to understand that no amount or quality of content will satisfy the ego for very long if the underlying egoic structure pertaining to that content remains in place. For example,

---

3. Odd as it sounds, thoughts and feelings are in fact examples of energy or "matter" (e.g., neurotransmitters moving across synapses), which can be measured by various contemporary technologies, such as fMRI or PET scans.

"wanting" is not content per se, but is part of the ego's basic structure; it is structural for the ego to want things, and so long as this structure remains in place, the person in question will go on wanting more and more content.

Identification with Objects

The compulsion to enhance one's sense of self through identification with objects is also built into the structure of the egoic mind; thus human beings the world over reflect this tendency to one degree or another. Indeed, identification with objects is one of the key mechanisms of the ego. A brief etymological analysis of the word "identification" shows that this realization is many hundreds of years old. During the early seventeenth century, the word was created by combining the Latin words *idem*, meaning "the same," with *facere*, which means, "to make." Thus, when we identify with something, we make it the same as that which is doing the identifying—namely, us (Tolle, 2008, p. 35). Identification is the extension of one's sense of identity onto other things, people, and so forth, which become incorporated into a person's definition of who he or she is (e.g., "*I* am a Beatles fan," "*I* am a psychologist"). The problem is not that we might find certain products or points of view entertaining, helpful, or resonant with our own experience, but that the ego is enlarged whenever we enmesh our sense of self with that which is "beneath," or less than, Ultimate Reality. In essence, this is what is meant by the term "idolatry": treating as ultimate what is less than ultimate, because anything less than Ultimate Reality must eventually fade.[4]

The egoic tendency to identify the self with objects is in many ways the backbone of the modern economy, which relies on the perpetual consumption of goods by consumers. The economy flourishes when consumers not only purchase those goods and services that they actually *need* (because needs are, in fact, limited), but when they spend money on products that correspond to their *wants*, because wants have no specific limits. One of the best ways to encourage human beings to spend according to their wants—or better yet, to conflate needs and wants—is to create within them a perception of deficit, dissatisfaction, or inadequacy, or in other words, to manipulate the fragile egos of consumers. This is accomplished through multiple means, all of which center on contrasting the consumer's person or life as it is with how it could be enhanced if it only included a particular product. Advertisers, whose *raison d' être* is to create artificial demand for products, accomplish this most

---

4. According to the Buddha, *impermanence* is one of the "three marks" or characteristics of all conditioned (or worldly) things, meaning that all such things are in a constant state of flux. The other two include *dissatisfaction/suffering* (i.e., nothing found in the physical world can bring deep, lasting satisfaction) and *not-self* (that which can be perceived by the senses cannot be "mine," and so should not be clung to).

often by showing the product being used or endorsed by a celebrity or otherwise appealing, attractive, "happy" person. The underlying message to the target audience is that their lives at present are currently missing something, and that by owning or using a certain product, they too can be happier, more attractive, more fulfilled, and so forth. Consumers, therefore, are not merely being encouraged to purchase a product, but to enhance their identities. In the case of Rickenbacker guitars mentioned earlier, the idea put forth in an early advertising campaign by the company was that by purchasing and playing the guitar, the buyer would then be capable of somehow having a unique experience not only with the music played, but with John Lennon, George Harrison, and the Beatles' fame and success.

Attachment

By identifying oneself with objects, we become attached to them, which is another structural aspect of the ego. By "attachment," we mean obsessive preoccupation or deep emotional investment with things. This is different from the recognition of "fact." For example, the Dalai Lama differentiates between two levels of interaction with objects: Level one is *recognition*, and level two is *attachment*. At the recognition level, there is a basic acknowledgement of a truth, such as, "I am an American," or "The lake is beautiful, and I appreciate it; it's a good thing." However, at the attachment level, the connection with the object is so deep that we believe we need it for our happiness or contentment (i.e., "America is *the* best place, *the* greatest country in the world; I couldn't possibly live anywhere else," or "The lake is so gorgeous I have to stay here in order to be happy or comfortable" [His Holiness, the Dalai Lama, 1986]). Attachment can also take the form of a negative or hostile emotional investment in people or things. For example, someone may be attached to holding a grudge or otherwise deeply invested in hating or resenting someone. Attachment is not necessarily involved when we obtain deep pleasure or satisfaction from the people and objects in our lives. Indeed, such relationships and objects can bring a great deal of authentic joy. Rather, attachment occurs when we know ourselves and identify ourselves primarily *through* the object or person, or perceive that we cannot live a reasonably happy life without the presence of the object or person. The central issue, therefore, is not so much the object or the person desired or despised, but the type and depth of the emotion invested in it.

Attachment is also a problem because the people or objects to which we are attached are not loved or appreciated just because they exist, but because of what they can do for us (this is more a problem in our relationships with human beings than with objects, of course). As a result, attachment encourages a sort of conditionality that can be a substantial stumbling block to achieving real intimacy in relationships. Attachment also predisposes a person to heightened suffering because of what the Buddhists call *anitya*: the impermanence of all things. This ancient observation is another way of describing the Second Law of Thermodynamics, better known as *entropy*: Things go from a state of order to a state of disorder all on their own. Over the course of a lifetime, institutions come and go; relationships change; human beings and animals age and die; objects are stolen, broken, fall apart, or lose their allure. Attachment constitutes a basic disavowal of or resistance to these facts. This is not at all to say that a person is better off not loving because of the inevitable losses that will result. However, it is to say that attachment predisposes a person to "love" others in unhealthy ways. The musician Sting (1985) put it well and succinctly when he sang, "If you love someone, set them free!" In other words, non-attachment allows for the highest form of love—that which recognizes and cherishes the inherent agency of our beloved, and also respects and honors the ephemeral, fleeting nature of life itself.

Another problem with attachment is that it encourages individuals to perceive of success or personal progress as being synonymous with *more* or *better* things. One of our current societal trends reflecting the collective ego of our times is the proliferation of "stuff"—the accumulation of surplus goods by many in the Western world, and the difficulty of finding a place to put it all. Consider this: The size of the average American house has more than doubled during the last 50 years, while the size of the American family has diminished during the same period of time (America's Homes, 2005; Adler, 2006). However, many home owners don't have enough room to store all of their possessions. Not surprisingly, there has been a dramatic growth in the storage facility industry, where customers pay monthly rent to procure additional space to hold all their surplus goods (Vital Statistics Self-Storage, 2011). And yet, despite this proliferation of purchased material goods and the increases in general income that it represents, human beings seem to be no more happy now than they have ever been (Are We Happy, 2006).

In order to determine one's level of attachment to things, responding candidly to certain questions can be helpful: Do certain things you own induce within you a subtle feeling of importance or superiority? Does the lack of them make you feel inferior to others who have more than you? Do you casually mention things you own or show them off to increase your sense of worth in someone else's eyes, and in your own? Do you feel resentful, angry, or somehow diminished in your sense of self when someone else has more than you or when you lose a prized possession? (Tolle, 2008, p. 38).

Wanting

The ego is identified with having, but as we've all experienced, the satisfaction that comes from possessing something new is short-lived. As was mentioned earlier, human beings have a remarkable ability to habituate, to quickly adjust, both emotionally and physically, to new conditions. This capacity has obvious adaptive benefits. Much as Victor Frankl described in his experiences of incarceration at various concentration camps, when human beings are faced with new, undesirable, adverse conditions that cannot be changed, they have the capacity to adjust and to make do (Frankl, 1984; Brickman, Coates, & Janoff-Bulman, 1978).[5] However, this capacity also means that the pleasures which come from one's latest acquisition will not provide a lasting satisfaction. Once the initial jolt of satisfaction fades, we are left unchanged and wanting another experience. Whatever our emotional set-point was before, we quickly revert to that same level as we come to see life through the lens of the new experience as being "normal," nothing special. This is one of the reasons that lottery winners, for example, are no happier a year after they won their prizes than they were before they won (Are Lottery Winners Happy, 2004). The desire to have, to possess more and more things in order to experience a brief sense of accomplishment or satisfaction, can be tantamount to an addiction. No amount of having ever satisfies the ego permanently, because wanting is part of the ego's very structure.

Separateness

As part of our earlier discussion on the developing ego, it was said that the ego was the product of increasing cognitive complexity—the use of language to symbolically identify with a name and the mental concepts of "I," "me," and "mine"—and identification of the self with thoughts, feelings, objects, and roles. When one's identity is founded upon the thoughts and emotions that comprise the ego, one's basis for identity is fragile, because thought and emotion are by their very nature ephemeral. Thus, each person's ego strives for repeated validation and ongoing expansion. To reinforce the perception of "I," the egoic self perceives the rest of existence in terms of "not I," or in Martin Buber's terminology, "it." The self, therefore, is defined to a large extent by what it is not. As Tolle (2008) put it, "The conceptual 'I' cannot survive without the conceptual 'other'" (p. 60). As has already been mentioned, a byproduct of this process of making distinctions between "me" and "not me" is that we create boundaries. However, every boundary line is also a potential battle line, and the most extreme manifestation of "otherness" is when we perceive others as enemies. This fundamental dynamic of the ego—its sense of distinction and separateness—makes objectification possible.

5. A classic study by Brickman and his colleagues (1978) showed that paraplegics do not differ in terms of overall happiness from other groups of normally functioning people.

Enemies can take many forms. Some varieties of "close" enemies might include those with whom we come into contact every day, such as coworkers, neighbors, family members, even ourselves, given the "unacceptable" thoughts and feelings we sometimes experience, not to mention some of our behavioral choices. "Distant" enemies, on the other hand, often include those we don't know personally but who have differing political or religious views, a different color of skin, a different nationality, or who represent ways of life that we frown upon. The ego is strengthened when we engage in behaviors such as complaining, resenting, name-calling, gossiping, and holding grievances, because these behaviors enhance the perceived separation between ourselves and others (Tolle, 2008). Such actions bolster the sense of separation the ego depends on because each time we complain, gossip, or resent, we are setting up a scenario in which we represent a perspective which *should* be the case; the person or thing complained about is wrong because it somehow thwarts our agenda or flies in the face of our personal preferences. Strongly felt grievances and resentments have the capacity to suffuse the rest of one's life with a sense of negativity or bitterness such that here-and-now experiences cannot be appreciated for what they offer.[6]

The Need to Be Right and for Others to Be Wrong

Perhaps no egoic structure strengthens the ego more than the perception of our being right and others being wrong. Resentment, complaining, and name-calling not only strengthen the sense of boundary and separation between oneself and others, but they encourage a sense of personal superiority while negating the validity or relevance of others. Notice, for example, how even complaints regarding nonhuman entities, such as the weather, the price of gas at the pump, or the amount of vehicular traffic on the freeway, set up a dynamic in which we have been personally offended or "put out" by the actions of Mother Nature or the decisions and actions of unknown others: We are right, but they are wrong for doing what they are doing. Such feelings come from identifying the self with a mental position—an opinion, a perspective, an idea, a judgment, a doctrine, or a story (Tolle, 2008). In order to perceive oneself as correct, some degree of assent or consensus from others is typically

6. It is important to point out that there is a difference between complaining and letting someone know they have made a mistake or that conditions are unpleasant or unfair. For example, letting a coworker know that you find his on-the-job sexually provocative remarks unpleasant or offensive is not complaining. You are simply stating a fact that his comments are not only illegal in the workplace, but unwanted by you personally. As Tolle points out, sticking to the facts avoids the presence of ego, but reactions that come from a desire to make others wrong and yourself right are typically infused with ego.

required, but there must also be someone or something else that is perceived as wrong. Pointing out the wrongness of others strengthens the ego because it enhances one's sense of self. Indeed, without the presence of "the wrong," it is nearly impossible to have a sense of being right.

Facts, of course, do exist. If you were to say, "Copper conducts electricity better than rubber does," or "Dinosaurs existed and went extinct long before human beings arrived on the scene," you would be correct. Basic experiments on electricity's conductivity via copper versus rubber, or rudimentary analysis of the convergence of findings from numerous scientific disciplines, such as geology, paleontology, biology, physics, and archaeology, would show that you are right. These assertions of fact could be infused with ego (as anyone who has raised a teenager who's recently discovered his intellectual prowess on the high school debate team knows very well), but they need not be. If one is simply stating what he or she knows to be true, such as "Dinosaurs pre-dated human beings," there is no ego involved. However, as soon as one identifies with or invests the assertion with a sense of self by saying something like, "Believe me, I know that. . ." or "You're being ridiculous if you don't believe me that . . .," such facts become personalized with a sense of "me" or "I," and are then in the service of the ego (Tolle, 2008, p. 68). The truth needs no defense; neither the action of electricity through copper versus rubber, nor dinosaur bones always being imbedded in sedimentary rock older or "lower down" in the strata than rock containing human remnants, is begging to be defended. We do feel a need to defend ourselves, however, when we are identified with a particular mental position.

The Ego and Time

The great thirteenth-century German mystic Eckhart Von Hochheim (aka Meister Eckhart) once said:

> Time is what keeps the light from reaching us. There is no greater obstacle to God than time. And not only time but temporalities, not only temporal things but temporal affectations; not only temporal affectations, but the very taint and smell of time. (Albert, 2009, p. 77)

It seems that most of us have a very literalist perspective on the meaning of eternity—eternity is thought of either as an endless stretch of years going back into the past and forward into the future, or at the very least, eternity is thought of as being a very, very, very long time. Such an understanding is consistent with the commonplace experience of reality as occurring concomitantly with the passage of time as measured by clocks. Most of us perceive life as being composed of discrete pieces or segments of measured existence—as seconds, minutes, hours, and so forth—which wait to be experienced ahead of us, or which stretch out as "spent" behind us for as long as we can remember. However, life as it's actually experienced is felt to comprise only a very brief segment of perhaps one or two seconds. Christian mystics called this perception of life the *nunc fluens*, or the "passing present" (Wilber, 2001, p. 64), which is felt to be a mere thin slice of experience existing between the mass of accumulated past time behind us, and the mass of potential time which lies ahead of us.

However, these perceptions of time and eternity are quite different from how the great contemplatives have understood it. For them, eternity does not make reference to time of an endless duration, nor to an unimaginably long expanse of time, but rather, *eternity is life experienced entirely outside or without time* (Huxley, 1970, p. 184). Lest this sound like an absurdity or an incidence of psychosis, let us remember that the contemplatives are speaking from the perspective of ultimate reality—unity consciousness—which, they tell us, is to experience life such that it ". . . is not temporal, not of time, but eternal, timeless. It knows no beginning, no birth, and no ending, no death" (Wilber, 2001, p. 56). To experience unity consciousness is to live radically in the present moment. Huxley (1970), in summarizing the perspective of the great mystics on the matter, had this to say:

> The present moment is the only aperture through which the soul can pass out of time and into eternity, through which grace can pass out of eternity into the soul, and through which charity can pass from one soul in time to another soul in time. That is why the Sufi and, along with him, every other practicing exponent of the Perennial Philosophy is, or tries to be, a son of time present. (p. 188)

While unity consciousness may seem beyond the possibility of most human beings to achieve or even experience briefly, a moment's reflection will likely affirm that there have been numerous occurrences, even in the least enlightened lives, that have had a timeless quality, where awareness of the past and the future collapsed into a seemingly endless present. Recall, for example, sensing peak moments of awe and wonder at the resplendent beauty of nature, or experiencing a transcendent sense of timelessness while in the midst of an enraptured embrace with one's beloved; or feeling oneself at the edge of the unfathomable depths of life itself as one's first child is born, or as we attend the bedside of a beloved as his or her life finally expires. Such experiences comprise what the mystics call "the eternal now." If we reflect on instances like these in our lives, then we realize that in the midst of them, there is no perception of time itself. The present moment indeed becomes a timeless moment, and a timeless moment is an eternal one; that is, it occurs outside the awareness of time. "If we take eternity to mean not infinite temporal duration but timelessness, then eternal life belongs to those who live in the present," said

Wittgenstein (2001 [1921], p. 6.4311). In truth, the present moment is the only thing that we can experience, for where is the future or the past that we can access it? Again, brief reflection will demonstrate that our awareness of the past results only because we have the capacity to remember; indeed, without memory, there would be no sense of things past at all. When we recall the first time we rode a two-wheeled bicycle without assistance, for example, we are not accessing the past as it was, but we're having a *present experience* of our recollection of past occurrences. It is the same with the future: It does not exist in any way apart from our present experience of anticipation of what may be. To be aware that the past and the future can exist only as a present experience is to realize that all time exists in the now.

It has been said that perhaps the best way to define the ego is simply to say that ego is a dysfunctional relationship with the present moment (Tolle, 2008, p. 201). What this means is that most people are not fully aware of the present moment, nor are they "at peace" with it; they don't fully accept it. Rather, the set-point for most human beings is to be distracted from the moment into the realm of thought, which typically has to do with some aspect of reflecting on the past or anticipating the future. This predisposes human beings toward suffering, both within themselves and between themselves and others. Huxley (1970) remarked, "The politics of those whose goal is beyond time are always pacific; it is the idolaters of past and future, of reactionary memory and Utopian dream, who do the persecuting and make the wars" (p. 10). Not being in accord with the present moment means that we are living in a mode of non-acceptance, which predisposes us to act in ways not called for by actual circumstances, but by our reaction to perceived past and anticipated future.

Recall Tolle's assertion that the ego is closely identified with form, which includes the thoughts and feelings that occupy consciousness at any given time (Tolle, 2008, p. 53). Most people's running stream of thought, when it is not preoccupied with random content, is often focused on anticipating or worrying about the future, or on reflecting on the past in a nostalgic or regretful way. Human suffering is impacted exponentially by our capacities to think in these ways. Says the Bhagavad Gita (2002) where Lord Krishna speaks to Arjuna,

I am come as Time,
the waster of peoples,
Ready for the hour that ripens for their ruin. (p. 94)

One of this passage's meanings is that the awareness of time, perhaps more than any other aspect of human experience, lays the foundations for human suffering. Another of the passage's potential meanings is that with the awareness of time comes the uniquely human capacity to focus on the past and future, and with that capacity, the eventuality of our physical demise. Charles Dickens made use of this singular human ability in his well-known work *A Christmas Carol*, where in an effort to save old man Scrooge's soul, ghosts of the past, present, and future visit him in turn one night. Scrooge's emotional pain is acute when he's presented with shadows of his past, which are filled with images of neglect, and regret over choices made and not made, but his pain turns to sheer terror when the ghost of Christmas yet-to-be shows him what lies in store for him should his present approach to life remain unchanged. Because of these traumatic yet poignant nocturnal visions, Scrooge is finally shaken out of his unenlightened way of living. More than anything else, Scrooge's newfound awareness of and connection to the immediate present become his salvation, as it empowers him to engage those around him in ways that prove to be transformative for all involved.

In my clinical work, I have come to realize that clients in distress are typically over-identified with the past and/or the future. I often remark to my clients that non-conflicted people never bother to walk through my door, but those who have intrapersonal or interpersonal conflicts are typically bothered by anxiety-provoking thoughts regarding possibilities that await them, or thoughts of regretful, unpleasant experiences they've already had. This is where the bulk of suffering resides—regretting the past or worrying about the future. Surprisingly, such pain and suffering is rarely present when the client is able to connect to her immediate, right-here-and-now experience. Accessing the present moment more consciously—getting out of one's thoughts and into one's actual experiences of the moment—allows individuals to increase the amount of acceptance they bring to their lives, which discloses heretofore unseen paths of action and relationship with others. This is not to suggest that focusing on the past or the future is always wrong, dysfunctional, or inappropriate for psychotherapy; on the contrary, the past and future can be important aspects of people's problems that need specific attention. But it is to say that in the immediate moment, people tend not to have problems—challenges maybe, but not problems—because problems require the ingredient of time perception and repetitive mind activity (Tolle, 2011). However, most human beings "live" in egoic reflection and anticipation, where the self is fused with thoughts about the past and future. Once again, our capacities to reflect on the past and anticipate the future are not inherently wrong. Indeed, these abilities allow us to accomplish a great deal—to learn from mistakes, to build upon accumulated wisdom, to imagine future possibilities, and then to work to achieve desired ends. We could not do well at all without these remarkable capacities of mind. But we cause ourselves and others to suffer when we confuse memory or anticipation with objective reality outside the present moment, as if it captured objective reality.

While the problem of death and how it contributes to the human tendency toward objectification will be addressed in depth in Chapter 12, a few words about the ego and fear of death are warranted here. Recall that the sense of "I" that comprises the ego begins at an early age and is the result of perceived separation between the self and the environment. This new awareness, which Wilber (2001) calls "the primary boundary" (p. 66), brings with it a psychological disposition of distinctiveness—*I am not that*—which continues in most people throughout the life span. As a result of the primary boundary, the world appears to be composed only of subject/seer (me) and object/seen (everything else), with subject/seer being synonymous with identity—thus making it, for the person involved, the most precious entity in existence. By contrast, the outside world is perceived as an object—less relevant, expendable, and a threat because of its capacity to annihilate one's body and mind. Recall also that the perceptual mode of "I am separate and distinct" typifies the lived experience of individuals at the *persona, ego*, and *centaur* levels of boundary transcendence (see Chapter 7), which include most human beings on the planet. The perception of separateness is less prominent for those at the *transpersonal* level, while for those at the level of *unity consciousness* the distinctions practically disappear. For those of us who are closely identified with the contents of our minds (i.e., thoughts and feelings), acutely aware of time, preoccupied with thoughts of the past and anticipation of the future, and deeply invested in the perpetuation of the body, death is the enemy *par excellence*. It is the greatest fear, the central evil, the perennial problem to be solved, which means attempting to postpone death or to avoid it at all costs. The fear of death, whether conscious or unconscious, motivates us to perpetually assume that tomorrow will come for us. The desire for an endless stream of tomorrows encourages ongoing thinking, planning, and yearning for the future. If death can be thought of as a condition of *no future*, then a man or woman who refuses death refuses to live without a future. In this way, the awareness and fear of death creates in human beings the heightened sensation or awareness of time (Wilber, 2001).

We can die in seemingly endless ways. Just a few might include death resulting from physiological malfunctions: a sudden heart attack, a stroke, an aneurism, or the slow growth of a stealthy tumor. Death can come from the amoral, impersonal, unpredictable, "pitiless" physical environment: earthquakes, tsunamis, hurricanes, avalanches, lightning strikes, floods, fires, mudslides, tornadoes, blizzards, thunderstorms, "micro-bursts," or over/under exposure to the elements, such as freezing to death (hypothermia) or over-heating (hyperthermia), dehydration, or hyper-hydration. Death can come from the unintentional actions of others: an auto accident or negligence on the job; death can come from the intentional actions of others, such as homicidal rage, or acts of war or terrorism. Death can come from mechanical malfunctions: failing brakes, sticking gas pedals, faulty wing rudders, and so forth. The vast majority of us have sufficient cognitive complexity to be aware of these realities—we know the precariousness of our situation. But to be continually aware of our tenuous footing in life would not be conducive to psychological equanimity. Therefore, we have evolved a variety of means to carry on living as if these and other threats to mortality were far away, if not nonexistent. The conscious mind is most efficient when it is focused on only one thing at a time. If death is not front and center in consciousness, it is not perceived to be an issue, almost as if it didn't exist at all. The ego is assuaged of death's reality through a variety of defenses, including repression, denial, distraction, and the creation of various "immortality projects"—seemingly lasting monuments to life that will go on long after our short life span has ended—such as writing a book, creating a work of art, building a house or monument, starting a family, establishing a philanthropic foundation, amassing a fortune, experiencing fame, or identifying ourselves with an "immortality ideology," either religious or secular. While much more will be said of this in Chapter 12, the central point is that the ego is not at all at peace with the reality of death, because ego identity is centered in the mind and body. That which brings an end to these entities brings an end to the ego itself.

CHAPTER 10

The Ego (Part Two)

Having versus Being

The difference between being and having is not essentially that between East and West. The difference is between a society centered around persons and one centered around things.

Erich Fromm *(1976, p. 17)*

EQUATING HAVING WITH BEING

A natural byproduct of living under the ego—that is, of identifying with and attaching to forms of various types—is to equate having with being. This egoic structure constitutes a quantitative perception of human existence; we "sum ourselves up" in terms of what we possess in order to prove that we have validity as individuals: "I have, therefore I am; and the more I have, the more I am" (Tolle, 2008, p. 45). In contrast, the "being" mode of existence grounds life on the authenticity, aliveness, or quality of experience. In this mode, we are not oriented toward having, nor do we crave any specific possessions, but nonetheless, we are peaceful and have access to a full range of physical, emotional, intellectual, and spiritual/intuitive faculties, which we utilize productively. In the being mode, we feel "at one" with the world.

The having and being modes have straightforward implications on our tendencies to objectify others. They represent opposing ends of a spectrum typifying our fundamental orientation to the world. Both are firmly rooted in human experience; we all live in both modes to one degree or another. However, having and being represent two fundamentally different kinds of character structure that impact our thinking, feeling, and acting. At the extremes, we could imagine that living entirely from the having mode would be as if one were morally and ethically "dead," a pathological or psychopathic person in every sense of those words, where other persons are "its"—mere objects—seen from the perspectives of extreme derivatization or dehuman-ization. By contrast, living entirely from the being mode would make one a saint: dwelling perpetually in the present moment, and experiencing the world as "Thou."

Contemporary Western society is more oriented toward the having than the being mode. This can be seen in a variety of ways, but perhaps most obvious is Western society's sanctification of the concept of private property. Indeed, the private ownership of property can be seen as one of the bedrock prin-ciples upon which contemporary "having" society is founded. The existence of private property is not necessarily problematic in and of itself—indeed, it seen by some experts as being an absolutely key ingredient in the develop-ment of a flourishing democracy (Bernstein, 2010). However, in the having mode, we easily come to identify ourselves *through* our possessions. For those of us whose identities are fused with our possessions, even slight, peripheral "threats" to private property—be it through proposed increases in property taxes, the possibility of restrictions on firearms ownership or use, or even just a census worker showing up at the front door to take collect data—can arouse feelings going far beyond the existing danger of being deprived of our pos-sessions. Indeed, the intensity of reaction against such perceived encroach-ments can be similar to what we would expect from an attack upon the self (Ferguson, 2010).[1] While the statement, "You can't take it with you when you die," is a well-worn cultural cliché in our society, most of us don't real-ize that the concept of ownership—the merging of the thought form *I* with the thought form *car, house,* or *building*—is ultimately a fiction until we are near death. At this point, it becomes obvious that there is *no thing* that holds any real, lasting value, and that we ourselves are not synonymous with, nor identified by, anything we might have owned during our lives (Tolle, 2008). In the Gospels, Jesus said, "Blessed are the poor in spirit, for theirs will be the kingdom of heaven" (Matt 5:3). One way of understanding this phrase is that "poor in spirit" means "unencumbered"—not weighed down with baggage of any kind, including pride, emotional hang-ups, or identification with things; in a word, with *ego* (Tolle, 2008). "Poor in spirit" is the antithesis of a life centered on "having." This does not mean that in order to be poor in spirit, we cannot own anything and must therefore be poor in a worldly sense. Rather, it has reference to our attitude or level of *attachment* to our possessions. Lack of attachment to things is the essence of a life centered in being.

1. One recent, extreme example includes a young census taker being threatened by a man with a blowtorch for coming onto his property. The man snatched the census worker's badge, ripped up his papers, and took his keys, according to police. The man then forced the census worker back behind his house where he took out a blowtorch, melted a can with it, and asked the young census worker if he knew what a blowtorch could do to human flesh. The man allegedly kept the census worker at his house for an hour before giving back his keys and letting him go with a warning: *"If any more census workers came back on his private property, they might not leave"* (Ferguson, 2010).

Examples of Having and Being: Erich Fromm on D. T. Suzuki's Comparison of Alfred Lord Tennyson and Basho

The twentieth-century psychoanalyst Erich Fromm spoke at length about the problem of having versus being (Fromm, 1976). In order to clearly illustrate the difference between these two life-orientations, Fromm made reference to D. T. Suzuki's "Lectures on Zen Buddhism" in which Suzuki contrasts two poems: one written by the English poet Alfred Lord Tennyson (1809–1892), and one by the Japanese poet Basho (1644–1694). Each describes different ways of viewing a flower. Tennyson captures his experience in these words:

Flower in a crannied wall
I pluck you out of the crannies
I hold you here, root and all, in my hand
Little Flower—but if I could understand
What you are, root and all, all in all,
I should know what God and man is.

Basho's haiku says the following:

When I look carefully
I see the Nazuna blooming
By the hedge! (Fromm, 1976, pp. 4–5)[2]

These poets' diverging approaches to "experiencing" are significant. Tennyson's poem depicts his coming into contact with the flower by uprooting it from its dwelling place. The poet comes to appreciate the "depth" that the flower represents, but he does so in the midst of ending the life of the flower. On the other hand, Basho's approach to knowing the flower is not invasive or destructive; he simply "looks carefully," not even touching the flower. Fromm speculates that Tennyson needs to possess the flower in order to understand it, and that by *having* the flower, he destroys it. On the other hand, Basho, desiring to understand and unite himself with a fellow living thing, studies the flower using primarily his sight; thus the flower is preserved. This contrast need not necessarily infer a fundamental difference in morality between the two poets, nor even a West versus East contrast, as human beings from both sides of the globe and from different eras of time have lived according to both the having

2. While Japanese, Basho's approach to nature is consistent with ancient Chinese thought, principally that of Lao Tzu, the author of the *Tao Te Ching*, the foundational text of Taoism, which says (29:1),
   Those who would take over the earth
   And shape it to their will
   Never, I notice, succeed.

and the being modes; but these poems do display two fundamentally different ways of living. One way emphasizes personhood based on quantity via incorporation, consumption, and possession, and is therefore much more in line with objectification and the ego. The other way emphasizes personhood based upon the qualitative nature of experience for its own sake.

Living according to the having mode presents a number of disadvantages. If we are defined by what we have and consume, then what becomes of us when what we have identified ourselves with is lost? Identity based in the having mode—be it through wealth, material goods, status, youth, beauty, strength, intelligence, power, or agility—is anxiety laden and precarious because of the very real possibility—even the inevitability—of loss. If we are what we have, and what we have disappears, *then we are not*. Innumerable historical examples of individuals who commit suicide in response to such losses bear witness to the fact that many human beings view their material goods as the measure of who they are.

An Example of Being: Victor Frankl

In contrast, short of a significant traumatic brain injury, identity rooted in the being mode cannot be taken from a person. The capacities to experience awe, wonder, and love can never be lost or destroyed, even in the most adverse or dire of external circumstances. The Viennese psychiatrist and Holocaust survivor Victor Frankl proclaimed these truths poignantly in his magnum opus, *Man's Search for Meaning* (Frankl, 1984).[3] Frankl, who survived over 43 months of imprisonment in the death camps of Theresienstadt, Auschwitz, and Türkheim because he was a Jew, asserts with rare clarity and credibility that after everything else has been stripped away, the one thing a human being can never lose is his capacity for *being*, which includes his capacity to chose his attitude toward his circumstances in any given situation. Frankl experienced this capacity in remarkable fashion on a many occasions while a prisoner. Once, when Frankl was quite ill and out on a work detail on a frigidly cold, early winter morning, a fellow sufferer working next to him whispered,

> . . . If our wives could see us now! I do hope they are better off in their camps and don't know what is happening to us. (Frankl, 1984, p. 48)

3. Victor Frankl's book, originally published in 1946 as *From Death-Camp to Existentialism*, was re-released in 1959 under the better-known tile, *Man's Search for Meaning* by Simon and Schuster. The central thesis of Frankl's book was also acknowledged directly in one of Jesus' most memorable sayings: "Lay not up for yourselves treasures upon the earth, where moth and rust doth corrupt, and where thieves break through and steal: But lay up for yourselves treasures in heaven, where neither moth nor rust doth corrupt, and where thieves do not break through and steal: For where your treasure is, there will your heart be also" (KJV, Matt. 6:19–21).

Frankl then recalls the following remarkable experience:

> That brought thoughts of my own wife to mind. And as we stumbled on for miles, slipping on icy spots, supporting each other time and again, dragging one another up and onward, nothing was said, but we both knew: each of us was thinking of his wife. Occasionally I looked at the sky, where the stars were fading and the pink light of the morning was beginning to spread behind a dark bank of clouds. But my mind clung to my wife's image, imagining it with an uncanny acuteness. I heard her answering me, saw her smile, her frank and encouraging look. Real or not, her look was then more luminous than the sun which was beginning to rise. [. . .] I understood how a man who has nothing left in this world still may know bliss, be it only for a brief moment, in the contemplation of his beloved. [. . .] I did not know whether my wife was alive, and I had no means of finding out (during all my prison life there was no outgoing or incoming mail); but at that moment it ceased to matter. There was no need for me to know; nothing could touch the strength of my love, my thoughts, and the image of my beloved. Had I known then that my wife was dead, I think that I would still have given myself, undisturbed by that knowledge, to the contemplation of her image, and that my mental conversation with her would have been just as vivid and just as satisfying. "Set me like a seal upon thy heart, love is as strong as death." (Frankl, 1984, pp. 48–50)

Frankl's ability to experience with such vividness and profundity emotions, images, and depth of meaning typifies a life grounded in being rather than having. In these most poignant and spiritual of life's moments, the terror and anguish more commonly associated with the potential loss of self or loved ones is nonexistent. The self is grounded in that which is formless and infinite, and perceiving proceeds out from this place.

Another Example of Being: Mohandas K. Gandhi

It is often difficult for those who are oriented toward the having mode to understand or appreciate the lives of those who live more according to being. They often accuse such individuals of "doing nothing," or at least, of not doing anything productive. I recall on one occasion an elderly acquaintance remarking that he could never quite understand why so many people thought that Gandhi was a great person, as it seemed to him that all he ever did was "lay around in the shade, doing nothing." This man came of age in the American South during the 1940s and 1950s when segregation and institutionalized prejudice against non-whites was the norm, and the American Dream and the Protestant work ethic were the dominant conventional wisdom of the day. Such a ruggedly individualistic, "pulling one's self up by the boot straps" cultural ethos lent itself well to the "having" perceptual mode, where the measure of a person was what he or she (mostly he) did or had to show for his life—family, property, wealth, status, and so forth. My acquaintance was largely unaware of what Gandhi had accomplished during his lifetime. This man (Gandhi) who, as a result of his simple diet and his numerous lengthy fasts weighed less than one hundred pounds, and had worldly possessions worth less than two dollars when he died, was nonetheless able to liberate hundreds of millions on the Indian subcontinent from the clutches of the British Empire without the intentional shedding of blood. Perhaps more significantly (though less well known), he erased a barrier more tenacious and formidable than that of race in America: He re-named the untouchables of India as *harijan*, "God's people," and elevated them to full human stature. In doing this, he instituted principles of nonviolence gleaned from his studies of Jainism, Christianity, and his native Hindu faith. Gandhi's insights and actions provided the inspiration that Martin Luther King, Jr., drew upon in his pursuit of civil rights for all human beings in the United States, seeking to vouchsafe rights specifically clarified in the Declaration of Independence, which had never been extended to many. Not only had my acquaintance minimized Gandhi's political significance, but more specifically, he was unaware of how Gandhi's power to inspire others and to accomplish such monumental tasks was largely drawn from his groundedness in being, which led to the gentle yet persuasive "forcefulness" of his personality. Gandhi himself put it this way:

There comes a time when an individual becomes irresistible and his action becomes all-pervasive in its effect. This comes when he reduces himself to zero. For a nonviolent person, the whole world is one family. He will thus fear none, nor will others fear him. It is no nonviolence if we merely love those who love us. It is nonviolence only when we love those who hate us. I know how difficult it is to follow this grand law of love. But are not all great and good things difficult to do? Love of the hater is the most difficult of all. But by the grace of God, even this most difficult thing becomes easy to accomplish if we want to do it. . . . You must not worry whether the desired results follow from your action or not, so long as your motive is pure, your means correct. . . . The last eighteen verses of the Second Chapter of the Gita give in a nutshell the secret to the art of living:
   . . . When you keep thinking about sense objects
  Attachment comes. Attachment breeds desire,
  The lust of possession which, when thwarted,
  Burns to anger. Anger clouds the judgment
  And robs you of the power to learn from past
  Mistakes. Lost is the discriminative
  Faculty, and your life is utter waste.
  But when you move amidst the world of sense
  From both attachment and aversion freed,

There comes the peace in which all sorrows end,

And you live in the wisdom of the Self...

He is forever free who has broken

Out of the ego-cage of I and mine

To be united with the Lord of Love

This is the supreme state. Attain thou this

And pass from death to immortality.

Love never claims, it ever gives. Love ever suffers, never resents, never revenges itself. Have I that nonviolence of the brave in me? My death alone will show that. If someone killed me and I died with a prayer for the assassin on my lips and God's remembrance and consciousness of his living presence in the sanctuary of my heart, then alone would I be said to have had the nonviolence of the brave. (Easwaran, 1978, pp. 101, 105, 108, 115, 121–122, quoted in Fowler, 1984, pp. 70–71)

Though disputed by some historians, according to biographers the last words emanating from Gandhi's lips as an assassin's bullets tore through his body were "He Rama" (Oh God), perhaps answering the question of whether he in fact possessed the "nonviolence of the brave" (Gandhi, 1962, pp. 234, 297–298; Nanda, 1997, p. 512; Brown, 1989, p. 382).

Subtler Modes of Having versus Being

Education

Fromm points out that there are many ways of living according to the egoic having mode that are not so obvious, and don't necessarily involve identification with objects or the accumulation of material goods. For example, students in the having mode tend to take a highly utilitarian approach toward their education. They approach the material as a means to an end, as the key to passing an examination, rather than as an end in itself: as content that could be incorporated into their own system of thought, broadening and enriching it. Such students' primary aim is to hold on to what they have learned via their memory or their notes. They do not feel an urge to produce or to create something new. Moreover, students in the having mode fear or resist new information, because it puts into question the sum of information they already have. Those in the having mode tend not to like ideas that may be complex, paradoxical, or multifaceted because these cannot be easily pinned or penned down (Fromm, 1976, p. 18).

In contrast, students in the being mode are intrinsically motivated to learn, because the experience of learning feels transformative. They recognize changes occurring within themselves as a result of the new ideas and information they've been exposed to. Such individuals often report the perception that they are "different" than they were last year (or even than they were last week), because their learning has altered their sense of who they are as a person and how they view the world. Moreover, students in the being mode will seek out opportunities to learn over and above what is prescribed.

There have been times in my own life when I have experienced the being mode of learning. I recollect the first few times, as a college student, I frequented an out-of-the-way, neglected Victorian house that doubled as a used bookstore in my home town. Though I had read little, my identity as college student was taking shape, and upon my first visit, I found the sight of all the books lining the bookshelves from floor to ceiling mildly exhilarating. The musty smell of the place and the creak of the hardwood floors underfoot served to enhance my fascination with the potential contents of the many disheveled, mismatched volumes. After I browsed a bit, the wiry-haired, bearded man behind the counter peered over his glasses at me and asked what I wanted. I mentioned something about Carl Jung or Hermann Hesse, two authors I was only vaguely aware of; he asked me who had sent me to find these books. I told him that I was just curious. He helped me find what I was looking for. Over the next few years, I returned many times, buying stacks of books, many of which he recommended for me (some of which I still have not read). The owner and I became somewhat friendly as time went by—as friendly as this man was willing to be with an intellectual novice such as myself, or perhaps with anyone. I learned that he was a difficult-to-please adjunct philosophy professor at a local college. It felt good offering what little financial support I could to his fledgling business, which existed at the tail end of elaborate retail sprawl some two or three blocks away, but I also felt good seeking out books by notable scholars all on my own without anyone telling me I had to read them. I remember one thing the man said to me: "I don't get many people like you coming in here anymore, just sampling books for the hell of it—not since the sixties and seventies anyway. . . ." Some of the books I bought from him literally changed my life—books by Hesse, Tillich, Becker, Jung, Niebuhr, Freud, Maslow, and others, to name a few. Ultimately, the explosion of the Internet and online book sales took what little wind was available for his business's small sail. After quietly closing, the house was soon bulldozed to the ground, and the lot has remained vacant ever since. Sadly, I also learned that the man was fired a short time later from the college where he was employed because he was deemed "too controversial."

Faith

If by faith we mean the expectation of a predictable, reliable, beneficent response from that in which we place our trust, then faith is a human universal, whether one is religious or not. We could not live without faith, for without it, personal relationships would fail, communities would cease to function, economies would come to a standstill, governments would collapse, and despair would reign. This notwithstanding, faith is lived and experienced differently by those in the having versus being mode. Fromm points out that in the having mode, faith represents being in possession of "truth" for which one has no substantive personal experience as evidence. It consists of taking upon oneself formulations devised by others, which one accepts because one submits to the authority of others who, most often, exist in a bureaucracy (Fromm, 1976, p. 30). Such "truth" can carry the feeling of certainty because the bureaucracy from which it comes exudes an impression of prosperity, power, and longevity, which is taken as evidence that the institution is adhering to true principles or is guided by divine providence.[4] Faith in the having mode gives certainty; it claims to pronounce certain, unshakable knowledge that is believable because the charisma, confidence, and power of those who promulgate and protect the faith seems unshakable (Fromm, 1976, p. 30).

Faith in the having mode can be thought of as *assensus* (Latin for "assent"), meaning that faith is synonymous with belief. This is faith as a "head matter," and it's all about having right beliefs instead of wrong beliefs (Borg, 2004, p. 28). Because faith in the having mode is equated with believing the right things, in religious contexts, this mode of being supposes that God's ultimate concern is the belief in people's heads, as if having correct beliefs is what will save people. As Bible scholar Marcus J. Borg (2004) puts it, the opposite of faith as *assensus* has both mild and strong forms. The mild form is *doubt*, and the strong form is *disbelief*. The conventional wisdom about both is that they are troubling or upsetting to God, and thus are to be avoided:

> [The conventional wisdom is that] if you have doubts, you don't have much faith. And disbelief is the absence of faith. And if one thinks that "belief" is what God wants from us, then doubt and disbelief are experienced as sinful. . . . If you have incorrect beliefs, you may be in trouble. [. . . Isn't it] remarkable to think that God cares so much about "beliefs?" (p. 30)

Faith in the having mode (*assensus*) encourages distrust in our own thoughts, feelings, and opinions, especially if they are not in line with established authority, doctrine, or orthodoxy. Faith in the having mode is used as a tool for those who desire certainty and closure—those who want easy or quickly available answers to life's difficult questions without taking the risk

4. Indeed, bureaucracies and institutions of all types seek to promote such an impression of themselves to buttress their credibility in the eyes of their constituents and prospective consumers. Consider, for example, how often banks and government institutions use as their decorative façade architectural devices from the temples of ancient Greece and Rome.

to search for them themselves (Fromm, 1976, p. 31). The irony here, suggests Borg, is that faith as belief is relatively powerless. One can endorse the sanctioned, orthodox perspective and still be "living under the ego." One can adhere to doctrinally correct principles and still be quite depressed and unhappy. One can believe all the right things and still be relatively unenlightened or unchanged. In other words, believing a set of claims to be true seems to have very little transformative power (Borg, 2004). Believing or endorsing a set of claims, for example, about "the importance of charity" or "the centrality of love" predicts little about one's actual behavior (Darley & Batson, 1973). This suggests that holding the "right" kind of beliefs is at best a superficial solution to such deep perceptual problems as objectification.

In contrast, faith in the being mode is not centered in belief, though it may include numerous assumptions as part of its totality; rather, it is an inner orientation, an attitude, a condition of the heart (Fromm, 1976, p. 31). It would be more accurate to say that if one's faith is rooted in being, then one is *in* faith, rather than one *has* faith. Faith in the being mode is "lived" rather than thought or believed, and is in many ways synonymous with a radical trust in the present moment of experience.

Love

Fromm points out that love has a dual meaning, depending on whether it is spoken of in the context of having or in the context of being. He makes the important point that, like *ego*, love is an abstraction; it cannot be possessed or had (Fromm, 1976, p. 32). While it is common to speak of love as an experience or a feeling of great fondness that one has toward another person, human wisdom has long recognized the folly of equating such feelings with the genuine article. Such wisdom realizes that while experiencing feelings of love can be of great significance to the one who experiences them, such feelings are easily confused with other states or conditions (e.g., infatuation, physical desire), are often fleeting and ephemeral, and are not necessarily predictive of loving behavior over time. Therefore, while feelings are quite meaningful and important to those who experience them, it seems most helpful to assert that love exists primarily in the *act* of loving—that love is synonymous with action, which may or may not be coupled with feelings of fondness or physical desire. When expressed in the being mode, love is expressed as ". . . the will to extend oneself for the purpose of nurturing one's own or another's spiritual growth" (Peck, 1978, p. 81). Thus, love in the being sense is productive activity. It implies ". . . caring for, knowing, responding, affirming, and enjoying. It means bringing to life, increasing his/her/its aliveness" and autonomy (Fromm, 1976, p. 32). In other words, the being kind of love champions the freedom and agency of the beloved to the extent that we would rather risk losing the relationship than place hindrances or constraints upon his or her will.

In contrast, love as experienced in the having mode is expressed in terms of ownership, possession, confinement, restriction, or the attempt to control the object one "loves." Perhaps the most extreme manifestation of love in the having mode would be what Robert J. Lifton (1989) referred to as *totalism*, a characteristic of extreme ideological movements and other cult-like organizations desiring complete control over their constituents' thoughts and behavior. More than just a problem of "love gone terribly wrong," totalism represents a perverted commitment to the betterment of humankind based on the belief that the group is in possession of absolute truths codified into rigid, dogmatic ideals for living. The misguided assumption is that strict, "mindless" obedience to such codes will be transformative in the lives of each member. Lesser manifestations of the having form of love are often justified under the guise of "loving them so much" or "just wanting what is best for them," but the result is that the other is impoverished or limited in terms of her agency, which diminishes her life, liveliness, and capacity for growth. Parents, of course, have a duty to protect, nurture, and guide their children, which may take the form of restricting or limiting the young person's activities, acquaintances, and so forth, but when done in the having mode, such actions are not done in a way that recognizes the gradually increasing capacity and need for autonomy which are concomitant with increasing age. Rather, such actions typically result from a fear of loss, a sense of ownership, or a desire to maintain possession of the other.

Knowledge

In a related fashion, knowledge is also easily subject to the egoic having mode. We can all likely remember a teacher or professor with impressive technical expertise in his or her field, perhaps possessing multiple degrees and having written articles or books, who taught without enthusiasm or personal connection to the material, thus leaving us without anything resembling real value. As a result, even those hearers whose minds were eager and receptive were not impacted in a way that was meaningful to them, and their lives were far from being opened or transformed by the experience. On the other hand, it is also likely we have experienced a seemingly simple person who, in worldly terms, had or possessed very little in the way of information or facts, but nonetheless was able to intrigue or delight her hearers through a sense of authenticity, aliveness, and personal relevance. As Fromm points out, there is a difference between "having knowledge" and "knowing." The first relates to taking in, keeping, holding on to, or possessing available information, whereas the latter involves the transformation of the self, because the material is incorporated into our productive, creative thinking processes (Fromm, 1976, p. 28).

Aldous Huxley's *Perennial Philosophy* (1970), which I have referenced numerous times, is a lengthy treatise on the being versus having modes of knowledge. His compilation of some of the world's great recurring pearls of wisdom underscores the assertions of Needleman's three observations mentioned earlier: specifically, that true knowing begins with realizing that our common-sense perceptions can be misleading; that our egoic "maps" of how the world works do not necessarily correspond to what actually exists; and, most important, that most people are, as both Plato and Fromm assert, half-awake, half-dreaming, and unaware that most of what they hold to be true and self-evident are often only shadows on the cave wall, products of the suggestive influence of the social world in which they live. Thus, knowing, in the being sense, begins with the shattering of illusions, with *dis*-illusionment (Fromm, 1976, p. 28). Knowing is not synonymous with "possessing the truth"; rather, it means that we penetrate the surface of things and then strive to critically and actively approach truth ever more closely. The great contemplatives—Jesus, the Buddha, Meister Eckhart, the Hebrew prophets, Lao Tzu, Saint John of the Cross, Teresa of Ávila, Boethius, Jalal-udin-Rumi, and others—and many of the great thinkers— Plato, Aristotle, Descartes, Freud, Marx, and others—were concerned with human salvation (Fromm, 1976, p. 28).[5] All of these individuals were critical of the conventional wisdom of their day, of socially accepted thought patterns. To these individuals, the aim of knowing was not the certainty of absolute truth with its attending security, safety, and complacency, but rather, the self-affirming process of reason coupled with intuition. The one who *truly* knows has not had her knowledge simply handed down to her; rather, she has undergone a gradual process of unfolding and refinement, which may have included so-called "dark nights of the soul" (May, 2005) and which led to previously cherished assumptions being discarded or reformed in light of new experience and information. For the person who *knows*, ignorance is as valid and good as knowledge, since both are part of the process of knowing, though ignorance of this kind is quite different from the ignorance of non-thinking. In the having mode, the ideal is to have more knowledge, whereas in the being mode, it is to know more deeply (Fromm, 1976, p. 29).

5. Freud, Marx, and other great thinkers who were professed atheists can be understood as individuals who had as their central aim the unshackling of the human mind from the chains of the enslaving, stultifying social conventions of their day; thus, "salvation," in a secular sense, was their primary concern. This notwithstanding, it's important to remind ourselves that each of the remarkable individuals mentioned above were nonetheless flawed, imperfect, fallible human beings.

Ignorance

He who does not know everything cannot kill everyone.
                    Albert Camus (cited in Lifton, 2003, p. 191)

Because of the ego's tendencies toward the having mode of knowledge and its deep investment in us being right and others being wrong, it tends to manifest certain attitudes toward that which it does not know. Much in the spirit of Erich Fromm on being's relationship to knowledge mentioned earlier, James P. Carse, in his excellent book, *The Religious Case Against Belief*,[6] elaborates on three varieties of ignorance that human beings experience. To his three I add one that I have noted in my own life experience. Ignorance and the ego are not necessarily always related to one another. Indeed, as Carse argues, one type of ignorance is in many ways synonymous with enlightenment. But when ignorance is used in the service of protecting and enhancing the self, or in defending a particular worldview with which we identify ourselves, it can be highly problematic. Ignorance of this type encourages human beings to pit themselves against one another and to view those who come from outside the cherished circle with suspicion.

Ordinary Ignorance

Carse's first type of ignorance is designated "ordinary ignorance" (Carse, 2008, p. 12). It is the most common type and is typical of our inability to know many things with certainty. For example, we do not know for sure who will win the next presidential election, nor do we know what next week's weather will be. In some respects, normal ignorance is trivial because there is literally no end to the number of things that we do not or cannot know, but we could eradicate most of these bits of ignorance if we had sufficient information. Ordinary ignorance can be more significant, however, when our ignorance relates to things that could have significant consequences for ourselves and others, such as a presidential candidate's hidden motives, an undetected tsunami, and so forth. With normal ignorance, there is no ego involved so long as we acknowledge that all of us are ignorant in this way.

6. Why the *religious* case against belief? Because the world's great religions transcend the manifold belief systems that derive from them. Belief systems have a great deal of difficulty tolerating ambiguity, paradox, ineffability, and ignorance, whereas the great religions, at their deepest (i.e., mystical) levels, are synonymous with such states.

The second type of ignorance I call "compound ignorance." It is not mentioned by Carse, but I believe it is deeply relevant to our conversation. Compound ignorance is the type of ignorance in which we are not aware that we are not aware. Ignorance of this type is so pervasive as to be nearly ubiquitous. It is the type of ignorance most typified by unenlightenment, and as such, it is a central feature of Needleman's three conditions mentioned in Chapter 4. If we unknowingly live in a "tissue of appearances"—not knowing our true selves, seeing only the surface relevance of things around us, and largely unaware of our connectedness to the Ground of all being that gives order and structure to the universe—then we are as Adam and Eve in the Garden of Eden, unaware of being unaware. I came to the idea of compound ignorance through a conversation with my wife as we reflected on our very confident son who was soon to be leaving for college on the East Coast. He insisted that he was uninterested in taking numerous required general education courses that did not speak directly to his declared major or his minor. My wife informed him that despite his belief that he was already interested in everything that was worth knowing (certainly an ego-laden position on his part), there was, in fact, a whole world of subject matter and learning out there that he wasn't even aware that he wasn't aware of.[7] Of course, he was incredulous, but this captures the essence of compound ignorance (my wife's term) quite well: Each of us is of the impression that our paradigm is complete because it feels comfortable. Because of our egotistical investment in being right, we are both consciously and unconsciously resistant to alternatives or challenges to our current collection of values or our paradigm of reality. Unbeknownst to us, there are a multiplicity of available perspectives that could, if we were aware of them, evidence themselves to be superior to our current model of reality. Yet we *don't realize that we don't know*. We have taken an important step on the path toward enlightenment when we become aware of the compound nature of our own ignorance, because as soon as this realization is made, the compounded nature of ignorance begins to fade, and one begins to open to new possibilities. Put broadly, educational experiences, close exposure to different cultures, and life crises of various sorts can act as catalysts for the type of growth that occurs as we make the humbling realization that our current paradigm is, of necessity, incomplete; that truth comes from multiple sources and from multiple cultural constructions; that our worldview is in many ways an accident of geography or birth and is only one of many possible models of reality available

7. Interestingly—and unbeknownst to me at the time of writing this—none other than Donald Rumsfeld made a similar observation in a press conference on February 12, 2002, regarding the assertion that Saddam Hussein's regime possessed weapons of mass destruction (video available at http://www.youtube.com/watch?v=GiPe1OiKQuk.).

to be known; and that we will likely never know the vast majority of truths that are possible to be known. The well-worn Shakespearean proverb from *As You Like It*, Act 5, Scene 1, addresses the issue well: "The fool doth think he is wise, but the wise man knows himself to be a fool." As a postscript, after three semesters of college, our son had gained an appreciation for subjects he previously saw little value in, and ended up changing his major to a drastically different subject as a result.

Willful Ignorance

Fraught with ego implications, "willful ignorance" is quite common, but it is more subtle, and more potentially dangerous than ordinary ignorance or compound ignorance. According to Carse, willful ignorance ". . . is a [contradictory] condition where we are aware that there is something that we do not know, but we choose not to know it. It is assuming ignorance when there is no ignorance" (Carse, 2008, p. 13). Examples of willful ignorance are manifold, with consequences ranging from the minimal to the substantial. One example might include the fact that my three sons have aspects of their lives of which I am completely unaware (as did I with my parents, as they did with theirs, and so on). I can imagine what some of these things might be, but I intentionally don't ask about them because there's a part of me that doesn't want to know. Another example consists of consumers who happily purchase mounds of cheap goods manufactured in foreign countries. While they vaguely understand that such low-priced commodities could only come from locales where labor costs are very low and worker and environmental protections are minimal to nonexistent, they choose not to think about the ramifications. Many of these same consumers enthusiastically eat hundreds of pounds of cheaply priced meat each year, but they choose to remain uninformed about the particulars of the living conditions of the animals, the amount of waste produced, and the environmental footprint created by the industry. Many religious fundamentalists think and behave as if they were unaware of the field of evolutionary biology; they likely know it exists, but they choose not to investigate its findings, or they flagrantly misrepresent the scientific facts. Heads of state declare and carry out wars while having some sense that their decisions will lead to the suffering and death of many civilian men, women, and children, but they suppress, minimize, or trivialize this realization. In all of these cases, there are complicating factors that we are perhaps dimly aware of, but we choose to remain ignorant; we choose not to know. We consider ourselves to be "sure" of our knowledge, yet we have subtle intimations suggesting that what we think we know is somehow incomplete. Nonetheless, we do not pay heed or pursue these loose ends lest they undermine our equanimity and self-confidence. For those of us who are willfully ignorant (and we all are to one degree or another), our egos and our way of life are centered so much in being at peace with what we know that we avoid becoming more conscious because of the dissonance it would cause.

Higher Ignorance

In contrast to the previously discussed types of ignorance, "higher ignorance" is paradoxically also a type of knowledge that forms the basis of the world's great wisdom traditions. Carse borrows the name from Nicolas of Cusa's fifteenth-century classic, *Di Docta Ignorantia* (Concerning Learned Ignorance), in which Nicolas says, "Every inquiry proceeds by means of a comparative relation whether an easy or a difficult one. Hence, the infinite, *qua infinite*, is unknown; for it escapes all comparative relation" (Cusa, 1990, p. 52ff, as quoted in Carse, 2008, p. 15). By "comparative relation," Nicholas means that one finite thing can be known or understood only by its association or comparison with another. Carse goes on to make the point that no matter how many of these relations we might discover, they will never add up to the infinite. Thus, we remain ignorant, to some degree, of what things truly are in themselves. No matter how many truths we may accumulate, our knowledge falls infinitely short of *the* truth (Carse, 2008, p. 15). Nicolas seemed to want his readers to understand that higher ignorance is not the kind of knowing we are born with, nor is it captured in the truism that "the more we know, the more we know we don't know." Rather, he felt that this type of ignorance could only be learned by a process of continued self-examination and in-depth reflection, coupled with a close reading of those thinkers who were already alert to such realities. We have to be *taught* to be ignorant in this way, and doing so is tantamount to the process of becoming awakened. The more we are aware of the limitations of our knowledge, the more awake we are to the world's enormous varieties (Carse, 2008, pp. 16–17).

Like other human character attributes, the having versus being modes exist on a spectrum rather than as discrete variables, and can represent the amount of ego present in our manner of existence. The having mode comprises a quantitative mindset toward living that emphasizes ownership and consumption. Thus, it is highly susceptible to the egoic structures of wanting, attachment, separateness, and identification with objects. Of course, in order to live satisfactorily in modern democratic societies, possessions such as homes, cars, clothing, appliances, and so forth enhance the quality of our lives and are necessary. We consume a wide variety of resources in order to maintain our standard of living. These activities need not be problematic in and of themselves. However, it is relatively easy for the ego not to be satisfied with "sufficient" ownership and consumption. The more we equate the measure of our lives with possessing things, the more we are susceptible to the ego and to objectifying the world, which obscures the true nature of ourselves and others. By contrast, the being mode emphasizes presence, experience, and relatedness over acquisitions and consumption. It sees the richness of experience as an end in itself rather than as a means toward some other, more desired end. Therefore, being is synonymous with enlightenment, which apprehends the depth of all existence. This provides us with one of the strongest antidotes to our tendencies to objectify others.

CHAPTER 11

Problems Stemming from Death Denial

The cradle rocks above an abyss and common sense tells us that our existence is but a brief crack of light between two eternities of darkness. Although the two are identical twins, man, as a rule, views the prenatal abyss with more calm than the one he is heading for (at some forty-five hundred heartbeats an hour).

Vladimir Nabokov (1989, p. 19)

Q: Of all the world's wonders, which is the most wonderful? A: That no man, though he sees others dying all around him, believes that he himself will die.

Yudishtara Answers Dharma (The Mahabharata, Vana-parva 313.116)

You are living amidst the causes of death, like a lamp standing in a strong breeze.

Nagarjuna (as quoted in His Holiness the Dalai Lama, 2009, p. 78)

Sigmund Freud plumbed the recesses of the human psyche more thoroughly and systematically than any doctor or philosopher who came before him; he postulated a groundbreaking theory of personality (the unconscious mind and its mechanisms of defense) that still has some relevance more than one hundred years later, yet his system of thought largely avoided the obvious. Carl G. Jung, Freud's brilliant understudy, who achieved considerable fame in his own right for the profundity of his insights into the spiritual side of human nature (such as archetypes, the collective unconscious, synchronicity, and dream analysis), also largely avoided the obvious. Other, more recent doctors of the soul, such as Frankl, Maslow, Fromm, Rogers, Erickson, and Ellis, achieved considerable fame because their contributions enhanced the capacities of human beings to understand themselves and to experience greater fulfillment and meaning in their lives, but they too largely avoided the obvious in their theorizing. It was Ernest Becker who finally situated death smack in the middle of his system of thought, and he did it in a way that was both frank and accessible to the masses. That it took so long for a great mind to do so is a testament not to the irrelevance or obscurity of the problem of human finality, but to its immensity and fearsomeness.

Great human minds have not always avoided the reality of death; indeed, it was the Roman philosopher, Cicero, who said that "to study philosophy is nothing but to prepare oneself to die" (Montaigne, 2006). Many other of the greatest philosophers and thinkers of ages past (e.g., Kierkegaard, Eckhart, Epicurus, and Socrates) held a similar perspective on death's centrality in gaining a truer understanding of life, but modern men and women have become largely unfamiliar with these thinkers and their insights. Becker, a voracious reader throughout his relatively short life, was heavily influenced by these and other luminaries. He was also deeply impressed by his experiences as a US soldier at the close of World War II, where he did not have the luxury of keeping death at a distance. After leaving Europe at the war's end, Becker decided to devote his life to developing a fundamental understanding of himself, the human condition, and the meaning of life. Toward this end, he took his doctoral degree in cultural anthropology because of its focus on understanding human nature as presented over the eras of time. His intellectual inquiries knew no disciplinary bounds, however, as he culled the very best wisdom from fields as diverse as biology, physiology, theology, philosophy, psychology, psychiatry, political science, sociology, and history. Many factors converged to lead Becker to conclude that the central problem humankind faced was an all too obvious one. Human beings embody a seemingly insoluble contradiction: We comprise both mind and body. In other words, we possess an incomparable brain, which imbues us with a felt sense of ourselves as godlike and eternal. At the same time, this mind allows its possessor to know that it is housed in a body that bears all the earmarks of an animal—hair that covers and insulates, a heart that pumps, lungs that gasp for breath, skin that perspires and exfoliates, a digestive system that creates body waste—an organism that, in its totality, is utterly dependent, fragile, and all-too-temporary. On this "animal" side of the equation, Becker referred to two problems that all human beings face: (1) *the problem of tragedy*, which is the fact that death can occur at any time for reasons that no one can fully anticipate or control, and (2) *the problem of anality*, which is that regardless of how much preventive maintenance we do, our bodies will inevitably remind us—via foul-smelling excretions, lost hair, reduced skin elasticity, fading eyesight, dimming memory, decreasing muscle tone, failing organs, and so forth—that we are subject to the processes of decay and death. Becker writes (1974):

> Anxiety is the result of the perception of the truth of one's condition. What does it mean to be *a self-conscious animal*? The idea is ludicrous, if it is not monstrous. It means to know that one is food for worms. This is the terror: to have emerged

from nothing, to have a name, consciousness of self, deep inner feelings, an excruciating inner yearning for life and self-expression—and with all this, yet to die. . . . It seems like a hoax, which is why one type of cultural man rebels openly against the idea of God. What kind of a deity would create such a complex and fancy worm food? Cynical deities, said the Greeks, who used man's torture for their own amusements. . . . (p. 87)

This is the great human paradox that has been appreciated by various keen, sensitive minds throughout the millennia—minds that have not been capable of remaining permanently under the protective layering of what the eminent sociologist Peter Berger (1969) called "the sacred canopy" of culture. Peering out from the protection of the canopy, some temeritous minds have seen the mirage of culture disappear before their eyes. Becker's own glances outside the canopy led to a perspective on human nature that was the first in the modern era to make the inevitability of death a *leitmotif* in understanding human motivational underpinnings. He unequivocally asserted that the evil human beings have done to one another throughout the centuries under the banner of their gods, their kings, and their countries has had, as one of its primary motives, something much less lofty, something more primal and basic: the desire to deny the ever-looming reality of death. As we will see below, our desires to triumph over death (either literally or symbolically) can have a dramatic impact on how we see and approach the world. Especially when reminded of our own mortality—as with the attack at Pearl Harbor on December 7, 1941, or the terrorist attacks on September 11, 2001—our tendencies to see others as objects and treat them accordingly can increase dramatically.

KIERKEGAARD'S CONTRIBUTION TO BECKER'S THOUGHT

Becker was highly influenced by the thought of Danish theologian Søren Kierkegaard, who was among the most eloquent of nineteenth-century voices acknowledging the realities of the human organism: that its seemingly incompatible union of opposites has the potential to lead to considerable suffering (Kierkegaard, 1957 [1844]). Kierkegaard argued that humankind's unique situation created the possibility of two quintessentially human emotions: *awe* and *dread*. Because of the human mind's capacities to be aware of itself, almost as if from an outside perspective, it knows, more so than any other creature we are aware of, *that it exists*. This awareness makes possible a vast array of positive experiences we often feel during the best moments of our lives, when we exult in the sublime privilege and joy of simply being alive. Awe is as good as it gets for human beings. It's the top end of the emotional spectrum, which can be brought on by a variety of means and stimuli—from subtle to the sublime—though its appearance is rarely one that is planned. Simply waking up after a good night's rest on a particular cloudless summer's morning, stepping into the backyard and feeling the warmth of the sun on your face, breathing in the cool, fresh, clean air, and seeing the sun's light glancing off the wetted surface of lovely flowers in full bloom may lead to you exclaim within yourself, "OMG. . . it is just awesome to be alive!" Nothing highly unusual, such as winning the lottery, or winning a Nobel Prize, happened that day. According to Becker, all of that is unnecessary because "the best things in life are indeed free"; you're simply basking in the ultimate human prerogative, which is to be alive and to know it (Solomon, n.d.).

Unfortunately, the capacity to experience awe comes at a price. Like all other human experiences, it has meaning only to the extent that its opposing condition can also be realized. *Dread* is the bottom end of human experience. Not necessarily synonymous with the depths of depression,[1] dread instead represents the shaking realization that one's very existence is tenuous and temporary, that all of one's meanings, relationships, and experiences will soon come to an abrupt halt, bringing with it one's ultimate negation as an entity. Becker, in his Pulitzer Prize–winning magnum opus, *The Denial of Death*, quotes Kierkegaard on dread:

> If man were a beast or an angel, he would not be able to be in dread. [That is, if he were utterly unself-conscious or utterly un-animal.] Since he is a synthesis, he can be in dread. . . man himself produces dread. [. . .] The spirit cannot do away with itself [i.e., self-consciousness cannot disappear] neither can man sink down into the vegetative life [i.e., be wholly animal]. [. . .] Thus, he cannot flee from dread. (Kierkegaard, 1957 [1844], pp. 139–140, quoted in Becker, 1974, p. 69).

Kierkegaard proclaims that human beings cannot flee altogether from the possibility of dread because its germ is built into the very fiber of our being. Becker, however, argues that this has not stopped our attempts at doing so. This grand *causa sui*[2] project has had profound implications for the human experience over the millennia. While anyone of adequate cognitive capacity will claim to know and understand death as a fact of life (Jim Morrison's memorable lyrical exclamation, "No one here . . . gets . . . out alive!" comes to mind), Becker asserts that most of us do not or cannot accept this reality straightforwardly at a deep, visceral level. Rather, he asserts that we deal with our existential dilemma by using our vast intelligence—our abilities to think abstractly and symbolically—and our innate social tendencies to buttress

1. Though depression can certainly be one result of the experience of existential dread, not all depression comes from this source.
2. *Causa sui* is a Latin term that Becker borrowed from the likes of Freud, Spinoza, and Sartre, meaning "cause of itself." It references the desire that human beings have to find for themselves an overarching system of meaning.

ourselves against the conscious reality of impending physical demise. While acknowledging many, Becker focuses more specifically on two defense strategies: the creation and maintenance of culture and the urge to heroism.

CULTURE AS A PLAUSABILITY STRUCTURE

Culture consists in the sum total of efforts we make to avoid being unhappy. . . . Defense systems against anxiety are the stuff that it is made of.

> Geza Roheim (cited in Becker, 1962, p. 130)

The great sociologist Peter Berger argued that society (i.e., culture) is a reciprocal, "dialectical phenomenon," meaning that society is a product of human beings, and that human beings are a product of society. He argued that there were three essential steps to this process: (1) *externalization*, which is the continuous outpouring of human thought and activity into the world; (2) *objectivation*, which is the attainment, by the products of such activity, of a reality that confronts its original producers as "a fact" external to and other than themselves; and (3) *internalization*, which is the deepening subjective ownership of this same reality by human beings who transform it yet again from the structures of the outside world into the structures of their subjective consciousness (Berger, 1969, pp. 3–4). In other words, culture is a human construction that acts back on its creators in profound ways. Human beings internalize and integrate their culture as part of their identity. Because of this, human beings typically see cultural constructions as representing not products of human mental and physical activity, but as "givens" of the objective world—their cultural worldview is simply reality as it is.

Becker extended these observations by making the assertion that culture's primary function is to help its constituents minimize the collective anxiety engendered by the uniquely human awareness of death (Solomon, Oct. 18, 2002). As novel as this description of culture may sound, Becker was not the first to think of it in this way (though he did make death more central to his overall thesis than any of his predecessors). Numerous astute observers have for some time been aware of culture's ability to cast a death-denying spell on its constituents (Rank, 1958, 1968; Brown, 1959; Roheim, 1971). Peter Berger (1969) put it this way:

> The worlds that man constructs are forever threatened by the forces of chaos, finally by the inevitable fact of death. Unless anomy, chaos, and death can be integrated within the nomos [i.e., structure] of human life, this nomos will be incapable of prevailing through the exigencies of both collective history and individual biography. To repeat: every human order is a community in the face

of death. Whatever the fate of any historical religion, or that of religion as such, we can be certain that the necessity of this attempt will persist as long as men die and have to make sense of the fact. (p. 80)

In other words, culture exists in order to buffer human beings from existential realities of life. According to Becker, the central mechanism by which culture diminishes anxiety about death is by covering its members with the protective ontological canopy mentioned earlier—that is, by granting its members the comforting perception of significance, meaning, and permanence in the face of mortality. One of culture's primary functions is to offer its constituents a "plausibility structure," or an explanation of the universe—why it's here and what role human beings play in it—and to provide them with social roles, the satisfaction of which allows individuals to perceive themselves as persons of value in a universe of meaning (Solomon, Oct. 18, 2002). The end result of this process is self-esteem, which, according to the Beckerian perspective, is a fundamental human need, allowing us to see ourselves as not merely another form of life upon earth, but as beings of transcendent value and importance (Landau, Solomon, Pyszczynski, & Greenberg, 2007). All of this can be quite helpful and adaptive, but it also sets the stage for conflict.

WHEN CULTURES COLLIDE

Because culture, worldviews, and self-esteem are symbolic constructions rather than universally accepted realities, they require ongoing acceptance and validation by others in order to be fully imbued with death-denying qualities. Those who share our worldview and agree that we are valued members of society help to allay death anxiety and bolster self-esteem. Our natural tendency as members of a particular culture or subculture is to view other members of the same culture in a more favorable light than those who are not members of our culture. Indeed, those who are considered "other"—outsiders or foreigners, who do not share our cultural worldview—tend to be viewed with suspicion, are seen as potential threats, and are more likely to be objectified. The reasons for this are understandable. Cultural beliefs provide their constituents with a protective, death-denying canopy. They give us concrete answers about who we are, why we are here, where we have come from, where we go after we die, what is moral, what is valuable, and what larger meaning and purpose the universe has. Being confronted by individuals who endorse competing or conflicting worldviews puts us in a predicament: If we accept that our culturally different neighbor's alternative construction of reality has validity, then we undermine the confidence that we have in our own belief system. This then exposes us to the very existential dread that our beliefs were designed to ward off in the first place. Literally hundreds of recent studies in what is known as *terror management theory*, a late twentieth-century research paradigm heavily influenced by Ernest Becker's earlier theorizing, have shown these dynamics to have real-world correlates (Solomon, Greenberg, & Pyszczynski, 1991; Burke, Martens, & Faucher, 2010). In controlled laboratory situations, when individuals are reminded of their own death (known as "mortality salience"), a short time later, the majority of them will be more likely to express increased hostility toward members of culturally different groups, and greater liking for culturally similar groups, than will those who have not received death reminders.[3] Moreover, some of these subjects even express increased willingness to behave aggressively toward culturally different others than do those subjects who have not received death reminders (Burke et al., 2010).

Rather than acknowledge the validity of alternative cultural constructions, human beings instead tend to engage in a number of compensatory mechanisms in an attempt to diffuse the threat posed by different worldviews (Shen & Bennick, 2005).[4] These run the gamut from the relatively benign to the blatantly hostile. On the more benign end of the spectrum, social groups may attempt to *assimilate* the perceived positive attributes of a rival cultural construction. A well-known historical example (which most of us learned in high school) is the Roman Empire's integration of the Greek pantheon of gods into its own theological constructions. Social groups can also attempt to *accommodate* or make room for alternative perspectives to exist side by side with their own. This is indeed asking much of human beings, who are existentially anxious social creatures craving consensus and validation for their tenuous perceptions of reality. The pluralistic societies of the West have utilized the accommodative tactic—with varied degrees of success—in an attempt to realize the Enlightenment ideal of peaceful coexistence within a multi-ethnic society. In such societies, periods of relative peace and calm have always been punctuated by periods of severe social unrest, conflict, even deadly violence, most often along lines of racial, economic, and ideological difference. Social groups may also attempt to *convert* those who subscribe to different constructions of reality, entering into a contest of ideas in an attempt to peacefully demonstrate the superiority of one worldview over another in the hope of persuading members of a rival group to adopt the persuader's belief system.

3. There are some exceptions to this finding. For example, subjects who score high on traits such as liberalism and tolerance (Greenberg, Simon, Pyszczynski, Solomon, & Chatel, 1992), a strong belief in an afterlife (Florian & Milkulincer, 1998), and a secure attachment style (Milculincer & Florian, 2000) show less reactivity toward those of different cultural backgrounds after mortality salience primes.

4. Terror management theory (TMT) has explicated each of these responses as versions of "worldview defense strategies." For a more in-depth analysis, see the award-winning Becker-inspired documentary *Flight from Death: The Quest for Immortality*, available in its entirety online for viewing at www.Flightfromdeath.com.

In the attempt to assimilate, accommodate, or convert others, the amount of conflict occurring in the interactions between the parties involved depends upon the spirit in which the activity is carried out. To pose a question in the phraseology of Martin Buber (1970), is one's approach toward the other person one of *I-Thou*, or *I-it*? If coming from the *I-Thou* mode—one of Subject relating to Subject—peaceful, respectful means of taking on admirable components of another culture, or attempting to persuade another person that our worldview has positives to be added to her own, or that she would benefit by substituting our worldview for her own, define the relational exchange. But if such efforts at change come from the *I-it* mode—one of Subject relating to object—the attempt to incorporate positives from another culture or to change others' points of view will be characterized by disrespect, hostility, even violence.

At the hostile end of the spectrum, our tendencies to objectify others who possess a different worldview become more obvious. Social groups routinely *derogate* rivals in an attempt to psychologically diffuse the threat that their alternative worldviews pose. Eminent twentieth-century anthropologist Mary Douglas (2002) has said that throughout the ages, derogation has taken the form of depicting the rival as being somehow dirty, contaminated, impure, inferior, subhuman, or evil—"matter out of place," given the boundaries designating "us" and "them" that most social groups draw around themselves. The psychologist Sam Keen, in his classic book *Faces of the Enemy* (1986), displays example after vivid example of politically motivated propaganda posters from the last century supporting Mary Douglas's claims. Nazi propaganda against the Jews is a classic example of derogation, but the polarized political Right and Left in America accusing one another of being somehow idiotic or morally inferior is a more routine, daily example.

Annihilation represents the ultimate extremity of an objectifying, hostile response to cultural difference, in which one or both parties involved decide that the rival construction is unworthy of continued existence. Despite our recent advancements as a species in terms of the spread of liberal democracies, our "universal" declarations of human rights, our understanding and growing appreciation of the fragility of the physical environment, our growing awareness of the need to respect and preserve many nonhuman species, our interventions in the developing world's epidemics and other catastrophes, and our utilization of science toward the betterment and prolongation of life for many, we continue to attempt to solve many of our perceived problems with culturally different others the same way our "less enlightened" ancestors did—only now we do so on a scale and with a deadly efficiency they could have only dreamed of in their worst nightmares. To wit: experts estimate that the total number of human beings slain in politically motivated conflict during the twentieth century alone is a staggering 200 million (Bassiouni, 1997;

Brzezinski, 1995; White, 2010). These four mechanisms (i.e., derogation, assimilation/accommodation, conversion, and annihilation) represent the tactics that cultures have utilized throughout history as they've attempted to protect themselves in the face of existential threat. However, the tactics are somewhat different at the level of the individual, and it is to these that we now turn.

THE DRIVE FOR HEROISM AND MERGER

The problem of heroics is the central one of human life. . . . It goes deeper into human nature than anything else because it is based on organismic narcissism and on the child's need for self-esteem as *the* condition for his life. Society itself is a codified hero system, which means that society everywhere is a living myth of the significance of human life, a defiant creation of meaning. Every society thus is a "religion" whether it thinks so or not.

Ernest Becker (1974, p. 7)

Human beings have always experienced the world as a theater for heroism (James, 1958 [1902], p. 281). This view, of course, is epitomized by the world's great mythologies, in which human beings are depicted as living their lives within a grand drama overseen by the gods themselves, with only the cleverest, bravest, and most virtuous of men and women going on to worldly fame and immortal glory, while the arrogant, the proud, or the cowardly are punished with ignominy. Throughout his lifelong study of mythology, Joseph Campbell underscored the now classic "hero cycle," which he asserted was evident in myths the world over, in which men and women undergo similar stages of divinely instigated proving in order to transcend mundane mortality (Campbell, 1949). In the mind of each of us, it is no different: Much like the professional athlete who's just scored a goal or a touchdown and gestures heavenward in acknowledgment of divine assistance, it's as if we are the focal figure on a stage, and our life is the main point of a compelling drama. However, in most cases, the drama—while vaguely symbolic of mythological figures and significant to us personally—isn't quite so high. Craving significance, acceptance, and approval in order to allay the anxiety of living, the more typical among us in the West pursue these desired outcomes by conforming to the societal ideals of hard work, independence, and self-sufficiency, and by performing satisfactorily in roles that the culture values, such as doctor, lawyer, teacher, electrician, father, mother, provider, nurturer, and so forth. In the Western world, this tends to happen in two ways: (1) standing out (*heroism*) and/or (2) blending in (*merger*) (Becker, 1974, pp. 150–154).

Standing Out

The heroic mode of behavior seeks to command the esteem of others by setting the self apart and above others—by being "better" in terms of creativity, beauty, performance, notoriety, power, prestige, and wealth. People living in the United States often refer to such desires by use of phrases like "the competitive drive" or "the urge to be number one." While dated, the opening scene from the 1970 Oscar-winning film *Patton* (Coppola & Schaffner, 1970) comes to mind, in which the general, played brilliantly by George C. Scott, stands before a giant US flag backdrop and speaks to viewers as if they were an audience of soldiers. Patton goes on to offer, in Scott's signature gravely voice, what has become an iconic monologue encapsulating some key aspects of conventional American "heroic" wisdom. In essence, Patton tells his hearers that dying for one's country does not help to win wars; rather, making "the other poor dumb bastard" die for his country is the key. He then asserts that it's not in America's character to avoid war. Rather, "real Americans" love to fight, they love to win, and they cannot tolerate losing. Patton himself says he "wouldn't give a hoot in hell" for someone who was okay with losing, because "the very thought of losing is hateful to Americans." In other words, *real* Americans are courageous, fierce, and victorious in ways that citizens of other nations are not. Such attributes are not claimed by Americans alone, however. Similar high rhetoric could be heard issuing from the mouth of Adolph Hitler to the adoring German masses before his armies blitzkrieged Poland; or from Iraqi Shi'a cleric Muqtada al-Sadr as he roused those who adhered to his apocalyptic vision of Islam, encouraging them to sacrifice their lives for the glory of Allah; or from contemporary rappers and hip-hop artists as they extol the virtues of their enclave over others. More routinely, the same sort of message can be heard issuing from parents the world over as they encourage their children to make the family proud by standing up to the neighbourhood bully or by setting themselves apart in some other way. The fictional character Willy Loman from Arthur Miller's (1949) classic play *Death of a Salesman* comes to mind as a prime example. Willy, an aging, self-deluded traveling salesman, is forever attempting to inspire his ne'er-do-well sons, Biff and Hap, with clichéd rhetoric about the importance of "being well liked," "rising to the top," and "leaving one's mark upon the world"—things Willy himself has been unable to accomplish, though he cannot admit this to himself. "Rising above the fray" is the timeless, universal human heroic myth, depicting what it means to be human at the highest level. According to this myth, defying convention, transcending superimposed limits, triumphing over others, and setting a new standard of excellence for others to admire makes a human life truly meaningful and gives it lasting significance.

Blending In

By contrast, the merger mode of behavior seeks to gain approval by immersing oneself in the group, seamlessly blending in; adopting the group's values, expectations, or perceptions of reality; by being "a good soldier." Here, too, the illustrious General Patton (as portrayed by Scott) had some things to say. He defines an army as a team in every sense of the word, and then says that "individuality. . . is a bunch of crap." Finally, he says that those who champion individuality ". . . don't know any more about real battle than they do about fornicating" (Coppola & Schaffner, 1970). Merger provides us with the perception of not only physical reassurance, but more important, psychological reassurance. It bolsters our confidence that our perceptions of the world are correct. Most social groups claim for themselves the same sense of specialness that individuals claim for themselves because of their narcissism. Thus, being a member of a group adds to our personal narcissism an additional layer of uniqueness and superiority. Think of any group—religious or secular—that you have belonged to and see if this perception of uniqueness is not true on some level. Gaining acceptance into a special group is a privileged association and confers instant status and an enhanced sense of identity. Almost all human beings want to be included as members of the "in" group; almost all human beings want to have the sense that they have been vetted and found worthy of inclusion in a rarified realm of social acceptability.

Strengths of Both Modes

To some extent, both the heroic and merger modes enhance the perception that we are people of value in a universe of inherent meaning, which has the effect of quelling existential anxieties (Becker, 1968). In the standing-out mode, our strivings to transcend ordinary existence can lead us to improve ourselves and society by continuing to learn, by improving current living conditions, by encouraging capacities to innovate and solve perplexing problems, by breaking through limiting barriers, and by creating that which never before existed—in short, to build a better life and a better world. Positive consequences of "standing-out strivings" are literally all around us, and comprise the forward thrust of creative and technological advances of all types. (For me, getting a doctoral degree and writing this book represent such strivings.)

In similar fashion, the blending in mode can also be quite beneficial. It brings us into contact with one another, providing us with a sense of common heritage and purpose. It encourages us to form new relationships that help us to better understand ourselves and the world we live in. Merger with others allows many of us to realize more of our intellectual, social, and creative tendencies, making is possible for us to surpass, in many instances, what we would be capable of accomplishing on our own. Merger allows us to feel a part of something larger and more permanent than ourselves. Ironically, it also provides us with a perennial problem to solve—how to get along peacefully with one another.

Weaknesses of Both Modes

But there are also costs related to both modes of heroism. While both work to suppress anxiety, they also create anxiety. Otto Rank (1884–1939) spoke at length about this paradox. In his *Art and Artist* (1932), Rank sees all forms of heroism as acts of will. By expressing our will, we differentiate ourselves and emerge from the group (standing out), whereas by suppressing our will, we minimize differences and blend in with the group (merger). Blending in creates guilt because we deny our creative individuality. On the other hand, expressing will and standing out from the group create guilt because we pull away from the family, or from society. The result is that no matter which way we choose, "willing" is inevitably a guilt-laden experience.

I have been aware of these processes at work in my own life. I was raised in a large, highly conventional, religiously devout family dominated by my father, in which children were not encouraged to trust their own feelings and thoughts—especially if such did not square with the ideology or opinions endorsed by my parents. In adult life, I have gravitated toward perspectives that are in many ways unorthodox given my upbringing. On one hand, I have felt compelled from within to explore modes of thought and perspectives that have brought me to what feels like a more authentic view of myself and the world. Not to "follow my own light" in these ways would be to suppress or deny my own lived experience. On the other hand, I have battled with occasional feelings of anxiety, self-doubt, and guilt because my moorings have pulled loose from those of my family. From the perspective of some of them, such feelings are indications that deep down, I know that I am in the wrong. From my perspective, I have come to realize that given the realities of my upbringing, occasional ambivalence and self-doubt are the price to be paid for independence and authenticity. As Rank (1932) suggested, the mature person—the creative person—is one who is able to will without too much guilt or inhibition. For most of us, giving birth to the true self is a lifelong process that may never really be complete.

Some specific shortcomings of the merger mode are depicted through George Orwell's (1949) characters Winston and Julia in his dystopian novel *1984*. These character's interiorities—their unique thoughts, feelings, perceptions, impressions, personal unorthodoxies, "heresies," and other nonconformist tendencies—are threatened and finally overcome by the immense pressure brought to bear by the system they are attempting to flee. The desire to be accepted by our fellows is not mere child's play, salient only when we are pimpled, insecure eighth-graders craving the affections and attentions of our peers. The urge to be approved of and to fit in remains a motivational force to be reckoned with throughout our lives. C. S. Lewis acknowledged this during a speech he gave toward the end of World War II:

> I believe that in all men's lives. . . one of the most dominant elements is the desire to be inside the local Ring and the terror at being left outside. . . . Of all the passions, the passion for the Inner Ring is most skillful in making a man who is not yet a very bad man do very bad things. (Lewis, 1944)

Individuals in the merger mode may also fall prey to the divisive, totalistic "isms" to which groups are prone (e.g., patriotism, nationalism, militarism, racism, conservativism, liberalism, capitalism, communism, etc.). Often, such "isms" have the same essential goal: the desire to remake humankind (Glover, 2001). The danger is that, in more malignant strains, such "isms" legitimize any means that bring about the desired end.

Because others are often seen as rivals, obstacles, or adversaries in the standing-out mode, our attempt to surpass and rise above others further exacerbates the intrinsic sense of separateness, enmity, and isolation that many of us experience at a deep level. For some, excelling at standing out contributes to the sense that others cannot understand what it is like to deal with the burdens of prominence, fame, or notoriety. The standing-out mode can also exacerbate humankind's inherent narcissistic tendencies, further inflating an ego that is already substantial and making it even more difficult for us to identify with or be empathetic with the experience of others. In fact, the heroic mode is the abode of the greatest despots and mass murderers in history: Genghis Khan, Nero, Ivan the Terrible, Hitler, Stalin, and Mao, to name just a few. Each of these men had gargantuan egos and was enthralled with power. In the name of their great vision for humanity, and toward the gratification of their own egos, no tactic was considered too extreme if it would advance the glorious cause.

In short, while the merger and standing-out versions of heroism serve the human species well in a variety of respects, they ultimately fail as solutions to the problem of finitude, as neither mode is able to deliver the truly authentic personhood that transcends intrapersonal and interpersonal conflict (Van Valin, 2009).

Ernest Becker articulated the realization that death is the issue *par excellence* for human beings. In an attempt to live in psychological equanimity despite our awareness of the reality of death, we have created cultures that provide us with a protective shield against the existential realities of life. Culture allows us to perceive of ourselves as persons of significance in a meaningful universe. It gives us an arena in which to strive for heroism in terms of rising above our peers or in seamlessly blending in with them in order to feel buoyed-up by our common vision of life. Culture gives us hope of immortality; it provides us with relationships and other endeavors that endow us with a sense of life purpose and the possibility of self-transcendence. However, in order to be fully imbued with death-denying qualities, we have to invest deeply in the worldviews that our cultures engender. This leads to a disposition of fear and defensiveness, as well as a desire to triumph over competing conceptions of reality. Indeed, we ask much of the anxious human animal to both invest psychologically in death-denying culture *and* to tolerate (let alone celebrate) the right of competing cultural constructions to exist side by side with his own, without resorting to damaging compensatory mechanisms.

PART FOUR
Who We Are

Situational Factors Contributing to Objectification

CHAPTER 12
Rising Awareness of Situational Power

Up to this point, our analysis has been centered on dispositional/internal factors that contribute to our tendencies to objectify others. However, an attempt to understand the problem of objectification and its attending evils would be incomplete without taking into account the substantial contribution (indeed, some would say the primary contribution) that situational/external factors play in influencing human behavior.

Most Westerners exhibit a strong cultural bias against acknowledging the power of situational influence. As Robert Bellah (1985) and his colleagues observed almost three decades ago, American culture contains strong elements of *individualism*, a value system that elevates the sovereignty of the individual to the level of the sacred. According to this view, an individual's right to think for herself, judge for herself, make her own decisions, and live her own life as she sees fit, is considered to be the highest good. Any forces that would curtail such capacities are considered to be not only morally wrong, but evil (Bellah, Madsen, Sullivan, Swindler, & Tipton, 1985, p. 142).[1] One variant of this perspective has been represented by the so-called "American Dream," a cultural mythology that emphasizes how life in the United States allows individuals the freedom, opportunity, and physical space to reinvent themselves (many times over, if need be) by using their own ingenuity, creativity, and hard work to transcend previous ceilings imposed by social class, ethnic background, or other perceived impediments to material success. The United States is thought to provide the raw materials necessary for any virtuous, hard-working, disciplined individual to go "from rags to riches," like the boys in Horatio Alger's nineteenth-century novels. This cultural ethos came out of a context of centuries-long struggle under monarchical and aristocratic

---

1. Not coincidentally, Bellah et al.'s work recapitulated conclusions drawn by French author Alexis de Toqueville (2001) [1838] 150 years earlier in his classic *Democracy in America*.

authority in Europe. These rulers wielded influence in seemingly arbitrary ways, and were often oppressive to those who dared to openly desire greater access to the rewards of their labor as well as the right to determine the direction of their lives. This historical context helps explain why the dispositional/ internal view of human behavior would predominate in the minds of many Westerners. Indeed, in the mid-twentieth century in the United States, not only was an emphasis on situational factors out of step with the conventional wisdom of the day, but to many, it seemed unwarranted, wrong-headed, even un-American in ways, especially given that it was in the pessimistic, deterministic theories of the adversary (e.g., Marx and Engels) that societal and situational forces received emphasis. However, world events soon coalesced in a way that would highlight the necessity for a different type of analysis.

Shortly after World War II, social scientists, along with the rest of the Western world, were trying to make sense of the shocking revelations emanating from both Europe and the Pacific Rim of the atrocities committed by Nazis against millions of Jews and other cultural minorities, and by the Japanese against thousands of Allied POWs, millions of Chinese civilians, and thousands of indigenous Pacific Islanders. Conventional wisdom, consistent with the deeply imbedded individualistic cultural strain, was that the Nazis were "monsters" and that the Japanese were similarly depraved, without conscience or moral scruples of any kind. Allied atrocities, on the other hand, such as saturation bombings of large civilian populations in Germany, or the use of two nuclear weapons against large population centers in Japan, were justified as responses to the Nazis' use of bombing earlier in the war against Britain, and as a way to avoid the catastrophe of invading Japan's mainland in order to force unconditional surrender. After the war, the desire of some to answer fundamental questions such as, "How could Auschwitz have happened?" led to a revolution in social psychological research, the likes of which the world will probably never see again.[2] The results of this research would turn the conventional wisdom upside down and cause many to fundamentally reassess their understandings of human behavior. Using the well worn metaphor of apples in a barrel (Zimbardo, 2008), it is true that there are some "bad apples" in the world who perpetrate evil. Society will be well served to identify such apples and to keep them a safe distance away from the remainder. But what about the barrel? Can't it also be true that a bad barrel can impact otherwise good apples housed within it?

2. I make this assertion based on the fact that the classic research from the early 1960s to the mid 1970s - utilized research paradigms that would not be allowed today given the heightened concern for the well-being of research subjects. Ironically, it was these very studies—designed to better understand why human beings are so willing to inflict harm on one another—that ended up sometimes doing emotional harm to some of their subjects. This outcome led to the creation of "human subjects review boards" whose task it is to safeguard the well-being of subjects participating in research.

At present, there are literally thousands of empirical studies verifying the barrel's power to impact the apples inside. What we now know is that "toxic situations" can contribute substantially to human beings' behaving in immoral ways. But perhaps what is less clear is whether or not toxic situations can amplify the universal human tendency toward objectifying others. In an attempt to answer this question, it is worth reviewing a few important, memorable lines of social psychological research. We will begin with two fairly innocuous early studies, which showed that situations do in fact matter, and then move quickly into a review of three landmark studies that some readers are likely to be familiar with. It will be meaningful to look again at these memorable studies through the lens of the objectification spectrum—a perspective none of these studies utilized as part of their original methodological planning or philosophical theorizing. Can certain situations influence or enhance our innate tendencies toward seeing others as objects? I assert that the answer to this question is a qualified yes—qualified because it appears that some toxic situations can induce us into behaving in highly immoral ways without necessarily enhancing our tendencies toward objectification (such as in Milgram's classic studies on obedience—more will be said of this toward the end of the next chapter), whereas other toxic situations show a clear capacity to catalyze our willingness to objectify others.

EARLY RESEARCH INTO THE POWER OF GROUP SITUATIONS ON THE INDIVIDUAL

Musafer Sherif

Perhaps it shouldn't come as a surprise that the man considered by many to be the founder of modern American social psychology wasn't born in America. The Turkish-born Musafer Sherif didn't come to the United States until after earning a bachelor's degree in economics in his home country. As a graduate student at Harvard, Sherif decided to shift his emphasis to psychology because the 1929 stock market crash showed him that "there was something very wrong" with the United States and its people, his adopted homeland (Sherif Obituary, 1988). Sherif hypothesized that Americans had more pressures to conform because of their strong beliefs in the ideal of democracy and its encouragement to band together socially and compromise in order to come to a workable consensus. As part of his doctoral dissertation at Columbia, Sherif had the ingenious idea to use what was known as the auto-kinetic effect to measure the conformity of individuals to group standards in a novel setting. The auto-kinetic effect is the tendency for individuals in a completely dark room who are shown a small dot of stationary light on a wall to perceive, after ten or twenty seconds, that the dot moves. This perception is thought to occur because the observer lacks a frame of reference for the dot due to the completely dark surroundings. Thus, the moving dot is an illusion generated by the mind. In Sherif's experiment, each subject was introduced individually into a dark room and asked to rate the degree to which the light moved; some saw it move a very small amount, whereas others judged that it moved more substantially. Each subject soon established a personal average range in which their reports of movement would fall. Then, subjects were put into the dark room with several other people. While reports of movement from the individuals in the group varied quite widely at first, after more trials, the group soon coalesced into an average range that all subjects seemed to agree upon. Then, after many trials, the subject was again put in the room by himself and asked to rate the light's movements. The subject's judgments now fell neatly into the range that his group had established previously, which often signaled a substantial departure from his own earlier individual judgments. Sherif then varied his protocols to include "insiders" who were trained by him to give certain specified judgments of the light's supposed movements, from very small to very large. Just as in previous trials, naive subjects' judgments were closely allied with that of insiders rather than with the sort of judgments they had previously made on their own.

Solomon Asch

Another foreign-born researcher, Solomon Asch of Poland, believed that US citizens were more independent than Sherif's research had suggested. Asch's assumption was that Americans possessed stronger wills than the average human being and would be independent, even when pressured by groups who had different perceptions of reality or how things should be done. He saw weaknesses in Sherif's research paradigm because the stimulus being examined was too ambiguous—it lacked any clear, obvious reference. As a result, research subjects never really committed very strongly to their own positions, so when under group pressure to conform, most just gave in. To genuinely assess the power of group pressure on the impulse to conform versus individual resolve to "stick to one's guns" despite being pressured to go along, Asch asserted that an individual would need to be presented with a stimulus that was *clearly* different from the others in the group, with group pressure then being brought to bear. Asch predicted that most American subjects under these conditions would hold firm to their own perceptions despite group pressures to conform.

Toward this end, at Swarthmore College in 1955, Asch came up with a simple research paradigm that involved two cards. One card depicted three lines of differing lengths: short, medium, and long. The other card depicted a copy of one of the three lines (this second card was randomly changed so that an exact copy of each of the varying line lengths would be presented). It was the subject's task to say which of the three lines on the first card dupli-cated the one on the single-line card—was the line the same as the short, medium, or long one? The task was very easy for subjects to complete cor-rectly (indeed, subjects made mistakes less than one percent of the time on their own). However, when seven "insider" subjects were added, and the naive subject was number eight in line to give his reply, things became more intriguing. Initially, naive subjects gave correct answers, just like their peers in line ahead of them. But when the insiders began to give unanimous wrong answers, naive subjects, some of whom were clearly a bit perplexed, began to change their responses to match their peers. (One can imagine how, as one of the insiders, it might have been hard not to snicker or chuckle when naive subjects, in response to obviously wrong answers, looked confused, but gave the same reply.) To Asch's surprise, 37 of 50 subjects conformed to the major-ity at least once, and 14 of them conformed on more than 6 of the 12 trials. When faced with a unanimous wrong answer by the other group members, the average subject conformed on 4 of the 12 trials. Asch was disturbed by these results, saying:

> The tendency to conformity in our society is so strong that reasonably intel-ligent and well-meaning young people are willing to call white black. This is a matter of concern. It raises questions about our ways of education and about the values that guide our conduct. (1955, p. 5)

Asch followed up his initial study with alterations in his methodology in order to determine at what point pressures to conform become salient. He found that when confronted by only one person whose judgment was dif-ferent, naive subjects exhibited some unease, but maintained their indepen-dence. Once the number of insiders rose to three, however, naive subjects conformed 32 percent of the time. Asch also learned that the presence of only one person whose views were in line with the naive subject greatly enhanced the willingness of the naive subject to hold his ground. Indeed, having the support of one subject diminished wrong responses to one-fourth of what they had been when there was no support, and this effect continued even after the supportive partner got up and left the research situation (Asch, 1955, p. 5).

The groundbreaking work of Sherif and Asch set the stage for a plethora of later research which would demonstrate in remarkable ways that situa-tional power often trumps individual power—that bad situations can over-turn an individual's typical disposition, personality traits, and character in certain contexts. Especially when the setting is new and unfamiliar, such situations can exert a disorienting effect on our moral compass, leading us to "do unto others" things we would never imagine ourselves capable of doing.

THE ADOLF EICHMANN TRIAL AND THE "BANALITY OF EVIL": AN OVER-CORRECTION

The spring of 1961 saw the notorious Nazi war criminal, Adolf Eichmann, finally being brought to trial for crimes against humanity. The trial took place in Jerusalem and was something of an international spectacle; given *carte blanche* by the Israeli government, news organizations from around the globe descended upon Jerusalem to broadcast the proceedings. The aging Eichmann, balding and bespectacled in thick lenses, sat inside a cubicle made of bullet-proof glass in order to protect him from family members of Holocaust victims should they attempt to kill him. Eichmann had been abducted by Israeli secret agents in a Buenos Aires suburb a year before. Offered the choice of death at the Mossad (Israeli Intelligence Agency) secret safe house in Argentina or standing trial in Israel, Eichmann opted for the latter (Holocaust Studies, 2011). Despite choosing what must have seemed as the lesser of two evils, and having been sedated for the duration of the transatlantic flight, Eichmann likely felt that he was walking off the edge of a great abyss as he stepped off the plane in the Holy Land. Now at age 55, the long-time Nazi bureaucrat who had become the "Transportation Administrator to the Final Solution to the Jewish Question"—the man who, from the fall of 1941 to the end of the war, was in charge of every train carrying doomed human cargo from occupied Europe into Poland—seemed to bear the brunt of the collective weight of the Holocaust on his shoulders. This same man, surely motivated to save himself, claimed throughout his trial that he was "only following orders," that he was merely a "transmitter" with very little power, that he ". . . never did anything, great or small, without obtaining in advance express instructions from Adolf Hitler or any of my superiors" (Baumeister & Bushman, 2010, p. 4).

Eichmann's last statements to the court included words that would find resonance a few short years later in a social science research laboratory at Yale. He said that he had never been a Jew-hater; that he had never willed the murder of human beings; that his guilt came from his obedience, though his obedience had been praised as a virtue. His obedience had been abused by the Nazi leaders, but he was not one of the ruling clique; he was a victim, and only the leaders deserved punishment (most of these individuals had already been put to death or had committed suicide) (Arendt, 1963, p. 247). Less than a year later, despite appeals made by his legal team and by a few notable Jewish intellectuals (Martin Buber being foremost among them) for a stay of execution (Arendt, 1963, p. 251), Eichmann died by hanging at the hands of the Jewish state for the role he played in the Nazi machine that consumed, as a pet project of Hitler's, more than 6 million Jews.

Eichmann's most prominent biographer, Hannah Arendt, wrote a lengthy treatise detailing his life and times, including specifics about his background, his family life, his work as a Nazi bureaucrat overseeing the transportation of Jews from various locales in Europe to death camps, his capture, his trial, and his execution. What made her work most notable was her assertion that Eichmann himself was not a monster, but was actually the most mundane of men. The implications of her perspective on Eichmann were that the greatest evils in the world are not only committed by charismatic, egomaniacal psychopaths, such as Hitler, but also by the most ordinary, mediocre, and "banal" of individuals. She asserted that her observations of Eichmann were supported by the experiences of most who attended the trials of war criminals after the war. Arendt (1963) writes:

> Nearly everybody who attended the trials of mass killers after the war, some of them respected doctors and pharmacists, came away with the disconcerting impression that the killers looked pretty much like you and me. The Israeli court psychiatrist who examined Eichmann found him a "completely normal man, more normal, at any rate, than I am after examining him," the implication being that the coexistence of normality and bottomless cruelty explodes our ordinary conceptions and presents the true enigma of the trial. (pp. xiv, xv)

In other words, for Arendt, the most remarkable and frightening aspect of the trial was her realization that Eichmann could not be dismissed as someone who was psychotic or in other ways fundamentally different from the vast majority of human beings—he was all too average and ordinary for that. His appearance was unremarkable; his comportment was unmemorable; his intelligence was middling at best; his personality was bland. If he were not on trial for crimes against humanity, he would have been utterly forgettable in almost every respect, and *this* was the frightening thought. It made so much more sense to the world that he be something else—something extraordinary in order to have played such a central role in so much suffering and death. But in all discernible ways, he was not unusual.

Arendt's analysis of Eichmann was important, but it was also flawed. On one hand, Arendt's stunning pronouncements, encapsulated by the now clichéd phrase "the banality of evil," served the important purpose of waking up the self-righteous masses to the fact that perpetrators of mass evil are not in fact monsters, but rather, are all too human. This meant that the conventional wisdom about evil and where it comes from—from within persons who are fundamentally different from the rest of us—is too often inadequate to explain the data and needs re-examination. On the other hand, Arendt's analysis minimized the facts of Eichmann's personal worldview, which was rife with the genocide-themed anti-Semitism of the Third Reich, despite the fact that he attempted to downplay these realities at his trial, especially during the early days, which comprised the portion of the proceedings that Arendt had attended (Haslam & Reicher, 2008, p. 17). Eichmann was not a mindless bureaucrat, a mere "pencil-pusher" who only followed orders without any malice intended toward the millions of nameless individuals whose deaths were all but guaranteed by the papers he signed and the orders he moved along. Indeed, he pioneered creative new policies to enhance efficiency and took pride in his "accomplishments," once proclaiming, "I shall laugh when I jump into the grave because of the feeling that I killed five million Jews; that gives me a lot of satisfaction and pleasure" (Goldhagen, 2009, p. 158).

A number of recent books have emerged that re-examine the perspective that Nazis were simply following orders, finding that relatively few can be exonerated on these grounds (Haslam & Reicher, 2007a). Contrary to popular belief, genocide is not inspired by images of human beings as mere numbers, abstractions, or products on an assembly line, as problematic as these perceptions can be. Genocide typically requires more than this; what is needed is a pervasive, vivid, dehumanizing perspective inveighed against the humanity of the intended victim embedded in a drama of the highest stakes imaginable (Smith, 2011, p. 104). Eichmann may have been a rather mediocre specimen of a man, but the beliefs that gave structure and direction to his actions were anything but banal. The dehumanizing beliefs that he endorsed were replete with the image of Jews defiling Aryan purity with their supposed genetic filth and corruption. Images of the Jews depicted as rats and lice—carriers of blood-borne infections, disease, and decay—had been prominent in Germany for years before Hitler marched into Poland in 1939. Such perceptions typified the view of reality that many "true believers" of the destiny of the Reich held. Arendt's verdict on Eichmann represents an over-correction from the previous dispositional paradigm which asserted that evil comes from within, that those who commit atrocities are fundamentally different from most ordinary human beings. Eichmann was apparently a very ordinary man in many respects, but he identified strongly with Hitler's ideology. The worst types of brutality occur when people strongly identify with groups that have a brutal ideology (Haslam & Reicher, 2008, p. 18). This perspective must be included in order to fully understand the motive for the evil Eichmann perpetuated. Contexts matter—and they matter a great deal—but so do worldviews. It is important, when attempting to accurately understand evil, to not lose sight of both.

CHAPTER 13

Situationally Induced Objectification

Three Relevant Classic Examples

When you think of the long and gloomy history of man, you will find far more hideous crimes have been committed in the name of obedience than have been committed in the name of rebellion.

C. P. Snow *(as quoted in Milgram, 1974, p. 1)*

Nearly one hundred years of social-psychological research shows that if we want to understand evil, we must take into account the role that situations play in influencing otherwise "normal" human beings to behave immorally. In numerous instances, the human tendency to objectify others—to disregard their totality, to relate to them as Subject to object rather than Subject to Subject—seems to be an experimental variable being manipulated, though few researchers ever seem to have been aware of this fact.

To underscore the connection between toxic situations and an increase in one's capacity to objectify others, we will briefly examine three classic studies—two conducted by Phillip Zimbardo and his colleagues, and another conducted by Albert Bandura. These three studies are in no way exhaustive; rather, they show what hundreds of similar studies show: that certain social psychological variables do indeed have the power to alter the way we view others, leading to changes in our willingness to behave immorally toward them.

A WORD ABOUT MILGRAM'S STUDIES

Many readers will be familiar with Stanley Milgram's groundbreaking research on obedience, which stunned the world with its results, and wonder why they are not included here as evidence regarding the role that situations can play in increasing objectification. For those unfamiliar with this line of research,

Milgram's experiments demonstrated—in the United States, and in the shadow of Adolf Eichmann's recently concluded trial in Jerusalem—that normal men and women (designated "teachers") were willing to give other pleasant, mild-mannered men and women (designated "learners") ever escalating levels of seemingly painful electric shocks simply because an anonymous authority figure told them to do so. These results flew in the face of what most would have predicted. Indeed, Milgram put the study's basic outline before a collection of 14 Yale undergraduate seniors in psychology, a professional group of his Yale peers, and 40 psychiatrists from the area to get their predictions regarding outcome. The groups were unanimous in asserting that they themselves would break off the experiment at some point long before the procedures reached their peak. They also predicted that less than one person in 100 would continue to the end of the experiment, and that most subjects would not go beyond the designation "very strong shock" (195 volts) (Milgram, 1974, p. 27). They were all quite wrong. While a few individuals did actually terminate their participation in the studies early, none of them did so until some point after the 300-volt level (Milgram, 1963, p. 375).

Most important for our analysis, there is no question that most if not all subjects were quite uncomfortable with the proceedings—that they were, in fact, behaving in ways contrary to their own deeply held belief systems and values. One observer, watching the proceedings behind a one-way mirror (in one of the 19 permutations on the original experiment) had this to say (Milgram, 1963):

> I observed [an] initially poised business-man [who] within 20 minutes [. . .] was reduced to a twitching, stuttering wreck, rapidly approaching a point of nervous collapse. He constantly pulled on his earlobe [. . .] twisted his hands. . . [and] pushed his fist into his forehead muttering, "Oh God, let's stop it." [. . .] Yet, he [. . .] obeyed to the very end. (p. 377)

In a recent conversation about Milgram with a close family member (a widely admired woman of impressive comportment and high moral character), she suggested to me that had she been in the Milgram experiments, given her pronounced, ingrained fear of authority (i.e., fear of their anger, fear of them somehow complicating her life), she would likely have—reluctantly—complied with the experimenter's wishes, not because she was objectifying the poor guy supposedly getting the shocks, but because she would have been more afraid of the authority figure's potential actions.[1] Indeed, the description

---

1. I consider this to be an enlightened admission on this person's part. Most people, when asked, tend to assert that they would be the exception to the rule—that they would be one of the precious few resisting authority pressure to inflict high levels of pain upon another person. However, we can't all be the exception to the rule.

of the "initially poised business man" above seems to fit just such a profile—he was deeply conflicted about what he was doing, he felt very badly for the man inside the box supposedly being shocked; nevertheless, because of the authority figure's pressure to obey, he did it anyway.

Given these observations, when analyzing these remarkable studies, it is hard to argue that Milgram's procedures somehow moved subjects along the objectification continuum, and that this is what accounted for their willingness to escalate the intensity of shocks given to the learner. The fact that most of Milgram's subjects evidenced at least some level of discomfort with what they were being asked to do—indeed, some manifested very high levels of discomfort and internal conflict—suggests neither that the learner had been deeply objectified by teachers, nor that the procedures increased whatever tendencies toward objectification the teachers might have had initially. However, the fact that *all* subjects were willing to participate in the study, even after they were told that they would be giving a series of escalating shocks to another person, suggests a number of possibilities about participants' dispositions: (1) subjects entered the experimental situation with more than a modicum of the "casual indifference" level of objectification already occurring within their psyches; (2) subjects underestimated or downplayed the severity of the shocks they would be administering, despite a demonstration that should have dispelled this misconception; or (3) despite realizing what they would be doing and feeling uncomfortable about the whole idea, subjects felt obligated to follow through with the procedures given that they had already entered the experimental situation and saw no evident way out. Whatever the case may be, Milgram's studies do not seem to represent a clear example of situational variables escalating people's native tendencies toward objectification.

THE POWER OF ROLES IN ENHANCING OBJECTIFICATION: THE STANFORD PRISON EXPERIMENT (SPE)

Listen carefully to me now—you are not #819. You are Stewart, and my name is Dr. Zimbardo. I am a psychologist, not a prison superintendent, and this is not a real prison. This is just an experiment, and those guys in there are just students like you. So it's time to go home, Stewart.

Phillip Zimbardo to one of the subjects designated "prisoner" (2008, p. 107)

Is it possible that an arbitrarily assigned role might have the power to influence our perceptions to the extent that we would be more willing to harm others? In the context of our larger analysis, might the adoption of specific roles have the power to move us further along the objectification spectrum?

The basement of Stanford University's Jordan Hall seems an unlikely location for an extended simulated prison experiment, but this is where Zimbardo and colleagues conducted such research during the early 1970s to determine if abusive prison situations were byproducts of the personalities of individual guards and prisoners, or were instead products of toxic situations. Toward this end, they decided to set up a mock prison where "prisoners" and "guards" would be provided the time and the space to interact in a largely unstructured way in order to see what impact the overarching structure of a "prison" would have on their behaviors. Seventy-five subjects were recruited from an ad placed in a local newspaper asking for "male college students interested in participating in a study on the psychological aspects of prison life."[2] All applicants were given thorough psychiatric interviews and personality tests to eliminate candidates with emotional problems, medical disabilities, or a history of crime or drug abuse. Ultimately, this left a sample of 24 young men who wanted to earn $15 a day by participating in a study. Based on all the criteria that the research team tested or observed, the remaining 24 subjects were "normal": healthy, intelligent, middle-class white males. This small sample was divided randomly into two groups—prisoners and guards—by a coin flip. Thus, at the beginning of the experiment, there were no discernible differences between the subjects assigned as guards or prisoners. Once expert consultants and skilled craftsmen helped alter the Stanford University Jordan Hall basement into a realistic facsimile of a small prison (Zimbardo, n.d.a.),[3] the experiment was ready to begin. The experiment was to take two weeks to complete, yet it ended up lasting only six days. This would seem to suggest that the experiment was a failure. On the contrary, the experiment evoked effects so strong that for the well-being of all involved, the study had to be aborted prematurely. In his book chronicling the study (2008), Zimbardo takes 175 pages to describe the occurrences of each of the six days of the experiment. For the sake of brevity, I will

2. This recruiting tactic, seemingly innocuous, may in fact have biased who signed up for Zimbardo's study. Canaghan and McFarland (2007) found that those who responded to ads to "participate in a prison study" were much more likely to accept or not have a problem with the harsh and hierarchical world that exists in prison than were those who responded to participate in a standard psychological experiment.

3. Each end of a main basement corridor was boarded up in order to create "the Yard," which was the only place where prisoners were allowed to walk, eat, or exercise, except to go to the toilet down a separate hallway (which prisoners did blindfolded so as not to know the way out of the prison). To create prison cells, doors were taken off some laboratory rooms and replaced with customized doors with steel bars and cell numbers on them. At one end of "the Yard" was a small opening through which a TV camera recorded the events that occurred. On the side of the corridor opposite the cells was a small closet designated "the Hole," or solitary confinement. It was approximately two feet wide and two feet deep, but high enough that a person could stand up. An intercom system was installed in order to "bug" the cells to monitor what prisoners discussed, and also to make public announcements to the prisoners. There were no windows or clocks to judge the passage of time.

only summarize a few of the main events of each day; much important detail will necessarily be left out.

Day One (Sunday): Subjects who've been designated "prisoners" are picked up early in the morning at their homes by police, often as concerned neighbors look on. Once at the station, each prisoner is formally booked, read their Miranda rights, fingerprinted, and photographed for a mug shot. The prisoner is then taken to a holding cell, where he is left blindfolded, in a state of bewilderment.

Before the prisoners arrive at the Jordan Hall prison, the guards are brought on-site. They are issued identical khaki uniforms, mirrored sunglasses, whistles, and billy clubs. They are given no specific training on how to be guards. Instead they are free, within limits, to do whatever they think is necessary to maintain law and order in the prison and to command the respect of the prisoners. Three rotating eight-hour guard shifts are instituted. Guards make up their own sets of rules, which they then carry into effect under the supervision of the warden. They are warned, however, of the potential seriousness of their mission and of the possible dangers in the situation they are about to enter.

Later that day, each prisoner is brought to the prison site to be greeted by the warden (a Stanford undergraduate), who conveys the seriousness of their offenses and their new status as prisoners. Each prisoner is then systematically searched, stripped naked, "deloused," and issued a smock (with no underwear), which he wears at all times. In the midst of this process, without any staff encouragement, some of the guards begin to make fun of the prisoner's genitals, making remarks about their small penises and uneven testicles. Zimbardo also notes that as soon as prisoners are put in their smocks they begin to walk and sit differently, and to hold themselves differently—more vulnerably, and more like a woman than like a man. On the smock is a prison ID number. A heavy chain, which is to be worn at all times, is affixed to each prisoner's right ankle. Flip-flop sandals are issued as footwear, and each prisoner is made to cover his hair with a nylon stocking cap.

At the conclusion of the degrading introductory process, prisoners are assembled together. Guards pronounce 17 restrictive rules regarding prison routines, prisoner obedience, personal hygiene, and cell orderliness, which the prisoners are forced to memorize and recite. Then, the first of many "counts" (i.e., requiring the inmates to assemble in a line to be counted) is initiated, presenting opportunities for guards to assert power over prisoners. Smiles, chuckles, and slack posture from prisoners are verbally reprimanded, and pushups are instituted as punishment. Among themselves, guards are already voicing concerns that certain prisoners are going to be trouble. Guards also differ in terms of how they feel about the "degradation rituals" of earlier that day. The night shift arrives and performs random counts throughout the night, accompanied by shrieking whistles and shouts. Prisoner idiosyncrasies in behavior soon begin to elicit a variety of creative, punitive responses from the guards. One prisoner is put into "the Hole" (a small closet) as an example.

Day Two (Monday): Early morning counts and reprimands from guards for petty disorganization (e.g., wrinkles in bedding) lead to "disrespectful behavior" from a prisoner, who is put promptly into the Hole. Another prisoner soon has an altercation with a guard who, despite rules to the contrary, punches the prisoner in the chest and then, with other guards, strong-arms the prisoner into the Hole, along with a fellow prisoner who complained (the two of them miss breakfast). Other prisoners begin to rebel, verbally testing the guards with profanity. In one room, prisoners remove their stocking caps, rip off their numbers, and barricade themselves into their cell, refusing to come out for mandatory counts. Voluntarily, the night shift guards stay on to help the morning shift guards deal with their predicament. Guards take out their frustrations on other prisoners by storming their rooms and removing their beds. Physical altercations ensue, as prisoners vehemently protest, "No, no, no! This is an *experiment*! Leave me alone! Let go of me, you fucker! You're not going to take our fucking beds!" Another exclaims, "A fucking simulation! It's a fucking simulated experiment! It's no prison!" (Zimbardo, 2008, p. 61). To get into barricaded rooms, guards use fire extinguishers equipped with skin-chilling carbon dioxide to spray barricaded prisoners away from their doors. Once inside, the guards strip the prisoners naked and take away their beds. Additional "hole" space is created so that guards can put the insubordinates into solitary confinement. Realizing that the situation is becoming more and more volatile, Zimbardo advises the warden to announce the possibility of prisoners forming a committee to voice grievances to "Superintendent" Zimbardo. A three-person prisoner committee is created. They complain that their contract has been violated in many ways: the guards are both physically and verbally abusive; there is an unnecessary level of harassment; food is inadequate; and guards have taken their books, glasses, and medications. Later that day, one of the prisoners decompensates: His thinking becomes disorganized, he cries uncontrollably, and he lashes out in rage. He demands to see the superintendent. The meeting is arranged, and Superintendent Zimbardo easily manages to talk the prisoner into staying. The prisoner returns to the yard and tells the other prisoners, "You can't leave; there's no way to quit." Later that night, the same prisoner (a leading antiwar activist in the Bay Area) continues to decompensate: "You're messing up my head, man! My head! This is an experiment. This is all fucked up inside! I can't stand it another night! I'll do anything I have to get out! I'll wreck your cameras, and I'll hurt the guards!" He then threatens to slit his wrists (Zimbardo, 2008, p. 77). After lengthy deliberation, the decision is made to release him from the experiment. Later, one of the guards overhears another prisoner talking about a possible break-in and liberation of the prisoners by the released prisoner and his friends. Elaborate and disruptive steps are taken by supervisors and guards to thwart such an attempt, which never occurs.

Day Three (Tuesday): The prison begins to smell like a camping latrine in mid-summer. Guards have turned toilet breaks into a privilege that has to be earned. Prisoner's rooms are issued buckets for toileting after lights-out, which are not allowed be emptied until morning. Realizing that they can't keep additional guards on duty at all times, the guards concoct the idea of "privilege cells" in order to use psychological rather than physical means to better control prisoners. Non-misbehaving prisoners are given beds and are allowed to wash and brush their teeth, but others are not. They are also allowed to eat special food in front of the other prisoners. Later, on a whim, the guards switch things up and allow the "bad" prisoners to go into the privilege cell and put the good ones into the bad cells. The effect is to break prisoner solidarity by causing prisoners to assume that some of their own are being bribed into being informants. The earlier prisoner rebellion serves to enhance solidarity among the guards. No longer viewing their role as "just an experiment," the guards now see the prisoners as real adversaries who are out to get them. In response, the guards increase their control tactics, surveillance, and use of aggression.

Day Four (Wednesday): A priest who's been an actual prison chaplain comes to give the experimenters feedback on how real he thinks their simulation is. As he interviews each prisoner individually, researchers watch in amazement as half the prisoners introduce themselves by number rather than by name. After some small talk, he asks, "Son, what are you doing to get out of here?" When the prisoners respond with puzzlement, he explains (bizarrely) that the only way to get out of prison is with the help of a lawyer. He then volunteers to contact their parents to get legal aid if they want him to, and some of the prisoners accept his offer. The priest's presence and his odd, stereotypical behavior further blurs the line between role-playing and reality. The only prisoner who does not want to speak to the priest is Prisoner #819, who is feeling sick, refuses to eat, and wants to see a doctor. Eventually, he is persuaded to come out of his cell and talk to the priest and superintendent so that decisions about intervention can be made. In the midst of talking, he begins to cry hysterically. His chains and his head covering are taken off, and he is told to rest while a ruling is made. Just then, one of the guards lines up the other prisoners and has them chant loudly, "Prisoner #819 is a bad prisoner. Because of what Prisoner #819 did, my cell is a mess, Mr. Correctional Officer." Their loud, repeated, in-unison shouts reduce #819 to uncontrollable sobs. Zimbardo suggests to #819 that he leave the experiment, but he refuses. Through his tears, he says that he could not leave because the others had labeled him a bad prisoner. Even though he is feeling sick, he wants to go back and prove he is not a bad prisoner. At that point, Superintendent Zimbardo says to him (Zimbardo, 2008):

> Listen carefully to me now—you are not #819. You are Stewart, and my name is Dr. Zimbardo. I am a psychologist, not a prison superintendent, and this is not a real prison. This is just an experiment, and those guys in there are just students like you. So it's time to go home, Stewart. (p. 107)

Zimbardo then reports that Stewart, ". . . stopped sobbing, wiped away the tears, straightened up, looked into my eyes like a small child awakened from a nightmare, and replied, 'Okay, let's go'" (Zimbardo, 2008, p. 107).

Day Five (Thursday): At the 7:00 a.m. count, prisoner #5704, routinely picked on by the guards, refuses to do sit-ups when he's commanded to. As punishment, the rest of the prisoners are forced to do them until #5704 relents. He doesn't give in and eventually is put in the Hole. Upon his release, he attempts to assault a guard, and it takes two other guards to restrain him and get him back in his cell. Later on, prisoner #416 (who was a replacement prisoner brought in when an earlier prisoner was released), dumbfounded by what he has witnessed since arriving only the night before, decides to go on a hunger strike and refuses to eat. Later that day, Zimbardo releases prisoner #1037 from the experiment because of the symptoms of "extreme stress." This is followed by the release of prisoner #4325 for similar reasons. That evening, a consultant (Christina Mislatch, Zimbardo's romantic partner and recently hired assistant professor at Berkeley) spends some time meeting with a few of the guards and consulting with staff. From the superintendent's office she happens to witness the last "toilet run" of the night which is, in effect, a chain gang parading past the open door of the office—ankle chains linked from inmate to inmate, paper bags over their heads, each prisoner's right hand holding on to the shoulder before him, with a guard leading the procession. Excitedly, Zimbardo exclaims, "Chris, look at this! She looks up momentarily, then turns her head away. "Did you see that? What do you think?" Her lack of fascination strikes Zimbardo as unprofessional, even inappropriate. He says to her, "Don't you understand that this is a crucible of human behavior, that we are seeing things no one has ever witnessed before in such a situation?" Clearly upset, with tears running down her cheeks, Mislatch replies, "I'm leaving. Forget dinner. I'm going home. . . . *What you are doing to those boys is a terrible thing.*" Out of the approximately 50 outsiders who have seen the prison on the inside, she is the only one to question the basic morality of the experiment. Zimbardo comes to the conclusion that perhaps it's time for the experiment to end.

Later that night, during counts, guards engage in blatant sexual harassment of the five remaining, bedraggled prisoners. They force prisoners to make sexually humiliating statements to one another. They then designate some of prisoners as "female camels," coercing them into bending over and exposing their bare buttocks. The other prisoners, designated "male camels," are then forced to "hump them" from behind, much as American soldier prison personnel at the Abu Ghraib prison in Iraq did over 30 years later (Clemens, 2010). With this, Zimbardo formally decides that it's time for the experiment to end, less than halfway through its intended duration.

Day Six (Friday): By lunchtime, the experiment is officially ended. Zimbardo's declaration is first met with disbelief, and then euphoria. Debriefing of both prisoners and guards soon commences, and group therapy–like encounters between the two groups occur over the next number of hours.

Guards

Before the experiment began, Zimbardo oriented those selected as guards to their roles. He spoke about the realities of prison life for prisoners and said that he wanted to create a "psychological atmosphere that would capture some of the essential features characteristic of many prisons. . ." (Zimbardo, 2008, p. 55). More specifically, he instructed them that:

> [w]e cannot physically abuse or torture them. We can create boredom. We can create a sense of frustration. We can create fear in them, to some degree. We can create a notion of the arbitrariness that governs their lives, which are totally controlled by us. . . . They'll have no privacy at all, there will be constant surveillance—nothing they do will go unobserved. They will have no freedom of action. They will be able to do nothing and say nothing that we don't permit. We're going to take away their individuality in various ways. They're going to be wearing uniforms, and at no time will anyone call them by name; they will have numbers and will be called only by their numbers. What all this should create in them is a sense of powerlessness. We have total power in this situation. They have none. (p. 55)

In other words, those who were assigned the guard role were primed with the expectation that they would behave in ways that would create a sense of powerlessness in the prisoners.[4] It is hard to argue that such instructions did not have some sort of impact on the guard's later behaviors. In addition, those designated as guards were also primed institutionally in ways that decreased their sense of individuality and common humanity with prisoners. The result was a situation that soon spiraled into general maltreatment of prisoners by guards, interspersed with incidences of violence and sexual abuse.

---

4. This is one of the main criticisms of the study: that subjects were not merely responding to the power of the situation, but were cued by researchers to behave in specific ways before they ever entered the "laboratory" (Haslam & Reicher, 2008, p. 18).

Those in the guard role seemed to coalesce into three types: (1) "tough but fair" guards who followed prison rules; (2) "good guys" who seemed to sympathize with the prisoners; and (3) "hostile, arbitrary, and inventive" guards who engaged in forms of prisoner abuse and humiliation. This last group of guards seemed to revel in the power they wielded. None of the pre-experiment screening procedures detected such tendencies. In other words, they looked no different from any of their peers on measures of psychological adjustment, but once these guards adopted their role, they moved rather quickly along the objectification spectrum into significant levels of derivatization where prisoners became mere extensions of their own whims and wishes. Indeed, the "hostile" guards (especially one nicknamed "John Wayne") descended into the realms of violence and sexual humiliation—some of which was not detailed above—with a rapidity that was remarkable for the experimenters to behold. It should also be pointed out that most of the guards were upset when the experiment was ended early, and that no guard ever came late for his shift, called in sick, left early, or demanded extra pay for overtime work (Zimbardo, n.d.a).

Prisoners

Those put into the prisoner role were first arrested in a rather unsettling way, then were subjected to experiences meant to humiliate them (being searched and stripped naked), degrade them (being deloused), de-masculinize them (being issued smocks—sans underwear—to be worn at all times), de-individualize them, anonymize them (having their names replaced with a prison ID and their hair covered with nylon stockings), and oppress them (wearing a heavy chain affixed to the right ankle at all times). For prisoners, the psychological impact of the above, combined with the loss of their personal identities and the incessant, arbitrary control tactics, as well as deprivations of privacy and sleep, led to a condition of passivity, dependency, and depression that resembled what has been called "learned helplessness" (Seligman & Maier, 1967).[5]

A few of the prisoners were able to maintain senses of themselves as separate from their designated role during the ordeal. One engaged in passive resistance by refusing to eat. Another, nicknamed "Sarge," stood up to the guard's domination and refused to yell obscenities at fellow prisoners when commanded to do so. Overall, he seemed to adjust the best to the rigid prison atmosphere.[6] Another, the most "evenly balanced" prisoner, said afterward that he survived by

5. *Learned helplessness*, a term coined by Martin Seligman (Seligman & Maier, 1967), refers to the behavioral phenomenon that occurs when human beings or animals learns to behave helplessly (i.e., passive resignation) when they perceive that their actions have no bearing on outcome.
6. Interestingly, Sarge was also the prisoner who ranked highest on pre-study measures of authoritarianism (Zimbardo, 2008, pgs. 198–199).

"turning inward" and not being as involved or helpful to the others as he might have been. However, none of these attempts represented any sort of coordinated effort, and so the effect on fellow prisoners was minimal. By the experiment's end, the prisoners had disintegrated, both individually and collectively. There was no group cohesiveness. Rather, single, isolated individuals tried to "hang on," much like many prisoners of war have described. The guards controlled every aspect of the prison, and they commanded the blind obedience of each prisoner (Zimbardo, n.d.a).

The Lucifer Effect

One might wonder why the subjects involved in the SPE didn't simply come together soon after the procedures began and say, "Look—this is going to be a long experiment. Let's make things much easier for all of us by coming up with some reasonable rules that everyone can accept and live by; that way, we'll all get along and things can go smoothly and quietly. We'll all earn our money with the least amount of hassle and get out of here." But this was not at all what the experimenters were interested in, and this is far from what happened. Powerful situational forces—such as convincing physical surroundings; de-individuating garb worn by both guards and prisoners serving to make them anonymous; ready objects of guard aggression such as clubs and whistles; absence of specific directives, protocol, or sanctions on guards from those in authority; arbitrary and restrictive rules governing guard/prisoner interactions; and, perhaps most significant, disorienting new roles—were brought to bear, affecting both the subjects and, ironically, the experimenters themselves. Zimbardo described this phenomenon as *the Lucifer Effect*, a term referring to the transformation of human psychology and behavior from pro-social to antisocial, resulting from certain situational forces, seemingly insignificant or benign in isolation, but synergistically malignant when combined together (2008; n.d.b).

The Corrupting Power of Roles

While each of the factors mentioned above played an important role in contributing to the toxic situation of the SPE, perhaps the most significant contributor was the provocative and powerful roles invoked at the outset of the experiment. Roles are "scripts," prescribed ways of behaving in certain situations. Human beings' lives comprise multiple roles at any given time, and while we may be better at fulfilling some roles than others, we generally have a good sense of what behaviors are called for in each case. No specific training is required. In the case of the guards and prisoners, the scripts for these roles likely came from the subjects' own experiences with power and powerlessness: from their observation of parental interactions (i.e., traditionally—and loosely—dad is guard, mom is prisoner); from their experiences with authority figures such as bosses, teachers, doctors; and finally, from their limited experiences seeing prison life depicted in films, television programs, or books. In Zimbardo's words, "Society has done the training for us" (2008, p. 216).

When we have accepted or given our assent to a role, it can be very difficult not to "play along" according to the implied script. The power of any role depends on the support system that demands it and prescribes it, not allowing alternate reality to intrude (Zimbardo, 2008, p. 217). In such circumstances, perceptions of self and others can drift out of the typical parameters that act as moorings for our assumptions, values, and moral codes. This can lead to behaviors uncharacteristic of us when we are in more common circumstances, enacting familiar roles. The SPE was a "total" system in this respect, in which outside influences were present from time to time but actual feedback was minimal, and the roles of prisoner and guard were starkly contrasted and relentlessly reinforced. The power of these roles to elicit new perceptions and behaviors became evident very quickly, as this SPE guard realized:

> Once you put a uniform on, and are given a role [. . .] then you're certainly not the same person if you're in street clothes and in a different role. *You really become that person* once you put on the khaki uniform, you put on the sunglasses, you take the nightstick, and you act the part. That's your costume and you have to act accordingly when you put it on. (Zimbardo, 2008, p. 213, emphasis added)

Clearly, when those designated guards put on their uniforms and took in hand the symbols of their status, they entered a role that enhanced their sense of personal power. Conversely, their perceptions of their peers now designated as prisoners went in the opposite direction: Prisoners were now devalued commodities. This, coupled with the other toxic aspects of the situation, made it much more likely that the guards would behave in ways that were, for them, out of character, just as those designated prisoners began a descent into a heretofore unprecedented role of powerlessness as they donned their sheer, wrinkled, emasculating smocks at the beginning of the experiment. The factors mentioned above combined as a catalyst to escalate some of the guards' native levels of objectification into realms that they had never before experienced. It's hard to imagine that any of those randomly selected as guards would have treated any of their peers with the kind of harshness and contempt that they evidenced toward them just a few days later. One of the guards offered some perspective:

> I would have really thought that I was incapable of this kind of behavior. I was surprised. . . . No, I was dismayed to find that I could really be a. . . That I could

act in a manner so absolutely unaccustomed to anything I would ever really dream of doing. And I . . . And while I was doing it, I um. . . I didn't feel any regret, I didn't feel any guilt; it was only after, afterwards, when I began to reflect on what I had done that this began to. . . that this behavior began to dawn on me and I realized that this was a part of me that I hadn't really noticed before. (Zimbardo, n.d.a)

Why this happened to some guards to a much greater degree than others is puzzling. One possibility is that in at least one case, the guard known as "John Wayne" may have identified much more strongly with Zimbardo's leadership role than anyone initially realized, even seeing himself as a quasi-experimenter in his own right, creatively inventing new ways to humiliate and torment his fellow subjects in an attempt to see just how far he could push them before they snapped (Zimbardo, 2008, pp. 192–194). Another possibility is that brutality can occur in people when they are subject to situational forces like those mentioned above, especially when they identify strongly with groups that have a brutal ideology. Like the case of Adolf Eichmann mentioned in Chapter 12, this identification encourages them to further that ideology knowingly, creatively, and even proudly (Haslam & Reicher, 2008, p. 18).

THE POWER OF LABELS IN ENHANCING OBJECTIFICATION: BANDURA'S ANIMALIZED COLLEGE STUDENTS

Nothing is more conducive to . . . brutalization of the modern world than . . . degrading definitions of man. . . . When people speak of people as. . . apes, all doors are opened to the free entry of bestiality.

E. F. Schumacher (1977, p. 22)

Life has not been devised by morality: it wants deception, it lives on deception.

Friederich Nietzsche (1879, p. 5)

"Kill a Gook for God."

message written on US soldier's helmet in Vietnam

In the mid-1970s, the renowned social psychologist Albert Bandura devised a remarkable experiment to test the power that dehumanizing labels have to encourage harm against others (Bandura, 1975). From the perspective of our analysis, Bandura was actually testing whether or not the use of dehumanizing labels could move people along the objectification spectrum, altering both their perspective of others and their behaviors toward them.

In pursuit of this end, junior college male volunteers were divided into "supervisory teams" of three members, whose task was to punish the defective decision-making of other college students. Naturally, the real subjects were those comprising the "supervisory teams" rather than those playing the role of decision-maker. On each of 25 trials, the "supervisors" were able to overhear the decision-making teams (supposedly in an adjacent room) formulating collective decisions. The supervisors were to evaluate the decisions of the teams based on criteria they had been given. Whenever a poor decision was made, the supervisory team was to provide punishment by administering a shock, which was supposedly given to each member of the decision-making team (of course, there were no actual shocks applied). They could choose the level of the shock's intensity, from a minimum level of 1 to a maximum level of 10 on any trial.

Bandura and his colleagues varied two crucial aspects of this situation: how the decision-makers were labeled, and how personally responsible the supervisors were for the punishment they administered. The supervisors were randomly assigned to three experimental conditions of labeling—dehumanized, humanized, or neutral—and two conditions of responsibility—individualized or diffused.

After the study was underway and procedures were moving along smoothly, each threesome of supervisors was led to believe that they were overhearing a conversation over an intercom ("accidentally" left on) between a research assistant and one of the primary experimenters about the questionnaires the decision-makers had supposedly completed. The assistant made a casual but candid remark about his impression of the overall qualities shown by the group of decision-makers. In the dehumanized (i.e., enhanced objectification) experimental condition, the assistant said, "These guys are an animalistic, rotten bunch." By contrast, in the humanized condition, the assistant said, "These people are a really perceptive, understanding, group" (Bandura, 1975, p. 258). In the neutral condition, no evaluative statements were made about the group. At no time did the subjects ever interact directly with the shock victims, and so they were unable to make such evaluations personally.

Not surprisingly, the labels stuck and had a substantial impact on how the victims were treated. Those labeled as "animals" were shocked most intensively, and their shock levels increased in a clear, linear fashion (meaning that their shocks climbed higher with subsequent trials, up to an average of 7 out of 10) over the 10 trials of the study. Those labeled "humanized" were given the least amount of shock, while the unlabeled fell between the two extremes.

It is important to point out that at the outset of the experiment, there were no real differences between the levels of shocks the three groups received for making errors. However, as the experiment proceeded and the mistakes began to mount, divergences between the levels of punishment dished out to the three groups began to be quite evident. Those shocking the "animals" shocked them more intensely over time. On the other hand, the fact that those who were labeled positively—and thus perceived as most human—were harmed the least shows that positively labeled individuals and groups will likely be treated with greater tolerance and compassion if someone in authority has labeled them as such. This suggests that the power of "humanization" to enhance forbearance and compassion is of similar weight, both theoretically and practically, to dehumanization.

Rather than being sadists, it's likely that the supervisory teams' willingness to increasingly punish the animalized subjects resulted from the sense of power and control they felt in a situation where they had dominance—where others were getting what they deserve; in addition, if the subjects had been labeled negatively, the disinhibiting, objectifying power of the label seemed to divest those so labeled of their human qualities, making them ripe for abuse.

Finally, with respect to responsibility, those who were told that the levels of shock they administered would reflect an average shock level of their threesome team tended to shock at the highest levels, whereas those who were told that their shock level depended on their own personal decision about how much pain to administer shocked less. Not surprisingly, shock levels were highest overall when subjects were in both the dehumanized and the diffused responsibility conditions. In other words, dehumanizing labels seem to enhance objectification, which enhances the likelihood of aggression against others, especially when people have a reduced sense of responsibility for the consequences of their actions. However, when differentiating between dehumanization and defused responsibility, Bandura points out that dehumanization makes a greater contribution than does diffusion of responsibility (1975, p. 266). In other words, according to Bandura, minimizing objectification is more effective than maximizing responsibility if you want to diminish the likelihood of violence toward others, all other things being equal.

THE POWER OF DE-INDIVIDUATION TO ENHANCE OBJECTIFICATION: THE SHOCKING BEHAVIOR OF ANONYMOUS WOMEN[7]

In a landmark study that set the stage for the Stanford Prison Experiment two years later, Phillip Zimbardo (1969) and colleagues devised an experiment which tested the degree to which de-individuation—the loss of a person's sense of individuality and personal responsibility—played a role in antisocial behavior and violence. They recruited 40 female college students and grouped them into 10 groups of four women each. These groups of women were told

7. Subtitle taken from Zimbardo, P. (2001), p. 299.

that they were to deliver painful shocks to dyads of women (half described as "very nice," half described as "bitchy") under the guise of a study analyzing creativity under stress. In essence, their job was to periodically administer painful shocks to two subjects while an experimenter in the next room administered a creativity test to the subjects. Of course, actors played the role of learners being shocked (unbeknownst to the subjects), and no shocks were actually given.

One of the key experimental variables was the condition of either anonymity or individuation. In the anonymous (de-individuation) condition, the women's identities were concealed by hoods, large jackets, and the issuing of random numbers in place of name tags. In the identity salience (individuation) condition, women wore the same hoods and jackets, but were issued name tags. The women in both treatment conditions were put into 10 four-women quartets; those in both treatment conditions were told to repeatedly shock each of two "learners" over the course of 20 trials. Unlike in earlier, groundbreaking obedience studies (Milgram, 1963), there was no authority figure directly pressuring the women to administer painful shocks—Zimbardo did not interact with the women at all during the shock trials. However, they could see him through a glass window, just as they could see the two women being shocked through another viewing window. Group conformity pressure was also kept to a minimum by each of the women being placed in separate, adjacent cubicles. Finally, as opposed to the Milgram study, there was no pressure on the women to perform their task out of concern that not doing so would invalidate the study; if any one of the four women in the group administered a shock, the learner would act hurt and upset enough to impair her ability to be creative. Therefore, for any of the four women, abstaining from administering a shock would not be disobedient or confrontational with the researcher; "[they] could simply be a passive observer of teammates' shocking the learner instead of an active perpetrator" (Zimbardo, 2008, p. 299). Before the actual experiment began, each subject was given a brief, actual shock of 75 volts so that she knew how unpleasant the shocks were. (75 volts is fairly uncomfortable.)

The criterion of greatest interest in the study was the *duration* of shock administered—not only *if* each subject would shock the learner, but *how long* each subject would hold down the lever to administer shock. While each subject had the freedom to not administer any shocks, none ever chose that option.

The results of the study were clear: The subjects in the anonymous condition shocked the learners twice as long as did the women who were in the identity salient condition. In addition, the women in the anonymous condition shocked both groups of learners—both the "very nice" and the "bitchy" learners—equally as long. They also prolonged the shock time for both types of learners over the 20 trials—continuing to hold their fingers down on the level for longer and longer intervals as the learners winced, yelped, and twisted before their eyes. By contrast, the women in the identity-salient condition discriminated between the two types of learners and shocked the likable learners less over time than they did the unlikable learners. Zimbardo's analysis of the surprising difference between the two groups was that the condition of de-individuation seems to bring about a substantial change in human psychology:

> The escalation of shock, with repeated opportunities to administer its painful consequences, appears to [cause] an upward-spiraling effect of emotional arousal that is being experienced. The agitated behavior becomes self-reinforcing, each action stimulating a stronger, less controlled next reaction. Experientially, it comes not from sadistic motives of wanting to harm others, but rather from the energizing sense of one's domination and control over others [. . .]. (2008, p. 300)

If Zimbardo is correct it also seems equally plausible to assume that those subjects in the de-individuated condition tended to self-identify less with all the learners as a whole. These subjects were less connected with the interior experience of both sets of learners; they were quite willing, and they were even satisfied by harming both sets of learners more and more, whereas those in the individuated condition seemed to self-identify more with the "very nice" learners than with the "bitchy" ones.

In conclusion, one finding seems to stand out from this line of research: Anytime we feel anonymous—that our reputation is not on the line, or that no one knows or cares to know who we are—seems to dramatically diminish the effectiveness of the breaks we all have on our capacities for immoral behavior. It's as if reducing our sense of accountability or concern about personal reputation lays bare our deeper tendencies to expand the innate sense of "I am not that" we all feel in reference to others, which makes it much easier to engage in immoral acts. This is especially so when either the situation at hand or some institutional influence gives us permission or encouragement to behave immorally.

SUMMARY: WHY SITUATIONS MATTER

We break no new ground by saying that personality and situations interact to generate behavior, or that human behavior always occurs within a variety of situational contexts. Yet, while we are substantially influenced by our environments, we also have the potential to influence the environments we encounter. Human beings are not mindless, passive objects moved around on life's chessboard by environmental contingencies. Most often, we choose the settings in which we participate. We can change circumstances by our presence and our behavior; we can influence others who are similarly situated; we can work to successfully transform environments. In many important ways, human beings are autonomous agents with the capacity to influence the direction of their lives and to shape their own destinies. Because of these facts, we have the tendency to believe in the essential goodness of our characters, the stability of our dispositions, our ability to rationally appraise situational pressures, and our capacity to unequivocally reject temptations to behave immorally. We seek to simplify the world by erecting clear boundaries between good and evil, with the good representing that which is known, familiar, and loved, and the evil representing that which is foreign, alien, or despised. What we all too often fail to appreciate is that the line separating good from evil runs through the interior of every human heart.[8]

However, when we assert that components of toxic situations have the capacity to change not only the way we treat others, but the way we view ourselves and others, we *are* saying something novel—that situations have the power to substantially alter our perceptions of reality. For the "man in the box" receiving the electric shocks, it makes no real difference whether the person sending the shocks is doing so out of reluctant but "blind" obedience to authority, or out of the belief that he deserves to be shocked because his humanity has somehow become less evident or relevant—he suffers the same either way. But to society, this difference should be significant. While the behaviors coming from both circumstances represent substantial weaknesses in human character, evil coming from the objectified condition represents the greater problem. To see the truth of this assertion, you need only imagine yourself stranded on an island peopled by two groups of individuals: one group that sees you as an equal but is milquetoast in the face of oppressive authority figures who encourage them to harm you, and a second group that has ready means of aggression and is convinced of your subhumanity. The first situation is analogous to being a prisoner in a P.O.W. camp staffed by sympathetic, guilt-ridden guards but overseen by a sadistic, ruthless commander. The second situation is analogous to being a visually obvious cultural minority member who finds himself surrounded by devotees of the KKK late at night. Both circumstances would be bad, but in the first situation, there would be a much better chance of escape or at least of "enlightening" the guards about the possibility of overthrowing their commander.

In the attempt to make sense of behaviors highlighted in the studies mentioned above, the dispositionalist perspective assumes that the most

---

8. Aleksandr Solzhenitsyn (1976) made this assertion when he wrote, "If only it were all so simple! If only there were evil people somewhere insidiously committing evil deeds, and it were necessary only to separate them from the rest of us and destroy them. But the line dividing good and evil cuts through the heart of every human being. And who is willing to destroy a piece of his own heart?" (p. 168).

important determinants come from within individuals and dramatically downplays the role of situations. The virtuous are thought to be those who resist inducements to behave unethically or antisocially whenever pressures arise to do so, while the morally weak are those who allow external pressures to influence them unduly. One flaw in such reasoning is that it denies the reality of universal human frailty and our vulnerability in the face of powerful situational forces. One important benefit of the situationalist perspective is that it helps encourage modesty and humility when we attempt to understand cases of human evil. Rather than adopting an attitude of moral superiority—creating artificial boundaries separating us from morally deficient others and thus effectively short-circuiting self-scrutiny—we would be well served to engage in "attributional charity" (Zimbardo, 2008, p. 212). In other words, we should attempt to understand the role that situational factors might have played before rushing to character judgment. Such an approach brings to mind a well-worn cliché, "There but for the grace of God go I." Henry Murray (1953) alluded to this truth when he memorably noted that every person is in certain important respects like no other people, like some other people, and like all other people. Vulnerability to engaging in evil behavior given the "right" kind of circumstance appears to be one of the universals Murray refers to.

Despite their methodological flaws and the difficulties inherent in generalizing results from the research laboratory to real life, the studies highlighted in this section show that human character can undergo a dramatic transformation in certain situational contexts. When immersed in the context of a powerful, toxic situation, otherwise good people can be "induced, seduced, and initiated" into behaving in mindless, antisocial, destructive ways (Zimbardo, 2008, p. 211). Moreover, some of these situational variables (e.g., toxic roles, toxic labels, and de-individuation, among others) seem to powerfully influence otherwise good people to move further along the objectification spectrum, altering the way they see their fellows and enhancing the probabilities that they will behave immorally toward them.

While many decades old, the results of this pioneering research should again sound out as a warning voice countering the conventional wisdom which asserts that *the good self* can always triumph over *the bad situation*. We will be best able to resist and potentially transform such negative situational forces only by humbly acknowledging the power that circumstances have to influence us. That situations can play such a large role in determining human behavior does not provide cover or excuse for evil deeds. Rather, these facts should help to democratize evil—making it the possible terrain of any of us, not just the psychopaths, the despots, and the deviants.

CHAPTER 14

Situationally Induced Heroism

Momentary Transcendence of Objectification

If there is any science man really needs, it is the one I teach, of how to occupy properly that place in creation that is assigned to man, and how to learn from it what one must be in order to be a man.

Immanuel Kant *(as quoted in Seidler, 2009, p. 12)*

Bad situations have the potential to draw out and enhance our innate capacities to objectify others. However, our history also shows that situations sometimes help to draw out what is best in us. Think of the few "good" guards who did not lapse into brutality and sexual degradation of the prisoners in Zimbardo's experiment; think of those subjects who terminated Milgram's experiments prematurely—without going "all the way" and administering the most severe shocks possible under the pressure of authoritative influence. What was it that allowed these individuals to do what they did? In the words of Ernest Becker, just what is the heroic individual?

Leaving for a moment the deeper, existential, "Beckerian" view of heroism, let's first focus on a more recognizable, practical version. Throughout this book, our proclivity for objectification has been approached from two perspectives: *what we are*, which refers to attributes endemic to human beings and how this contributes to the problem; and *who we are*, which makes reference to our situatedness in life and how this contributes to the problem. There are those rare and remarkable individuals who have lived what could be termed *the heroic life*—individuals such as Mother Teresa, Mohandas K. Gandhi, Martin Luther King, Jr., Nelson Mandela (to name a few more recent examples) who create "zones of liberation" (Fowler, 1981, p. 200) for others—spiritually, psychologically, and otherwise—literally putting their lives on the line on a daily basis for complete strangers. According to some who have made in-depth studies of world-class heroes like those mentioned above, such persons, though certainly not perfect, have undergone transformative processes that involved some substantial degree of ego transcendence, but they have also been individuals situated in a particular place and time where the "exigencies of history intersected with the providence of God" at work in their lives (Fowler, 1981, p. 202).[1] Gandhi, for example, was a young lawyer visiting South Africa and traveling by train— a dark-skinned man sitting in a first-class cabin. When the conductor discovered him, Gandhi was publicly humiliated by being thrown off the train. Had he not been steeped in the doctrine of *ahimsa* (non-injury) by his Jain mother, the outrage might not have inspired him to begin an openly confrontational but nonviolent campaign against the unjust system of Apartheid. Martin Luther King, Jr., was raised in the Jim Crow American South by a family that included a long line of charismatic, social-justice-minded Baptist preachers. Were it not for this, he may never have inherited a pastorship in Montgomery, Alabama, at the same time that Rosa Parks was arrested for refusing to give up her seat to a white man on a Montgomery bus. This confluence of events in time effectively catalyzed King's heroic imagination and set him on a path to become the greatest civil rights advocate the United States has ever known.

Just as *who we are* and *what we are* often collide to bring more evil into the world, these factors can combine to bring to the fore latent possibilities of heroism lying dormant within individuals. Indeed, most heroic action, when analyzed, is not engaged in by lifelong heroes like those mentioned above, but rather by average human beings who become "heroes of the moment" (Zimbardo, 2007, April 2) when an unusual situation calls forth extraordinary behavior from an otherwise ordinary person. In other words, there is no evidence that such "heroes of the moment" are different in a substantial way from other people. Rather, atypical circumstances, such as simultaneous "bird strikes" causing the loss of forward thrust in both jet engines on an airliner (Rivera 2009),[2] can ignite what Zimbardo (2007, April 2) calls, "the heroic imagination" within ordinary people. Almost to a person, when such individuals are queried about their actions, they deny the moniker, "hero," claiming they simply went into action as the situation demanded; they insist that anyone in their shoes would have likely done the same thing.

1. Of such individuals, James Fowler (1981) said, "It is as though they are selected by the great Blacksmith of history, heated in the fires of turmoil and trouble and then hammered into usable shape on the hard anvil of conflict and struggle" (p. 202).
2. Capt. Chesley Sullenberger, realizing he had lost all power to his aircraft due to birds being sucked into his engines, decided immediately to splash down his massive airliner, filled with 155 people, in the nearby Hudson River. After splash-down, Sully went through the passenger cabin three times to make sure no one was left on board. He was the last person off the plane as the aircraft sank deeper into the frigid waters of the Hudson River near New York City.

A classic example includes the 2007 case of a New York City construction worker and Navy veteran, Wesley Autry. On January 2, Autrey was waiting for a subway train in Manhattan with his two young daughters. At around 12:45 p.m., Autry and two other women standing nearby noticed a young man having a seizure, causing him to stumble from the platform and fall onto the tracks. As the young man lay convulsing across the tracks, Autrey saw the lights of an oncoming train. One of the women held Autrey's daughters back away from the edge of the platform as Autrey jumped down onto the tracks, assuming that he would be able to move the young man off the rails. However, he quickly realized there was not enough time to drag him away because he was too heavy. Instead, he thought it might be possible there would be enough room for the train to pass safely over both of them. He protected the flailing young man by laying his own body down over him in the drainage trench between the tracks. In the few seconds before the train's arrival, Autry said to the young man, "Please sir, don't move. If you move, one of us is going to lose a leg or die" ("If You Move," 2007). Though the operator of the train attempted to stop before reaching Autry, he couldn't, and all but two cars passed over them at some speed before the train was able to stop, close enough over Autry's head to leave grease on the top of his cap. Autry's young girls were panic-stricken, thinking their father had been crushed by the train, but he called out to them from under the train, telling them that he was okay. Autrey later told the *New York Times*, "I don't feel like I did something spectacular; I just saw someone who needed help. I did what I felt was right" (Buckley, 2007). Heroic actions such as these are not the domain of any one country, culture, or "type" of individual—a crisis presents itself, and an individual or group responds.

Or perhaps they don't. For every instance of awe-inspiring heroic action, there are likely countless others of non-response. Research has attempted to decipher situational variables that play a role in whether or not people will act in a sociocentric rather than an egocentric fashion. What seem on the surface to be minor factors can make a big difference. For example, whether or not the person is in a hurry makes a big difference, as hurried people are much less likely to help (Darley & Batson, 1973). Whether or not people are alone or are in a group makes a big difference, as people who are situated in groups are less likely to help (Darley & Latane, 1970). Whether or not there's been prior social contact makes a big difference; help is less likely to occur without it (Moriarty, 1975).

Heroism of the moment apparently depends on the presence or absence of many factors, only one of which is the character of the potential hero; and while heroism of the moment may make the difference between life and death, such acts do not necessarily imply any degree of lasting, substantive ego transcendence on the part of the hero. Once the crisis is resolved and the moment fades into the past, the memory of the event may indeed linger for the rest of the hero's life, impacting the way he or she views both self and others. But much in the way that lottery winners' lives are not permanently transformed due to a sudden windfall of wealth, it also seems quite likely that engaging in brief, extraordinary action does not fundamentally alter the hero's character. Who she or he was before the action is likely who she or he is afterward.

Moreover, it is important to emphasize that heroic acts, such as Autry's, while wonderful, should remain the end goal of larger-than-life comic book figures rather than flesh and blood human beings. Comic book figures, because they are fictional, can personify "the benevolent gargantuan ego" in action without causing collateral destruction, whereas real human beings have a much harder time combining heavily ego-laden strivings with moral behavior. The very worst human behavior is made manifest when a would-be hero—one who has *not* largely died to self—feels called upon to put into play his or her glorious vision for what human kind ought to be. Too often, this involves pursuit of the goal by any means necessary. One need only call to mind the typical cast of characters—Mao Zedong, Adolf Hitler, Joseph Stalin, or Idi Amin—for vivid examples. Hundreds of millions of human beings have lost their lives because they were deemed less valuable than the hero's ego as symbolized by his illustrious cause. Truly heroic human beings, on the other hand, do not engage in heroic acts to buttress their egos. Rather, their heroism can be said to be "universal" in that they seek to validate and include every individual, especially those who oppose them, in order to pave the way for a larger, more inclusive, unified circle of humanity.

We must also acknowledge other versions of heroism—much less heralded, but equally life-altering for many—which are called forth by circumstances, both foreseen and unplanned. Take, for example, the woman who—without the benefit of a partner, and in the face of countless sacrifices—raises her children to be well-adjusted, contributing members of society; or imagine the man who gets up early every day for decades to work at jobs he doesn't enjoy so that his family can have a home, food on the table, bills paid on time, and perhaps some music lessons for the children; or consider the illegal immigrant who risks life and limb to find back-breaking work in the hot fields of a foreign land so that his parents back home can have the medicine they need, and that his children in their care can have the possibility of a better future than his. This is the sort of heroism that is much more typical and mundane, but it is also the type of heroism that we would miss the most were it not the norm for our species. In this, there are shades of the Beckerian, universal version of heroism mentioned earlier: the type of heroism typified by the likes of Martin Luther King, Mother Teresa, Gandhi, or Mandela. Heroism of this sort is represented by *the consecration of one's existence to meanings that transcend the self despite creatureliness—despite the looming reality of death*. The mothers and fathers mentioned above make the sacrifices they do because they see their own biological necessity—in the form of their children and other relatives—and they respond to it. Yet, this type of sacrifice, impressive and important as it is, is only part of the process of enlightenment, because one's sense of self-in-other extends primarily to one's blood kin, but not elsewhere.

The expansion of our boundaries of self to include those who are not in our immediate family is the great next step in the process. The transformation from living as a being with a narrow circle of inclusion, where objectification looms as an ever-present reality, into one whose boundaries of self have expanded to incorporate the whole is indeed the work of a lifetime. While this type of cosmic heroism may seem outside the realm of what is possible for the vast majority of human beings, in truth, such a "journey to the interior" is a type of heroism that is available to almost all. The psychology of the ancients knew this and saw all human beings as "pilgrims," "wayfarers," and "wanderers" who could reach the heights of the loftiest peaks of enlightenment, salvation, or liberation if they were willing to pay the price. By contrast, modern psychology (recent theoretical adjustments notwithstanding) has largely seen human beings as neurotics, narcissists, and codependents, and therefore has been concerned with merely helping sick people become normal. As important as this work is, it is not the path of self-transcendence on which already normal people undergo successive transformations in order to become supernormal. For this, each would-be hero must undertake the afore-mentioned journey, which requires us to display a willingness to turn our back on the mundane, often trivial preoccupations of everyday life in order to begin a process of deeper self-awareness, much as Joseph Campbell described in his classic work *The Hero with a Thousand Faces*. This path, according to Campbell (1949), takes forms symbolized by the world's great mythologies, which "do not hold as their greatest hero the merely virtuous [i.e., morally excellent] man or woman. Virtue is but the pedagogical prelude to the culminating insight, which goes beyond all pairs of opposites" (p. 35).

"Know thyself" was the inscription on the Oracle at Delphi and still represents the starting point for the processes of self-transcendence. The paradox is that in order to ultimately transcend our limiting boundaries of self and thus to overcome the human tendency to objectify others, one must first gain a deep understanding of oneself, and this is not easily accomplished. There are many different strategies available to help achieve this goal—participating in religion, various forms of psychotherapy, acts of service, meditation, yoga, tai chi, travel, the arts, reading scripture, reading the "Great Books," reading self-help books, listening to podcasts, watching TED talks, journaling, going on retreats, among many others. Unfortunately for us, self-transcendence is not guaranteed by any of these admirable pursuits, practiced alone or in tandem. This is in part because the individual brings remarkable complexity and resistance to the process; but it also seems to be true that the experience of enlightenment involves inexplicable elements, which some have referred to as "acts of grace." Perhaps only after the questions of God's existence and whether or not the self survives—in any real way—the physical death of the body, the processes of "dying to self" while one is still ensconced in the world has to rank near the top of the great puzzles of life. It is to this that we now turn.

PART FIVE

Pathways toward Transformation

Trails Leading Out of Plato's Cave

CHAPTER 15

The Problem of Enlightenment

. . . However humiliating the path may be, man, beset by anarchy, banditry, chaos, and extinction, must at last resort turn to that chamber of horrors, human enlightenment; for he has nowhere else to turn.

Robert Ardrey *(1970, pp. 352–353)*

No god is a philosopher or seeker after wisdom for he is wise already. Neither do the ignorant seek after wisdom; for herein is the evil of ignorance, that he who is neither good nor wise is nevertheless satisfied with himself.

Socrates, from Plato's *Symposium (as quoted in Ross, 1994, pg. 58)*

To be properly human, you must go beyond the merely human.

Scholastic maxim *(as quoted in Schall, 1998, p. 221)*

THE CHALLENGE OF INTERPRETING ONE'S OWN ILLUMINATION

Throughout our history, precious few human beings have realized (in a transformative way) their interconnectedness with all that exists, making it possible for them to transcend the problem of objectification. The process of enlightenment includes what Maslow called "peak" or "transcendent" experiences. Such experiences are typically described in many ways, only a few of which include "rapturous," "beautiful," "perfect," "resplendent," and "complete" (Maslow, 1970, pp. 91–96), which causes "the whole person [to] resonate [to] the experience the way a crystal lampshade reverberates every time a C sharp is struck on the piano" (Steindl-Rast, 1989, p. 12). Enlightened by what they have experienced, and desiring that others should taste the same delicious fruit of liberation from the prison of self, such individuals have often striven to communicate their illuminations, their "great awakening," their experience of enlightenment and liberation, to others. These attempts have often been problematic for many reasons. One of these is that the enlightened person first must come to terms with the experience of transcendence—interpreting

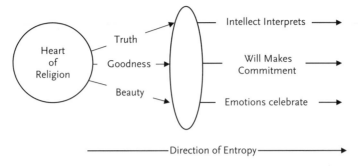

Figure 15.1: Mystical Core of Organized Religion, Part 1

what it means in the context of his or her previous paradigm, which inevitably exerts a distorting influence. This process is depicted well in the first part (Figure 15.1) of an insightful diagram by David Steindl-Rast depicting the illuminative process, which I have broken down into three sections for ease of explanation (1989).[1]

Steindl-Rast makes the point that we do with our mystical experiences what we do with all our experiences: We try to make sense of them. This is especially so when we have a disorienting experience of self-transcendence, which he calls "the heart of religion." Our intellect "swoops down" almost immediately afterward and begins interpreting the experience within the frame of our time, place, and previous experiences in its search for truth. If we are part of a particular religious worldview, we may already have a vocabulary for such experiences before we have the experience. Thus, when such an experience occurs, we tend to recount it and understand it in the vocabulary already accepted as appropriate (Laski, 1961). Koestler (1960) put it this way:

> Because the experience is inarticulate, has no sensory shape, color, or words, it lends itself to transcription in many forms, including visions of the cross, or of the goddess Kali; they are like dreams of a person born blind. . . . Thus a genuine mystical experience may mediate a *bona fide* conversion to practically any creed, including Christianity, Buddhism, or Fire Worship. (p. 353)

While some of us may be more intellectually inclined than others, all of us interpret our experiences by thinking them through to some extent. We then form an opinion either for or against the experience; we accept it or we reject it. In the case of the transcendent experience, the bliss of universal belonging brought on by such experiences inevitably leads to our saying "yes" to it.

---

1. To Steindl-Rasts's original diagram, I have added the lower arrow showing the "direction of entropy," or the tendency for the original illumination to gradually dim as more interpretive elements and the passage of time are brought to bear.

Because we recognize the experience as inherently good, we desire more of it, and we commit ourselves to willingly go after it. According to Steindl-Rast, this is the process that lies at the root of ethics, as all ethical systems can best be understood as the quest for "right behavior" coming out of a feeling of belonging (Steindl-Rast, 1989, p. 12). The more responsive we are, the more we are likely to hallow and celebrate the experience, perhaps recalling the particular preparations engaged in that remarkable day, the precise moment of the day, the particular calendar day, or the particular place of the illumination. The intention is to commemorate the experience again and again through repeated pilgrimages or repetitions of behavior, though the experience may never occur again. This is the beginning of ritual, as all rituals have as their basis the quest for belonging that points toward that ultimate belonging experienced in moments of transcendence (Steindl-Rast, 1989, p. 12). In short, one of the problems of enlightenment is that there is a process of distillation and distortion that occurs in the mind of the newly illuminated as he or she grapples with the meaning of what has been experienced.

THE CHALLENGE OF SUCCESSFULLY PASSING ONE'S ILLUMINATION ON TO OTHERS

Perhaps even more problematic, however, is the difficulty that the enlightened person has in communicating effectively his or her experiences to unenlightened others. Who would be capable of understanding truths as profound as those gleaned through the Buddha's 49 days of intense meditation, for example? How can speech-defying transcendence be translated into words, or illuminations that shatter previous categories be housed in language? Because experiences of transcendence are ultimately ineffable, even the best possible verbal descriptions and phrasings are quite inadequate to capture the totality of the experience (Maslow, 1970, p. 72). Joseph Campbell (1991) put it this way:

> All things in the field of time are in pairs of opposites (e.g., being and not being, many and single, true and untrue). We always think in terms of opposites [but] the mystery of life is beyond all human conception. . . . There is a plane of consciousness available where you can identify yourself with that which transcends pairs of opposites. . . . We want to think about God. God is a thought. God is a name. God is an idea. But its reference is to something that transcends all thinking. The ultimate mystery of being is beyond all categories of thought. As Kant said, the thing in itself is no thing. It transcends thing-ness, it goes past anything that could be thought. *The best things can't be told because they transcend thought. The second best things are misunderstood, because those are the thoughts that are supposed to refer to that which can't be thought about. The third best things are what we [can actually] talk about.* (pp. 56–58, emphasis added)

Ineffable though it may be, the mystic's experience of transcendence is too good not to share. Indeed, one of the hallmarks of genuine enlightenment—in addition to being truly loving, pure in heart, and pure in spirit (Huxley, 1970, p. x)—is the desire to assist in other's progress toward the same realization (His Holiness, the Dalai Lama, 2009, p. 215), whereas those who are falsely enlightened or too immature in their own characterological development will either hoard their realizations, or they will try to convert others to their new-found perspective by any means necessary. The essence of the problem is that those with whom the enlightened attempt to share their illuminations are "non-peakers" (Maslow, 1970, p. 22)—in other words, those who tend not to have peak experiences. Non-peakers also tend to be more managerial and legalistic in temperament; therefore, their natural bias is to distill and codify the original mystical experience into a formula that is more accessible and practical to the masses (Maslow, 1970, pp. 19–22). As Joseph Campbell suggested, much gets lost in translation, but such attempts have coalesced into the world's great faith traditions, which all started from an original mystical experience had by a lonely mystic. Each of these traditions had at their base the aim of transforming human consciousness away from the self and toward a more inclusive circle of being. With time, however, layer upon layer of cultural and other historical influences were added, giving the experience of the original mystic a uniquely "local," more complicated flavor that contains remnants of the peaker's original illuminations, but with substantial overlay. The masses tend to emphasize this overlay—the localisms, peculiarities, and ethnocentric phrasings—rather than those elements that all authentic transcendent experiences have in common (these will be addressed in the latter part of the next chapter).

Figure 15.2, which shows the middle portion of Steindl-Rasts's diagram, depicts these processes. The intellect's interpretations of the original mystical experience coalesce into more crystalized meanings, which become statements of "fact" (i.e., doctrines). Over time, these facts are re-interpreted from the perspective of more individuals and their historical influences; commentaries form upon commentaries, and with every new interpretation, there is

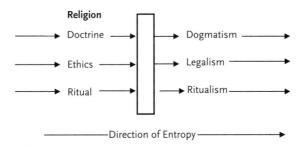

Figure 15.2: Mystical Core of Organized Religion, Part 2

movement further away from the experiential source. As Steindl-Rast puts it, "Live doctrine fossilizes into dogmatism" (1989, p. 13).

A similar process takes place with ethics. Initially, moral prescriptions tell us how to transfer the sense of mystical belonging experienced in the great awakening into our daily lives. These prescriptions remind us to treat one another as if we are truly one. Out of a desire to express unwavering commitment to the goodness glimpsed in mystical moments, we "carve prescriptions in stone," making our expression of commitment unalterable. However, when circumstances inevitably shift, calling forth a more nuanced, altered expression of the same commitment, the "thou shalts" and "thou shalt nots" remain carved in stone. Rigidity replaces fluidity, and morality turns into legalism (Steindl-Rast, 1989, p. 13).

Finally, ritual starts out as a genuine celebration of the sense of belonging experienced in the mystical illumination. Each time such a celebration occurs, it brings back grateful remembrance and a sense of renewal of our ultimate connectedness. This is why, when we engage in such celebrations, we desire those closest to us to be present. Because of the significance of these celebrations, we want to give them perfect form, and over time, form comes to be placed ahead of that to which the ritual originally pointed. When form becomes formalized and content becomes less relevant, "ritual turns to ritualism" (Steindl-Rast, 1989, p. 13).

However, as Steindl-Rast (1989) points out, there is a silver lining to these seemingly inevitable problems of enlightenment. Despite the gradual deterioration of the flow of original mystical light, it is possible that it again can be purified and renewed. The final portion of Steindl-Rast's diagram (Figure 15.3) depicts this process, which occurs:

> . . . whenever a faithful heart recognizes, in spite of all distortions, the original light. Thus, the [neophyte's] mysticism can become one with the Founder's. The heart of religion can find itself in the religion of the heart. The two can become one. (p. 13)

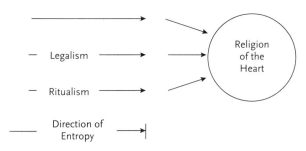

Figure 15.3: Mystical Core of Organized Religion, Part 3

Again, individuals such as these are likely to be peakers—those closest to the spirit that preceded the structures in the first place—and they will have reverence and respect for these structures. However, these individuals are also likely to be those who demand that the hardened structures be renewed, reformed, or transformed. They become the "uncomfortable agitators" of the system. How authentic their enlightenment is will be evidenced by their degree of compassionate understanding for those who guard the status quo, because genuine enlightenment proceeds from the experience "where we and they are one" (Steindl-Rast, 1989, p. 14).

The challenge of coming to terms with one's own experience of enlightenment and then attempting to successfully pass that wisdom on to unenlightened others represents the secondary and tertiary problems of enlightenment. The primary problem is, of course, becoming more individually enlightened to begin with. This has been the bailiwick of the great religious and wisdom traditions of the world, and it is to these we now turn.

CHAPTER 16

Theistic and Nontheistic Approaches to Transcending Objectification

In the broadest terms, religion says that there is an unseen order, and that our supreme good lies in rightful relations to it.

William James *(1903, p. 58)*

The glory of God is a human being, fully alive.

Irenaeus *(Against Heresies,* Book 4, 20:7)

If one is not oneself a sage or a saint, the best thing one can do. . . is to study the works of those who were, and who, because they had modified their merely human mode of being, were capable of a more than merely human kind and amount of knowledge.

Aldous Huxley *(1970, p. 14)*

Our greatness and our wretchedness are so evident that the true religion. . . must account for such amazing contradictions.

Blaise Pascal *(1995, p. 46)*

HUMANKIND AS *HOMO RELIGIOSUS*

It is well established that humankind has a very long history with religion. Some of the world's best students of the human condition (e.g., Alister Hardy, Mircea Eliade, Edmund Burke, Wilhelm Röpke) have gone so far as to rename the species *homo religiosus* because the religious impulse appears to be ubiquitous in the human experience throughout time. A simplified version of the naturalistic perspective asserts that religion is itself a byproduct of many other social adaptations that enhanced the early human capacity for survival (Atran, 2002; Boyer, 2002; Guthrie, 1995; Kapogiannis, Barbey, Su, Zamboni, Krueger, & Grafman, 2009; Kirkpatrick, 2004; Shermer, 2012;

Thomson, 2011).[1] These include our ability to engage in complex social interactions with hypothetical or invisible others (*decoupled cognition*); the perception that unknown forces—such as the wind or shadows—are in fact human agents (*hyperactive agency detection*); our ability to "read" or attribute mental states—such as feelings, beliefs, intentions, and knowledge—to others, and to understand that others have mental states different from our own (*theory of mind*); and the tendency to detect patterns in ambiguous stimuli (*patternicity*), to name only a few. Though research in these areas is still in its infancy, a unified, scientifically testable model of the human origins of religion is now taking shape. From the naturalistic paradigm, religious experiences (including unity consciousness) appear to represent instances in which—often because of an emotional crisis or other "extremity" experience—activity in the brain's frontal and right temporal lobes is dramatically heightened, while activity in the left parietal lobe is lowered (Newberg, Alavi, Baime, Pourdehnad, Santanna, & d'Aquili, 2001; Newberg, Pourdehnad, Alavi, & d'Aquili, 2003). Psychologically, we may experience this as "hearing God's voice," or otherwise having our awareness freed from its typical confines, allowing us to make contact with an ever-present stream of higher consciousness available within the human psyche that far transcends everyday consciousness. Thus, the naturalistic perspective asserts that the experiences and insights coming from instances of unity consciousness are genuine, but they do not represent contact with or intervention from a supreme being. Various nontheistic religious perspectives, such as Buddhism, also make this claim.

On the other hand, the perspective of *theism* asserts that the ubiquitous religious impulse results from a divine source having instilled within the human species a yearning for union with its creator. This source is the origin of all that exists; its essence or spirit fills the immensity of space (i.e., it is transcendent—"out there") and infuses all living things with life (i.e., it is immanent—"right here"). Transcendent, mystical experiences represent instances in which humankind makes divinely assisted contact with higher

1. Here, I prefer the so-called *biproduct* theory of religion due to its current preponderance of empirical support. There are, however, competing naturalistic theories of the origins of religion. One is the *group selection* theory, which says that religious beliefs enhance a group's capacity to cohere, thus giving them a survival advantage (Wilson, 2002; Wade, 2009; and Haidt, 2013). Another is the *behavioral* theory, which asserts that giving one's accent to another's supernatural claims promotes cooperative multigenerational social relationships. A willingness to accept unskeptically the influence of another person's beliefs is similar to a child's acceptance of the influence of a parent. Thus, religions survive by taking on the guise of a family (e.g., brother, sister, Father, Mother, etc. [Steadman & Palmer, 2008]). Finally, there is the *brain size* theory, which argues that gradual increases in the size of our ancestor's brains ultimately led to self-consciousness. With self-awareness came the ability to contemplate mortality, which made the creation of religion and other manifestations of culture a psychological necessity (Becker, 1974; Gould, McGarr, & Rose, 2007). While more speculative in nature, I find this last theory to be the richest in terms of its ability to illuminate important aspects of human nature.

levels of consciousness within the self and/or with the spirit of the divine, which provides illumination.[2] One result is a transformation of human consciousness from self-centeredness to a broader, more inclusive circle of being. The various theistic religious traditions in the world represent the legacy of certain individuals' experiences with the divine, as expressed through differing cultural contexts.

My intention here is not to make an argument for the veracity of the naturalistic or the theistic perspective. Rather, it is to say that, in most instances, enlightenment experiences and the unity consciousness that attends them have themselves evolved into religions, or they have been co-opted by extant religions, both theistic—such as Christianity, Islam, Judaism, and Hinduism—and nontheistic—such as Buddhism, Taoism, and Jainism. This is likely because such experiences move awareness beyond typical self-boundary confines, inspire awe, defy adequate description, and transport the experiencer into a rarified, otherworldly realm of spirit. As Koestler (1960) and Laski (1961) suggest, the experiencer uses whatever vernacular she has available to make sense of such an illumination, both for herself and with those she attempts to communicate with. Historically, with few notable exceptions (e.g., ancient pockets of atheism such as Diagoras of Melos and Lucretius in ancient Greece, and nontheist contemplatives in Buddhism, Jainism, and certain sects of Hinduism), the cultural backdrop has been theism. This then becomes the framework for how most of these experiences have been understood.

Whether theistic or not, each "revealed" religion has at its center a mystical core that has translated into all religions' attempt to improve upon human nature as it typically manifests itself in the world. When at their best, each of the world's religious traditions centers around a desire to create in its constituents the seemingly simple attributes that Huxley (1970) mentions as requirements for enlightenment: "becoming loving, pure in heart, and poor in spirit" (p. x). However, one of the great paradoxes of human history is that the world's religions have also been primary sources of subjugation, domination, violence, and destruction throughout human history. Whenever this has been the case, the illuminations of the original mystics have been forgotten or perverted—oftentimes many centuries later—in the hands of their unenlightened followers. For example, Jesus' simple teachings bear no resemblance to later doctrines giving rationale for the establishment of the Holy Roman Empire, let alone the Crusades, the Inquisition, the Thirty Years' War, or the Salem Witch Trials. The Buddha's teachings fly directly in the face of various Zen sects giving support to Japanese imperialists in World War II, or the recent Myanmar junta government committing atrocities against thousands of its own people, including many monks. While there's controversy over whether or not he encouraged violence

2. In many religious systems of thought, higher consciousness within the self is thought to be synonymous with the spirit of the divine.

against those who did not convert to the faith, the Prophet Muhammad likely would not have countenanced the Muslim part of the widespread bloodshed occurring during the late 1940s partition of India into Pakistan, the spiraling, violent conflict currently occurring between Israel and Palestine, or the terroristic strategies of Al-Queda and its offshoots.

When practiced in an enlightened manner, each of the world's great religions addresses four central concerns: (1) *the problem* (something is wrong with the status quo of human existence); (2) *the solution* (there is a way to remedy the problem); (3) *the method* (there are specific practices that help achieve a desired outcome); and (4) *the result* (there is a specific, reachable end that will be attained given proper implementation of the method). Thousands of volumes have been written on the major religious traditions of the world. Space will not permit anything more than a most superficial analysis of five of the most influential religious traditions—Hinduism, Judaism, Buddhism, Christianity, and Islam—with respect to these four central concerns (I have chosen this particular order insofar as it represents the relative ages of these traditions, from oldest to youngest). Brief summaries are bound to leave out, under-emphasize, or over-emphasize particulars of these faith traditions. These limitations notwithstanding, such an analysis will help us better appreciate some of the ways that human beings have utilized religion—whether theistic or nontheistic—in their attempts to solve the problem of objectification through boundary transcendence.

A BRIEF REVIEW OF FIVE RELIGIOUS TRADITIONS

Hinduism

The oldest currently extant major faith tradition on earth comes from the Indian subcontinent. It has no single founder, as it comprises various related strains of illuminations received by numerous individuals stretching over many hundreds of years (Osborne, 2005). Hinduism in its modern form is a remnant of the Iron Age "Vedic" tradition, the Vedas being a large collection of scriptures that were written between 1700 and 1100 B.C.E. According to Huston Smith (1991), if Hinduism is taken as a whole—its vast literature, its varied collection of rituals, its myriad folkways, and its resplendent art—and is compressed into one single message, it would be, "You can have what you want" (p. 13). Perhaps this sounds like a hedonist's dream, but in reality, it puts the burden of the answer back into our own laps: Just what do we want?

Hinduism begins by proclaiming that human wants occur on two separate strata: The lower strata are those that come most readily and naturally to conventional levels of awareness, and the higher strata are those which may arise somewhat later on. The former include pleasure, worldly success, and the fulfillment of duty. While each of these has its legitimate place in life, each also has drawbacks: Pleasure is all too fleeting; wealth and power are inherently competitive, insatiable, self-centered, and ephemeral; and duty, while bringing respect and gratitude from our peers, ultimately leaves the human spirit unfulfilled, as our capacities to perform and make a difference are limited in scope and of short duration. Higher level desires arise only when having immersed ourselves in what the world has to offer, we nonetheless come to recognize a sense of emptiness and hollowness within ourselves. Echoing the sentiments of the ancient preacher who penned Ecclesiastes, Simone Weil speaks for many such persons when she observes:

> We all know that there is no true good here below, that everything that appears to be good in this world is finite, limited, and wears out. . . . Every human being has probably had lucid moments in her life when she has definitely acknowledged to herself that there is no final good here below. But as soon as we have seen this truth, we cover it up with lies. (Diogenes, 2010, p. 194)

According to Huston Smith (1991), the moment when we finally come to the point of asking, "Is this all there is?" is the juncture that Hinduism has been waiting for, because what we *really* want runs at the deepest levels of our being. Humankind's deepest yearnings include: (1) *being* (ongoing, fulfilled existence); (2) *knowledge* (penetrating, genuine, crystalline truth); and (3) *joy* (unbridled enthusiasm for life). For Hinduism, these three represent the holy trinity of existence—*sat* (being), *chit* (full consciousness), and *ananda* (rapture).

The Problem

According to Hindu sages, our central problem is also triple in nature: We are limited, ignorant, and restricted beings (Smith, 1991). First, we are limited in our capacities to experience being, knowledge, and joy. Physical pain, aging, and general world-weariness and boredom all impact our capability to experience joy. Second, our pervasive ignorance about ourselves and the world seems to suggest that we will always be groping in the dark for answers to the most fundamental of questions—who are we, why are we here, and what is our destiny? After millennia of efforts, we seem to be no closer to the answers. Finally, our being is restricted—the scope of reality with which we identify all too often goes no further than the boundary of ourselves or our own kindred or clan. All of this is true of us, yet Hinduism asserts our practically limitless potential:

> For what is a human being? A body? Certainly, but anything else? A personality that includes mind, memories, and propensities that have derived from a unique trajectory of experiences? This too, but anything more? Some say no, but Hinduism disagrees. Underlying the human self and animating it is a reservoir

of being that never dies, is never exhausted, and is unrestricted in consciousness and bliss. This infinite center of every life, this hidden self or *Atman*, is no less than *Brahman*, the Godhead. Body, personality, and *Atman-Brahman*—a human self is not completely accounted for until all three are noted. . . . But this eternal is buried under the almost impenetrable mass of distractions, false assumptions, and self-regarding instincts that comprise our surface selves. (Smith, 1991, pp. 21–22)

In other words, Hinduism asserts that we all have within ourselves a true self (*Atman*), composed of the same substance as the universal Spirit (*Brahman*), which originated and supports the universe. However, this deepest reality is encrusted with the residue of temporal existence. Like a light bulb covered in dirt and grime, we cannot shine forth our true brilliance. This is the source of life's problems.

The Solution

According to Hinduism, all such barriers are removable. Perhaps Hinduism's most startling assertion is not only that liberation (*moksha*) is possible, but that human beings already have *sat, chit*, and *ananda* within themselves, waiting to be released. The remedy for these ailments is *yoga*. A Sanskrit word meaning both "to unite" and "to place under discipline," yoga represents various methods of discipline designed to lead to integration of the human spirit with the spirit of the divine lying concealed within. Hinduism clarifies four primary types of yoga meant to correspond with four types of personality predilections and strengths:

1. *Jnana yoga* is the discipline for those who have a tendency toward introspection and reflective thought. It represents the path to God through knowledge—not knowledge of facts and figures, but knowledge representing the ability to discriminate between surface self and deeper self, which allows for detachment from surface elements of self (e.g., egoic thoughts and feelings (Smith, 1991). This is accomplished through various forms of meditation. One prominent approach is called *neti-neti*, which means "not this, not this." When a distracting thought or feeling arises, the meditator simply says, "Not this, not this," and dismisses it. All such thoughts and feelings are discarded, over and over again if necessary, until the mind is clear and deeper self is revealed (Ledgerwood, 2010).
2. *Bhakti yoga* is the discipline for those who desire to find God through the path of love (Smith, 1991). Like *Jnana* yoga, *Bhakti* is also a meditative practice in which we visualize God sitting or standing before us. We pour out our love and adoration toward God, until we experience a flow of love and life force occurring between us and God. In *Bhakti*, the aspirant typically has a heightened awareness of two-ness. However, the devotee may

also lose self-consciousness and become aware only of God. With *Bhakti*, the goal is for God's spirit to move into the meditator, suffusing us with peace, warmth, and light. Whether in two-ness or oneness, transformation occurs: our character deepens and improves. With continued practice, periods of higher consciousness come more frequently, and we can live in a sense of permanent relationship with the divine (Ledgerwood, 2010).

3. *Karma yoga* is for those who are drawn toward a more active approach to life. It is the uncovering of God through the exertion of work (Smith, 1991). Opportunities for work abound; God can be found in our daily tasks as well as anywhere else. If we immerse ourselves in our work in a mindful way, without regard to the personal benefits it may bring us, great rewards will follow—not just in terms of the temporal benefits of industry (e.g., order, cleanliness, and other desired outcomes), but in terms of learning that every movement, if engaged in mindfully, can connect us to the divine that exists right here, right now. Says the *Bhagavad Gita*,

He who does the task
Dictated by duty
Caring nothing
For the fruit of the action
He is a yogi (6:1)

Meditations in the *Karma* tradition tend to focus on surrendering selfish motives for reward, and dedicating our actions to God (Ledgerwood, 2010).

4. *Raja yoga* is perhaps the most rigorous and demanding of all forms of yogic practice. It represents the way to God through psychophysical experiments, presenting aspirants with a series of psychological, intellectual, and physical endeavors to be attempted (e.g., physical postures coupled with meditations), which have, as their aim, reintegrating the fragmented self (Smith, 1991).

Hinduism recognizes that no person is exclusively prone to one type of yoga over another. Therefore, we should test all four and combine them as best suits our needs.

The Result

Hinduism's depiction of the end goal is *nirvana*, a word literally meaning "to blow out"—not a blowing out of existence per se, but rather a blowing out of the fires of greed, hatred, self-delusion (Gombrich & Keegan, 1988, p. 63), and the boundaries of the finite self (Smith, 1991, p. 113). In this, Hinduism shares much in common with its spiritual descendent, Buddhism, but in Hinduism, nirvana represents union with the Supreme Being in a state of blissful egoless-ness. This state is beyond words; it is described as ". . . no world at all, for here, every trait that characterizes the world as normally perceived—its multiplic-ity and materiality—vanishes" (Smith, 1991, pp. 69–70). Noted ambassador for the Hindu faith Satya Pal Sharma says that the ultimate goal of Hinduism is "perfection," and by perfection he means:

> . . . To become the perennial child of God, to become *arya*. . . to make the soul the real master. It means to be perfect spiritually—to be above the senses, to be above the passions, to be above other concerns. It means to be oneself—one's true self [. . .] is perfection. Once you attain [. . .] perfection, you [become] part [of] God. . . . That is Hinduism. (Ledgerwood, n.d.)

Judaism

Unlike the other faiths profiled in this section, Judaism is not oriented toward the enlightenment of the individual as such. It does not offer specific prescriptions for personal salvation or overcoming the world. Rather, Judaism orients itself around the transformation of the world itself through performing one's unique role in the world in such a way that the glory of God is made manifest. This creative impulse can be seen in Judaism's orthodox expressions, where in addition to strict obedience to divine law as revealed to the prophet, Moses, discerning subtle nuances of meaning from God's divine law is stressed. Remarkably, this creative urge is especially pronounced in Judaism's numerous less observant (or non-observant) individuals who have gone on to have a substantial impact on the world far out of proportion to their numbers (Beit-Hallahmi, 1988; Rector & Rector, 2003).

Despite being by far the smallest of the world's major religions in terms of adherents,[3] Judaism may be perhaps the most influential, inasmuch as it is the progenitor of the world's largest faith—Christianity—and to a lesser extent Islam, the world's second most populous religion. Moreover, some experts have opined that at least one-third of Western civilization bears the mark of Jewish influence: Our basic moral code, our ideals of liberty and freedom, our greatest literature, our highest artistic triumphs, even many of our given names bear the indelible mark of Judaism (Smith, 1991). More impactful than all of these combined is the Jewish contribution of monotheism: the notion that there is one God—*Yahweh*—who stands supreme and transcends nature. In this, the Jews were unique among all their Middle Eastern neighbors, who

---

3. Current estimates are that there are approximately 14 million Jews worldwide (Adherents, 2007).

were decidedly polytheistic. For the Jews, asserting the existence of a Supreme Being had a dramatic impact on life's focus. If God represents that to which we give ourselves unreservedly, then to have more than one God is to live a life of divided, competing loyalties. Centering one's attention, devotion, and affections on only one God made *fidelity* a hallmark of the Jewish life: "Hear, O Israel: The Lord our God is one Lord" (Deut. 6:4, KJV).

But perhaps most revolutionary of all was the character that the Jews envisioned for this most high God. God created the world as a home for the human species and pronounced it *very good* (Gen. 1:31). He gave human beings agentive choice and dominion over the world; thus, the world also became a theater for human action (Gen. 1:26). *Yahweh* is a God who cares—he is righteous, and he demands the moral behavior of human beings. This concept is especially remarkable when placed in the brutish "might makes right" context of the Middle Bronze Age out of which Judaism sprang. Said Huston Smith (1991):

> ... The supreme achievement of Jewish thought [is] not its monotheism as such, but in the character it ascribed to the God it intuited as One. The Greeks, the Romans, the Assyrians [. . .] would have said two things about their god's characters. First, they tend to be amoral; second, toward humankind, they are preponderantly indifferent. The Jews reversed the thinking of their contemporaries on both these counts. Whereas the gods of Olympus tirelessly pursued beautiful women, the God of Sinai watched over widows and orphans [. . .]. God is a god of righteousness, whose loving-kindness is from everlasting to everlasting and whose tender mercies are in all his works. (p. 275)

This most remarkable, philanthropic God formalized his interests in human history through the use of covenants—contractual obligations between deity and human beings—first extended to the man Abraham:

> Now the LORD had said unto Abram, Get thee out of thy country, and from thy kindred, and from thy father's house, unto a land that I will shew thee: And I will make of thee a great nation, and I will bless thee, and make thy name great; and thou shalt be a blessing: And I will bless them that bless thee, and curse him that curseth thee: and in thee shall all families of the earth be blessed. (Gen. 12:1–3 KJV)

What, then, to conclude when life goes disastrously wrong, as it so often has for the Jews? According to ancient thought, there are essentially two alternatives. One conclusion, quite prevalent among the Jew's ancient Mediterranean neighbors, was to ascribe misfortunes to the fates: Drought, untimely death, and other forms of suffering were the inscrutable will of the gods who were predominantly unconcerned with human lives. This led to a largely passive, resigned, helpless approach to altering outcomes.

The Jewish alternative was to attribute such events to oneself—more specifically, to some misstep taken in one's covenantal relationship with the divine, thus incurring divine displeasure. While in the midst of his great suffering, Job's friend Eliphaz underscores this aspect of the Jewish perspective:

> Remember, I pray thee, who ever perished, being innocent? Or were the righteous cut off? Even as I have seen, they that plow iniquity, and sow wickedness, reap the same. By the blast of God they perish, and by the breath of his nostrils are they consumed. (Job 4:7–9)

Attributing misfortune to estrangement in one's relationship with the divine led to a creative approach to suffering—one that emphasized *meaning*, no matter the circumstances (Frankl, 1984), and a desire to heal the relational rift through creative means, often necessitating sincere repentance "in sackcloth and ashes" (Jon. 3:8). Part of the intense hunger for meaning in Judaism included the desire to understand fully what it means to be human—to understand human nature not in terms of mere biological fact, but in terms of the deepest truths of human life. The Jews wanted to comprehend the farthest reaches of human nature in order to transform the world and usher in the coming of the Messiah, who would vanquish their enemies and exalt the righteous.

The Problem

The Jews developed a decidedly complex view of human nature. On one hand, they saw that human beings were little more than mere animals:

> I said in mine heart concerning the estate of the sons of men, that [. . .] they [. . .] themselves are beasts. For that which befalleth the sons of men befalleth the beasts. . . . As the one dieth, so dieth the other; a man hath no preeminence above a beast: For all is vanity. (Ecc. 3:18–19, KJV)

On the other hand, they asserted that human beings were endowed with attributes of the divine: "For thou hast made him a little lower than [God], and hast crowned him with glory and honor" (Ps. 8:5).[4] Thus, human beings are a complex mixture of animal and divine, and from this seemingly impossible mixture of opposites stems the root problem of humanity: Created free and

---

4. The word *elohim* used in the original Hebrew in this verse does not designate "angels," as was used in the KJV, but rather "God(s)." Some scholars assert that the King James translators used "angels" instead of "Gods" in this verse because they likely felt that the Hebrew author was overly bold (Smith, 1991, p. 250).

meant to be noble, we are divided, disintegrated, and double (Hos. 10:2; Ps. 12:2); we *sin*—we "miss the mark" (Vine, 1996, p. 576). The Garden of Eden narrative portrays human beings in all of their nobility, but it's also a narrative of human lapse—". . . Meant to be noble, we too often amount to much less; meant to be generous, we withhold from others; created more than animal, we often sink to being nothing less" (Smith, 1991, p. 281). Betrothed to *Yahweh* as a bride to a groom, we hide ourselves (Gen. 3:10), we play the harlot (Hos. 4:15); we are unfaithful (Ps. 78:57). This is done by forgetting *Yahweh* and his laws, but also, by extension, mistreating our neighbors—neglecting the plight of the poor, the widow, and the orphan (Jer. 5:28).

The Solution

Given that the Jewish conception of the human problem involves straying from the covenantal relationship with the divine due to double-mindedness, conflictedness, and lack of integrity, it should come as no surprise that the solution to these problems is simply "turning" toward that to which we have become estranged. In essence, we must search the depths of our hearts and make a course correction, which moves us more in the direction of peace, wholeness, and authenticity. Said Martin Buber (1966):

> . . . Turning stands at the center of the Jewish conception of the way of man. Turning is capable of renewing a man from within and changing his position in God's world. . . . Turning means something much greater than repentance and acts of penance; it means that by a reversal of [the] whole being, a man who had been lost in the maze of selfishness, where he had always set him as the goal, finds a way to God; that is, a way to the fulfillment of the particular task for which he has been destined by God.

The Method

Judaism does not emphasize a life to come. Instead, emphasis rests squarely on our doings in this life. The path toward integration, peace, and enlightened living is not spelled out in concrete, specific steps as it is in some Eastern faiths (e.g., Buddhism). Rather, illumination comes as a byproduct of searching our hearts, committing ourselves to purposes that transcend the self, and devotedly studying God's revealed word—commandments to holy prophets (the Torah); the inspired commentaries on the Torah written by Jewish sages (the Talmud); and, for some, the great mystical writings of Judaism (the Zohar and the Kaballah). The inspiration that comes from prolonged, diligent searching of self and the divine word brings with it an understanding of how to perform our particular work in the world. Judaism asserts that each person's soul is a serving member of God's overall work of creation, which, by inspired human effort, is to become the Kingdom of God. Therefore, none of us is to make our own salvation our primary focus. True, each of us is to come to know ourselves, to purify ourselves, to perfect ourselves (in so much as is humanly possible), but none of this is for the sake of the individual, not for our own temporal happiness, nor our own eternal bliss, but for the sake of the work we are destined to perform in the world (Buber, 1966).

The Result

The potential end result of performing a "turn," of diligently searching our souls and the revealed word, is to come to know firsthand—through divine illumination—the non-dualistic truth of existence. One contemporary scholar of Judaism (Michaelson, 2010) lists a variety of conclusive statements of Jewish sages through the ages, comprising what he calls "Jewish enlightenment." These affirm the reality that "God fills and surrounds all worlds"; "He fills everything and He is everything"; there is no place devoid of God; that God ". . . surrounds all, and fills all, and is the life of all; You are in All." A particularly apt sixteenth-century summary of the highest intuitions coming from a life dedicated to endeavors larger than the self reads:

> God is the existence, the life, and the reality of every existing thing. The central point is that you should never make a division within God. . . . If you say to yourself, "[the Endless, Infinite One] expands until a certain point, and from there on is outside of It," God forbid, you are making a division. Rather, you must say that God is found in every existing thing. One cannot say, "This is a rock and not God," God forbid. Rather, all existence is God, and the rock is a thing filled with God. . . . God is found in everything, and there is nothing besides God. (Michaelson, 2010)

In other words, unity consciousness is the result. Judaism has its classic "representative men," such as Abraham and Moses, who epitomize the ultimate possibilities of human existence, but perhaps more applicable to our daily lives would be the numerous examples through the centuries of notable yet relatively unknown rabbis and mystics who were men (always men) of deep learning, but who also possessed great insight and wisdom for life. Michaelson (2010) points out that the mystical wing of Judaism (i.e., Hasidism) understood enlightened consciousness not as a "steady state" but as what they called *ratso v'shov*, literally "running and returning." It was understood that a mystic would have to experience these shifts in awareness as he perceived the highest unity during moments of meditative clarity, but that he would also need to operate on a much more mundane, practical level as he tended to the needs of his family and the community. Thus, the *tzaddik* (the leader of the Hasidic community) was expected to have the capacity and flexibility both to enter the highest states of consciousness and to be readily available to provide for the community's material and spiritual needs—the glory of God made manifest in both. In Judaism, the experience of enlightenment is one of oscillation between what one Hasidic master called "God's point of view" and "our point of view" (Michaelson, 2010).

Buddhism

Of all the world's religious figures, perhaps only Jesus is more well known than the young man, Siddhartha Gautama, who later "woke up" and became the Buddha. Raised a prosperous prince, Siddhartha had all the luxuries one could imagine in the sixth century B.C.E, and, according to various sources, was "extremely handsome, trust inspiring, stately, and gifted with great beauty of complexion and fine presence" (Sri Dhammananda, 1993, p. 1). At 16, he married his regal cousin Yasodhara, who bore him a beautiful son. Yet despite his seemingly great fortune, the young Siddhartha would, by his mid-twenties, renounce his worldly position and comforts in order to begin a quest that would come to its culmination during his thirty-fifth year, beneath the Bodhi tree in Bodh Gaya, India. After utilizing the meditative techniques of Hinduism's *raja yoga* without ceasing for 49 days, he received enlightenment and became the Buddha—*one who has woken up*. The Buddha spent the remainder of his life traveling in Asia as he attempted to facilitate the enlightenment of others.

What could possibly lead a strapping young man from the lap of worldly pleasures, luxury, and leisure to an uncertain life of seeking and wandering? Siddhartha was intentionally sheltered by his father, but he was naturally inquisitive and remarkably intelligent. In Buddhist tradition called the "Four Sights," the young Siddhartha saw, from his chariot on four separate occasions, a decrepit, elderly man, representing old age; a diseased person lying in agony on the side of the road, representing illness; a human corpse, bloated and rotting in the sun, representing death; and a Hindu monk with shaven head, clothed in an orange robe, extending a wooden bowl for alms, representing renunciation of the world. This gradual exposure to life's existential realities started the young Siddhartha on a journey toward enlightenment. Though likely mythical rather than historical in nature, this story tells a basic truth embodied in the heart of the Buddha's teachings: The body's gradual, inexorable movement toward death as epitomized by aging, disease, and decrepitude shows that lasting fulfillment on the physical plane is an impossibility. Worldly pleasures and distractions are merely temporary; all corporeal things fade. On the cusp of leaving his princely life behind, the young Siddhartha said, "[So] life is subject to age and death [. . .]. Where is the realm of life in which there is neither age nor death?" (Sri Dhammananda, 1993, p. 1)

The Problem

Some of the great strengths of the Buddhist formula for enlightenment include its clarity, specificity, and comprehensiveness. Thus, reviewing even superficially its basic points will require more space. These strengths are mirrored in the Buddha himself, a man who possessed perhaps one of the greatest personalities of all time—a man who had the rare combination of a very rational, cool head and a warm, compassionate heart. When he finally rose from the rapture of his enlightenment underneath the Bodhi tree, he walked toward the holy city of Banaras, India, which was over one hundred miles away. On the outskirts of the city, he stopped to speak to a group of Hindu ascetics. The subject of his first discourse was the "Four Noble Truths," which epitomize the foundational principles of enlightenment as he'd come to know it.

The first Two Noble Truths diagnose the problem. The first of these is that *life is dukkha*. While the traditional rendering of *dukkha* is "suffering," in truth, there is no adequate one-word synonym in English. As used in the Pali language, the word *dukkha* implies a wheel whose axle is off-center, or bones that are not quite situated in their sockets (Smith, 1991, p. 101). Thus, rather than simply saying, "life is suffering," it may be more accurate to say that life as experienced by human beings is dislocated, out-of-joint, and gone wrong. Like the wheel whose hub has been knocked out of true center, we wobble, rub, chafe, and wear thin at painful points of contact with life. Given the analytical bent of his mind, the Buddha was not content to leave this first Noble Truth in such generalized form. The Buddha went on to innumerate six ways in which life's chafing is especially apparent: (a) the trauma of birth (psychoanalysts from Freud [1935] to Rank [1924] specified this experience as the prototype of all later anxiety); (b) the pain of sickness; (c) the stresses of being an adult and the painful emotional realizations and physical limitations of advancing age; (d) fear of death; (e) binding ties to what one loathes, such as undesirable physical characteristics, an incurable disease, or character defects; and (f) the pain of separation from what one loves (Smith, 1991, pp. 101–102).

The Second Noble Truth is that *dukkha comes from tanha*: What is always present when the chafing of life is present, and absent when such suffering is absent? The answer is *tanha*. Traditional renderings of *tanha* are "thirst," "craving," or "desire," but again, it is inadequate to leave it at this, because the Buddha did not see all desire as being problematic. *Tanha* is the egoistic drive for separate existence, the desire for private fulfillment, the wish to have or obtain what one does not have, or the wish to not have what one does. When we have transcended selfishness, then we are truly free to act. However, the primary issue is this: How is one to maintain such a state? It is *tanha* that ruptures such moments of selflessness.

The Solution

The last two Noble Truths prescribe the solution and flow naturally from the first two. If the cause of life's dislocation is selfish desire and craving, then the solution lies in transcending such states. Buddhism is often mistakenly perceived as a pessimistic philosophy, most likely because of a misunderstanding or over-generalization of the first Noble Truth. Buddhism's inherent optimism is evident in the affirmation that there is a solution to life's suffering. The Third Noble Truth points the way: *To overcome tanha, one must first overcome the drive for separate existence* (Smith, 1991, p. 104). This is quite simple to say, yet as if to put a very fine point on the immensity of the task, Buddhism posits the doctrine of the transmigration of souls (i.e., reincarnation), suggesting that many lifetimes may be required in order to fully transcend the problem of *tanha*, but the pathway is clear—the Fourth Noble Truth points the way. *To overcome the drive for separate existence, follow the Eightfold Path.* It is only intransigent human nature that holds us back: This is the point at which Buddhism becomes quite prescriptive, as a specific method is explicated. The Eightfold Path can be seen as a course of treatment for the human condition, but it is not a treatment in the typical sense. The initiate is no mere passive recipient of a medicinal cure. Rather, we must exert ourselves in a conscious, intentional effort over time. The Buddha proposes a series of eight foci or endeavors designed to release the individual from "ignorance, unwitting impulse, and *tanha*. . . . By long and patient discipline, the Eightfold Path intends nothing less than to pick one up where one is and set one down as a different being. . . ." (Smith, 1991, p. 104).

The Method

Before briefly outlining the Eightfold Path, it's important to point out that the Buddha knew firsthand how difficult the remedy for *tanha* was. Therefore, he prescribed what he called *right association* as a preliminary step. Just as negativity, pessimism, anxiety, and depression are contagious (Joiner & Katz, 1999), so are health, virtue, and cheerfulness (Bono & Remus, 2006). The Buddha knew that human beings are social creatures whose associations help set the floor or ceiling for what is both permissible and possible. He knew that we should "associate with truth-winners, converse with them, serve them, observe their ways, and imbibe by osmosis their spirit of love and compassion" (Smith, 1991, p. 105). With the right supports in place, we are then in the best position to make real progress. The eight objectives constituting the path toward enlightenment are as follows:

The first two have to do with having the correct paradigm for living.

1. *Right views*: In order to proceed in the correct direction, one must have an accurate understanding of the true nature of the problem and the solution. A deep understanding of the Four Noble Truths (i.e., the reality of our suffering, the cause of our suffering, the fact that our suffering can be transformed, and the path toward transformation) provides this.

2. *Right thinking*: Whereas Western thought has been profoundly influenced by Descarte's maxim, "I think, therefore I am" (i.e., thought is proof positive of existence), the Buddhist view regarding thought is that much of it is counterproductive. Thus, learning how to quiet our thinking and be fully aware of the present moment is, paradoxically, the right way to use the mind. Mind and body come together as one in *right thinking*. Thich Nhat Hanh (1998, pp. 60–62) suggests four practices to encourage this tendency:

   a. *"Are you sure?"* We must ask ourselves this question again and again as we are easily deceived; wrong perceptions cause incorrect thinking and unnecessary suffering.

   b. *"What am I doing?"* We must ask ourselves this question in order to pull ourselves out of our mental focus on the past or future and back to the present moment.

   c. *"Hello, habit energy."* When we recognize dysfunctional patterns of thought recurring, we can say "hello, habit energy" to ourselves to identify ingrained ways of thinking while not beating ourselves up for having them.

   d. *Bodhichitta*. The motivational force for mindful living is most effective when it's centered in improving the self for the purpose of bringing more happiness to others, rather than benefiting the self. This is the mind of enlightenment.

The next three steps have to do with the practicalities of our daily lives.

3. *Right speech*: The words we speak can help us to become aware of our character as nothing else can. For example, rather than assuming that we speak the truth at all times, we will be well served instead to notice how many times we overstate or understate the truth, asking ourselves why we did so. Also, we can observe in ourselves incidences of unkind speech and the motives behind such speech. Once we understand the ego-enhancing function of these behaviors, we can then proceed toward the goals of right speech: *speaking truthfully, not speaking duplicitously* (i.e., not misrepresenting the truth depending on who you're speaking to), *not speaking cruelly*, and *not exaggerating or embellishing*.

4. *Right conduct*: The basis of right conduct is to do all that we do mindfully. Four areas are especially relevant:
   a. *Reverence for life*. Not only is human life sacred, but animal life is also. (Buddhists are vegetarians.)
   b. *Generosity*. Not only should we not exploit other living things, but our attitudes and actions should encourage justice and well-being in society.
   c. *Sexual responsibility*. We should not engage in sexual relations with another unless there is true love and long-term commitment. We respect our own commitments and the commitments of others.
   d. *Mindful eating, drinking, and consuming*. We should "consume" things (i.e., food, drink, entertainment media) only to a degree that encourages peace, well-being, and joy in our body, consciousness, family, and society.
5. *Right livelihood*: Our life work takes up a substantial portion of our waking time and attention. Spiritual progress will be very difficult if we earn our living in ways that are antithetical to inner growth. Since few of us will feel so inclined toward the pursuit of liberation that we will devote our lives to it in the form of entering the monastery, most of us have to attempt further enlightenment while being engaged in mundane activities. The key for *right livelihood* is to engage in occupations that promote or enhance life and goodness instead of detracting from or destroying them.
6. *Right effort*: The Buddha placed tremendous emphasis on the importance of the will. Only a strong and steady desire for liberation will lead us closer toward its fruits. He likened *right effort* to an ox that walks deep into a mire carrying a heavy load, looking forward, but not relaxing completely until he comes out of the mire (Matanga & Gobharana, n.d.). Yet the Buddha also endorsed *the middle way*, which encourages living between the extremes of austerity and sensual indulgence (he had tried both and found both had major weaknesses). If our spiritual practice does not bring joy, we are not practicing correctly. Lack of diligence stems from not yet finding a true way to practice, or from not yet feeling a deep need to practice. Paradoxically, practices that embrace suffering (rather than fleeing from suffering) will lead to the transcendence of suffering; such a willingness epitomizes *right effort* and will lead toward liberation. Physical exercise is but one manifestation of this principle.
7. *Right mindfulness*: In Buddhist thought, mindfulness is everything; it is "cultivating the Buddha within," which is analogous to the Christian's goal of abiding in the Holy Spirit. In Sanskrit, mindfullness (*smriti*) means to "remember"—in other words, to come back to the present moment. Mindfulness allows us to truly access our lives, because the present moment is the only place in which our lives are occurring. Mindfulness brings with it "seven miracles," which have a dramatic impact on our quality of life (Thich Nhat Hanh, 1998, pp. 64–67):
   a. *The first miracle*: To fully experience our lives as they happen.

b. *The second miracle*: To make the other—the sky, a flower, a child—fully present, alive, and "deep"—an end in itself rather than a means to an end.

c. *The third miracle*: To genuinely nourish our beloved.

d. *The fourth miracle*: To relieve suffering in our beloved.

e. *The fifth miracle*: To look deeply, allowing us to see the truth.

f. *The sixth miracle*: To have understanding because of our presence and deep looking. Understanding is synonymous with loving.

g. *The seventh miracle*: To undergo transformation of our own and others' suffering.

8. *Right concentration*: To engage in *right concentration* is to cultivate a mind that is singularly focused rather than scattered or fragmented (which is precisely how most of us experience our minds much of the time). Over the course of more than two millennia, Buddhists have devised and refined hundreds of meditative techniques, all toward the same end: to learn how to become *one* with the present moment. At the highest levels of meditative practice, we see deeply into reality and come to realize *impermanence* (i.e., all things fade), *inter-being* (i.e., nothing can exist by itself alone), and *non-self* (i.e., nothing—not even what I call "me"—has a separate self).

The Result

Similar to its spiritual parent, Hinduism, Buddhism asserts that the ultimate outcome of enlightenment is *nirvana*. The Buddha resisted a positive description of *nirvana*, saying it was beyond the capacity of thought to describe or imagine, saying only that "[*nirvana*] is the highest happiness" (Dhammapada, vs. 204); "Bliss, yes bliss, my friends, is *nirvana*" (Smith & Novak, 2003, p. 53). *Nirvana* is also synonymous with enlightenment—being fully awake as to the true nature of reality. It is not a place (e.g., heaven), but rather, a state of emptiness where the true human personality, the self that is non-self, becomes reality (Guenther, 1949, pp. 156–157). Thus, we can attain *nirvana* without dying. When we die after having finally realized *nirvana*, our death becomes the last link in the cycle of death and rebirth (*samsara*), and we will not be reborn again. What happens to a person at this point cannot be explained, as it is outside all conceivable experience. However, the *bodhisattva* principle is one which says that individuals on the cusp of realizing enlightenment can choose to delay their full realization in order to—out of compassion for others—continue to return to earth in life after life in order to assist others toward greater levels of enlightenment. His Holiness, the Dalai Lama (2009) said, "Bodhisattvas. . . out of compassion, take rebirth so that they can help sentient beings. By abandoning any aspiration for themselves alone, they advance for the well-being of others" (p. 176).

Christianity

Perhaps more than any other world faith tradition, Christianity roots itself in actual historical events. Foremost among these is its central figure: a Jewish carpenter who was born in the humblest of circumstances in an insignificant corner of the Roman Empire between the years of 7 and 2 B.C.E. (Carson, Moo, & Morris, 1992, pp. 54, 56). Apart from a possible brief foray into Egypt (only one Gospel mentions this tactic used by his family to evade Herod's alleged kingdom-wide infanticide), he never traveled more than perhaps four dozen miles from the place of his birth. He owned no property, received no formalized education, never married, had no offspring, left no writings, and at the age of 33 was ignominiously executed as a state criminal. Yet the legacy of this man's brief time on earth permeates the lives of more human beings than any other world faith—more than 2 billion adherents represent tens of thousands of denominations (Religions ranked by number, n.d.; Christianity today, general statistics, n.d.). This man is Jesus called *"Christ"* (Greek for *the anointed*), whom Christians profess as God manifested in the flesh. During his brief life, Jesus proclaimed by word and deed that he was infused with the spirit of God ("The spirit of the Lord is upon me"; Luke 4:18), that he was able to subdue the powers of hell ("I cast out demons by the spirit of God"; Matt. 12:28), and that he ushered in the long-awaited coming of the kingdom of God (". . . Thy kingdom come, on Earth; Matt 6:10), all of which had the power to transform humanity from base creaturliness to compassionate saintliness.

For all of its emphasis on history, Christianity may also be the most "literary" of the world's religions, for its theology emerges from a story of irony, tragedy, and triumph that is perhaps unrivaled in history. In this story, the very God of the universe, out of a desire to redeem his fallen creations, condescends to take upon himself the form of an ordinary man. He walks among his fellows largely unrecognized, speaking of a revolutionary ethos of love, spiritual transformation, forgiveness, and redemption. He performs miracles, not as a brash show of strength or power, but out of compassion for those at the margins of society; he heals the leprous and restores sight to the blind, hearing to the deaf, mobility to the lame, and life to the dead—all richly symbolic of his intense desire for humanity to experience a renewal of life and a reconciliation with the very Ground of their being. In response, the religious and political powers-that-be—not recognizing his true identity, and threatened by the potential appeal of his message of love, forgiveness, and reconciliation—put him to death in the most feared manner imaginable at the time. With his last tortured breaths, this God in human form, voluntarily allowing himself to be slain, utters a plea unto heaven for his tormentor's forgiveness. The great paradox is that by executing him, those who conspire and actively participate in his torture and death unwittingly assisted in bringing salvation not only to themselves, but to the entire human race, permanently bridging the chasm between humanity and divinity. This is so because Jesus' innocent death, after a life of perfection, brings about *the atonement*: the re-uniting of humanity with God.

The Problem

From the Christian perspective, human nature is "fallen," which predisposes human beings to act in ways that are contrary to divine will. Such actions lead us into a state of deeper disconnectedness and estrangement from the divine, and toward that which seems appealing on the surface, but ultimately doesn't satisfy—the self. Such a condition has been referred to as a type of "spiritual bondage" (Acts 8:23; Gal. 5:1), which traps us in attachment to ourselves. The more we are attached to self, the more likely we are to sin (i.e., to knowingly act contrary to God's will) and the less we are able to love others; yet, we do not like ourselves much either. The result is a life experience typified by an underlying sense of guilt, fear, dissatisfaction, and despair.

The Solution

Divine omniscience foresaw the human predicament and sought to liberate humankind from the prison of self. "For God so loved the world that he gave his only begotten son, that whosoever believeth in him should not perish, but have everlasting life" (John 3:16 KJV). In other words, in order for a reconciliation to occur, God came to earth disguised in human form to show humanity the way to salvation—how to find release from the prison of self in this life, and inherit eternal life in God's presence in the next—and to ransom humankind, to "pay the price of sin" (Alexander, 1847) through his suffering in Gethsemane and his death on Golgatha.[5] In his teachings and in the conduct of his life, Jesus showed the way that God would have us live our lives on earth:

> Ye have heard that it hath been said, An eye for an eye, and a tooth for a tooth: But I say unto you, that ye resist not evil: but whosoever shall smite thee on thy right cheek, turn to him the other also. And if a man will sue thee at the law, and take away thy coat, let him have thy cloak also. And whosoever shall compel thee to go a mile, go with him twain. Give to him that asketh thee, and from him that would borrow of thee turn not thou away. Ye have heard that it hath been said,

---

5. There are, of course, numerous Christian models of atonement (e.g., sacrificial, satisfaction, moral influence, reconciliation, etc.); ransom is one of the more commonly utilized.

Thou shalt love thy neighbor, and hate thine enemy. But I say unto you, Love your enemies, bless them that curse you, do good to them that hate you, and pray for them which despitefully use you and persecute you, that ye may be the children of your Father which is in heaven. (Matt 5: 38-45, KJV)

The fact that revolutionary precepts such as these are so central to Christianity, yet are so often ignored by Christians (whether in deed or in their politics), shows just how tenacious and powerful the prison of self is. God foresaw that enlightened teachings and human effort would be inadequate to breach the spiritual divide on their own. For this reason, Jesus allowed himself to suffer and die, though he was innocent of any sin (2 Cor. 5:21; 1 John 3:5), in order that an atonement be made on behalf of humanity, spiritually cleansing them, and making them fit for eternal life with God.

The Method

In order to avail themselves of the redeeming power of the atonement and be reconciled to God, human beings must come unto Christ with a "broken heart and a contrite spirit" (Ps. 51:17), acknowledging from the depths of their hearts that Christ is their savior and redeemer. Such a condition of humility allows human beings to become the vehicles of God's spirit (i.e., the Holy Ghost), which manifests itself in them through their love of all creation and their lack of desire for sin. While Christians vary on how much human effort (if any) is necessary in order to avail oneself of the atonement of Christ, all will agree that Jesus Christ acts as the bridge between God and humankind, and that human beings must participate in some degree of ongoing "relationship" with Christ in order avail themselves of the influence of the Holy Spirit. Christians also differ in their belief that their relationship to the divine is a purely personal matter versus one requiring an institutional intermediary. The sacraments of the church and the covenants made in connection with these represent the physical tokens of one's personal relationship to Christ. Regular participation in such ordinances and renewal of the covenants associated therewith, along with frequent prayer, scripture study, and charitable action toward others, helps humanity express "good faith" in the relationship and retain the influence of the divine spirit.

The Result

The earliest respondents to Jesus' message of "good news" found that their lives had been transformed. Otherwise ordinary men and women had found, in Jesus and his message, the secret to living. They had become "born again" (John 3:3); they were "new creatures in Christ" (2 Cor. 5:17). Early church father Tertullian (c.a. 200 C.E.) observed outsiders remarking of Christians, "'Look,' they say, 'how they love one another (for they themselves hate one another); and how they are ready to die for each other (for they themselves are readier to kill each other)'" (Tertullian, 1932, 39:7). The early Christian apostle Paul described "the fruits of the Spirit," or the attributes of those who had undergone the drastic change of heart spoken of by Jesus this way: ". . . love, joy, peace, long-suffering, gentleness, goodness, faith, meekness, temperance: against such there is no law" (Gal. 5: 22–23). What was it that produced such universally desired but rarely obtained traits? Huston Smith (1991) points to three intolerable burdens that had been lifted from the shoulders of Christians, allowing them to lives epitomized by love and joy: (1) the fear of death, (2) the onus of guilt, and (3) the cramping confines of the ego. One can easily imagine how release from these ubiquitously oppressive weights could feel like a rebirth, and how the one held responsible for such liberation would be hailed as a savior, the very epitome of God on earth (p. 333).

Jesus disclosed the ever-present, overpowering reality of God's love for humanity. Indeed, the only power capable of affecting a transformation of the order described above is love. Locked in the human heart is a slumbering treasure trove of love, which partakes of divine love and can only be activated by "love's bombardment":

> A loving human being is not produced by exhortations, rules, and threats. Love only takes root in children when it comes to them—initially and most importantly from nurturing parents. Ontogenetically speaking, love is an answering phenomenon. It is literally a response. (Smith, 1991, p. 334)

The experience of God's love is the transformative power in the life of a Christian. This love was disclosed in the words and deeds of Jesus during a time when life was cruel, short, and cheap. As Joseph Klausner (1997) observes, if we take the teachings of Jesus one at a time, we can find parallels for each of them either in the Old Testament or in the Talmud. However, when taken as a whole and as given by one person at the height of Rome's crushing domination of the world, they have a singularity, clarity, beauty, urgency, and revolutionary character unmatched by the words of any other person in history. The Apostle Paul describes in words that continue to astound us today the type of love that Jesus conveyed—divine love. Humans have the capacity to express this same type of love to the world once they have had awakened within themselves their *imago dei*, their God within:

> Charity suffereth long, and is kind; charity envieth not; charity vaunteth not itself, is not puffed up, doth not behave itself unseemly, seeketh not her own, is not easily provoked, thinketh no evil; rejoiceth not in iniquity, but rejoiceth in the truth; beareth all things, believeth all things, hopeth all things, endureth

all things. Charity never faileth. . . . For now we see through a glass, darkly; but then face to face: now I know in part; but then shall I know even as also I am known. And now abideth faith, hope, charity, these three; but the greatest of these is charity. (1 Cor. 13:4–8; 12)

In terms of representative figures in Christianity, Jesus, of course, has no equal. In the mind of Christians, the notion of that a person could undergo a Spirit-of-God mediated transformation of character such that he or she comes to equal the moral perfection of Jesus is tantamount to blasphemy. While Jesus represents *the goal* for Christians, he remains an unreachable archetype of perfection in human form. Having said this, it is also important to note that many men and women over the centuries have indeed been transformed in remarkable ways through the methods outlined by various strains of Christianity. The effect of their lives can be seen as a ripple emanating out over generations, impacting for good not only relationships within individual families but indeed throughout entire nations.

Islam

Islam's central human figure, Muhammad, was born into Mecca's leading tribe in approximately the year 570 C.E. Despite his early life being marked by the untimely deaths of many of his caregivers, he is described as a young man of remarkable attributes: pure-hearted, beloved, gentle, and sensitive to suffering, especially given these early loses (Smith, 1991, p. 224). By the time he was a young man, he is described as a person troubled by the pervasive inter-tribal strife that was so prevalent among his contemporaries; as a result, he became more inward-looking, more self-reflective. After his marriage to the deeply devoted, supportive, and inspirational Khadija (who was 15 years his senior), Muhammad would occasionally visit a cave on nearby Mount Hira for solitude and reflection. It was there, in the midst of a deep contemplation, that he received a manifestation from the divine: The angel Gabriel, on errand from Allah—the one and only God—commanded Muhammad to "proclaim" the following words:

Proclaim! In the name of thy Lord and Cherisher, Who created-Created man, out of a (mere) clot of congealed blood:Proclaim! And thy Lord is Most Bountiful,-He Who taught (the use of) the pen,-Taught man that which he knew not. (Koran, Sura 96, 1–3)

Over the course of the next 23 years, Muhammad continued to periodically receive the words of the angel into his mind. Others who became devoted to this new prophet—first and foremost his wife, Khadija—either memorized the words or wrote them down. These sayings later became known as the Koran. This lengthy revelation is not explicitly metaphysical, nor is its theology embedded in a dramatic narrative, as are the Indian epics. It is not a historic narrative, like the Old or New Testaments, nor is God revealed as an anthropomorphized being, as in the *Bhagavad-Gita*. Rather, the Koran is predominantly doctrinal and only marginally historical. As Huston Smith puts it, "When the Lord-servant relationship is the essential point to get across, all else is but commentary and allusion. . . . In the Koran, God speaks in the first person; he describes himself and makes known his laws" (Smith, 1991, pp. 234–235). For Muslims, the Koran "is not *about* the truth, it *is* the truth" (Cragg, 1988, p. 18). The Koran outlines the way to submit our will to Allah in this life—indeed, Islam itself is an Arabic word meaning "submission"—in order to transform our life in this world and gain eternal life with Allah in the next. By the time of his death in 632 C.E., Muhammad's revelations and the faith he proclaimed had spread over Arabia in a manner unprecedented at that time.

The Problem

According to Islam, we as human beings are of divine origin ("Surely, We have created humanity of the best stature"; Koran 95:4), which predisposes us toward Islam as a means toward oneness with Allah. However, as human beings enmeshed in the vagaries of the temporal world, subservient to their surroundings, and captivated by their lusts and animal impulses, we are also prone toward *ghaflah*—forgetfulness, negligence, and heedlessness—in which our own selfish desires reign supreme. In such a condition, we are estranged from Allah. These tendencies are further complicated by the fact that children are often raised in faiths other than Islam. These same children, as adults, may turn in a variety of directions in terms of their lifestyle and their approach to the divine, perhaps in the direction of disbelief altogether.

The Solution

The solution to heedlessness and forgetfulness is, of course, to remember. One way of understanding Islam is that is represents a collective of practices and rituals that are designed to assist us in the act of remembering—remembering who we are, remembering from whence we came, and remembering why we were created. In short, human beings need to remember Allah and his path, which is the path of diminishing individual will in favor of submission to divine will. Remembering is so important that Islam's basic structure creates a new way of life for its adherents, requiring a level of repetition and observance for the layperson which surpasses that of any other monotheistic faith. This need to remember is why Allah sent prophets, such as Adam, Abraham, Moses, and Jesus to remind us of the reality of the divine and to proclaim his will to us. However, in each dispensation, the message was misunderstood, distorted, or forgotten. Finally, Muhammad was sent to humankind as the great and last Prophet, to solidify and proclaim the pure message contained in the Koran.

The Method

If a Muslim was asked to declare in one statement how Allah admonishes us to live our lives, the answer would likely be, "He teaches us to walk along the straight path" (Smith, 1991, p. 242). The metaphor of "the straight path" comes directly from the opening words of the Koran, which often are included in the prayers that Muslims offer five times each day:

In the name of Allah, the Beneficent, the Merciful.
All praise is due to Allah, the Lord of the Worlds.
The Beneficent, the Merciful.
Thee do we serve and Thee do we beseech for help.
Keep us on the right path.
The path of those upon whom Thou hast bestowed favors. Not the path of those upon whom Thy wrath is brought down, nor of those who go astray. (Koran 1:1–6)

Of what, then, is this path composed? Through Muhammad, Allah revealed what has come to be known as the *Five Pillars of Islam*. The first pillar is the *shahadah*, a simple statement grounding everything else: "There is no God but Allah, and Muhammad is his prophet." This is not only a foundational article of faith, oft-repeated in the life of a Muslim, but it's also a phrase, though brief and simple in construction, that has the power to transform one's life when it is uttered with complete conviction.

The second pillar is *salat*, consisting of the five daily prayers that Muslims are to offer at specific times of the day (i.e., before the sun rises, when the sun is at its peak, when it's in mid-decline, when it sets, and before one retires for the day) as they kneel in the direction of Mecca, wherever they may be in the world. These five prayers merely represent outwardly what Muslims are admonished to do inwardly in terms of keeping a prayer "constant" in their hearts (Koran 29:45).

The third pillar is *zakāt*, or charity, which is a principle predating the modern welfare state by centuries. It mandates that Muslims in good standing before Allah are required to give 2.5 percent of the value of all they possess annually to the poor and needy.

The fourth pillar is *sawm*, or fasting, most notable during the month of *Ramadan*, the month when Muhammad received his initial revelation and later made his trek from Mecca to Medina. Commemoration involves able-bodied Muslims abstaining from food or drink from dawn until dusk, at which time food and drink can be partaken of in moderation. This practice enhances our thoughtfulness and self-discipline, underscoring the reality of our dependence upon Allah, and also encourages compassion for those who suffer.

Finally, the fifth pillar is the *hajj*, or pilgrimage to Mecca, which all Muslims are admonished to complete at least once in their lives, regardless of where they live. The pilgrimage heightens one's devotion to God, but it's also a reminder of the great truth of human universality and equality, as all pilgrims don the same plain white garments for the entirety of the *hajj*, regardless of ethnicity, country of origin, social class, or gender.

The Result

Just as the Buddha epitomizes enlightenment resulting from the internalizing of the Four Noble truths and living according to the Eightfold Path, and Jesus embodies enlightenment in the form of divine love and compassion resulting from his oneness with the Spirit of God, so Muhammad could be considered a "representative man" for what is possible when humans live according to the Five Pillars of Islam (Nasr, 1989). First, he represents the quality of *piety*— complete devotion, dedication, and fidelity to one's relationship with Allah. This means that one's personal will is perpetually subservient to the will of Allah, as revealed in the Koran. Second, he represents the quality of *engagement*, of being constantly engaged with all that negates truth and disrupts its harmony. Most significantly, this is epitomized by the "great holy war" (*al-jihād al-akbar*), the continuous battle with our carnal nature, which tends toward the negation of God and his will.[6] Finally, he represents the quality of *magnanimity*—largeness of spirit, generosity in forgiving insult or injury, and freedom from pretty resentfulness or vindictiveness. This is as an attitude of charity toward all human beings, of giving rather than receiving, of

---

6. The Arabic word *jihad* has multiple meanings within Islam. As used in this context, I refer to "the greater *jihad*," which according to Islamic tradition refers to the inner struggle of submitting one's will to Allah. The "lesser *jihad*" refers to the physical (i.e., violent) struggle with Islam's opponents, often emphasized by extremists.

remaining serene and peaceful in the face of adversity (Nasr, 1985, pp. 72–74). These three attributes, epitomized by the prophet Muhammad, display the full-flowering of Allah's spirit within a human life as submission to divine will becomes an integral part of our nature.

COMMONALITIES IN THE WORLD'S FAITH TRADITIONS

In each of the world faiths briefly reviewed above, the solution to the problem of self and the tendency to objectify others looks very similar: We are required to submit our will not just to something other than ourselves, but to something larger than or transcending ourselves. The act of engaging in such a process over an extended period of time is not synonymous with perpetual, white-knuckled, willful exertion. Rather, it is more akin to surrendering—giving up our resistance to uncontrollable forces and/or ceasing to strive to impose our will in ways that enhance our ego. Whether we surrender to the present moment of experience, to the reality of ever-present divine grace and mercy, or to the recollection of our natural affinity for the divine, the process is the same. The result of surrendering our will over time is that, paradoxically, change occurs—the self is cleansed, refined, even reborn as a new creature. This new self is not a self in the traditional sense of the term (i.e., defined by social scripts and roles, socioeconomic status, accomplishments, the possession of certain objects, and so forth), but rather, the new self is "at one" with the world. The self's limiting boundaries have been transcended to a point where we no longer identify solely with our body, family, nation, or species, but rather with all of existence. As we move in the direction of this more enlightened condition, our tendencies toward objectification diminish concomitantly because we no longer doggedly pursue our self-interests. We are more aware of the impact our choices and behaviors have on others, and we live more peaceably with the world.

This universalizing process can be observed in remarkable cases of individuals experiencing transformation through the implementation of the "inspired" methods encouraged by their particular culture's spiritual traditions. A few examples from Hinduism might include Mohandas K. Gandhi (1869–1948) and Swami Vivekananda (1863–1902). In Judaism, Rabbi Joseph Gikatilla (1248–1305), Moses ben-Maimon (Maimonides) (1135–1204), and Martin Buber (1878–1965) show these tendencies. In Buddhism, Cheng Yen (1937–), Thich Nhat Hanh (1926–), and His Holiness, the Dalai Lama (1935–) are representative. Christianity's examples could include the likes of St. Francis of Assisi (1181–1226), Thomas Merton (1915–1968), and Mother Teresa (1910–1997). In Islam, Al Hallaj (858–922) and Khwaja Abdullah Ansari (1006–1088) are good examples. While the traditions differ in terms of doctrines, rituals, and deities worshipped, the end result of the highest spirituality attainable by each religion looks very similar. The individuals mentioned above, while representing different eras, geographies, and cultural worldviews, would find themselves, if suddenly placed together in the same room, among kindred spirits with respect to personality, life experience, and conclusions drawn regarding the meaning of existence and how human life is best lived.

This should not come as a surprise. While no one will dispute that there are enormous differences between the world's spiritual traditions, we should also appreciate perhaps more deeply than we do that there are a handful of very important similarities upon which the world's great religions agree. These similarities are important for two reasons: (1) they suggest the presence of objective realities in the universe that human beings can access; and/ or (2) they suggest a more enlightened level of consciousness available within the human psyche, regardless of epoch or culture, which can be accessed through various methods. Experience has shown that accessing these realities—be they objective or subjective in nature—has the power to catalyze an inner transformation, fundamentally changing how the experiencer views and interacts with the world. As Wilber notes, it seems evident that human beings are "hardwired for spiritual realities," and that "any practice that would help individual human beings attune themselves to these patterns would increase humanity's understanding of, and attunement with, the spiritual patterns of the universe" (Wilber, n.d.). What are the agreed-upon similarities mentioned above? Wilber mentions a tentative seven (Schwartz, 1995):

1. Spirit, by whatever name, exists (i.e., there is a Force or Presence extant in the universe which does not lend itself to direct analysis by empirical science, but is available to other methods of knowing).
2. Spirit, although existing "out there," is found "in here," and is revealed within to the open heart and mind.
3. Most of us don't realize this Spirit within, however, because we are living in a world of sin, separation, or duality—that is, we are living in a fallen, illusory, or fragmented state.
4. There is a way out of this fallen state of sin, illusion, or disharmony; there is a Path to our liberation.
5. If we follow this Path to its conclusion, the result is rebirth or enlightenment, a direct experience of Spirit within and without, a supreme Liberation.
6. This Liberation marks the end of sin and suffering.
7. This Liberation manifests itself in social action of mercy and compassion on behalf of all sentient beings. (p. 354)

Wilber (n.d.) makes two additional points. The first is that authentic spirituality must *transcend and include* the findings of modern science. In other words, authentic spirituality does not deny, resist, or disregard science, but instead integrates its findings and then moves beyond the merely sensory. Science does not place a cap on authentic spirituality; rather, it acts as its grounding (the Dalai Lama's deep fascination, love, and respect for science is an excellent example of this perspective). For example, authentic spirituality accommodates the facts of evolution as part of its perspective. It accepts natural selection as a fundamental process that orders the natural world; it also sees and understands the necessity of deep time for species and geological change to occur. Authentic spirituality then moves on to explore and specify how humanity might continue to evolve its consciousness—expanding and refining it to include an ever-widening circle of concern. Authentic spirituality is not, however, limited by the assumptions of "scientism" (e.g., the notion that the scientific method is the only valid way to access truth, and that sensory data represent the most fundamental aspects of reality), because authentic spirituality assumes that interior, non-sensory modes of knowing also have validity. Second, ordering our psychological life—that is, working through our emotional hang-ups and character flaws—can help enhance our spiritual capacities. For example, a woman can engage in a regular practice of meditation and increase her ability to find release from the prison of her thoughts, but if she hasn't worked out her troubled past with her family, her progression will likely be stymied. Jack Kornfield, world-renowned Buddhist philosopher and mindfulness meditation expert, said it this way (Schwartz, 1995):

> My meditation [. . .] helped me very little with relationships; I was still emotionally immature, acting out the same painful patterns of blame and fear, acceptance and rejection, that I had before my Buddhist training, only the horror was that now I was beginning to see these patterns more clearly. [. . .] I had used the strength of my mind in meditation to suppress painful feelings, and all too often I didn't even recognize that I was angry, sad, grieving, or frustrated until a long time later. I had very few skills for dealing with my feelings, or engaging on an emotional level, or living wisely with my friends and loved ones. There were big dimensions of [my] life [. . .] that were quite uncooked and unfinished. (pp. 314–315)

Each of the spiritual traditions acknowledge that human spiritual evolution is a lifelong process, and that while human perfection is a virtual impossibility, lesser degrees of perfection can be attained through a gradual process of refinement. They also assert that this refining process occurs as individuals participate in a structured, supportive community, continue to internalize the deepest ideals of their faith tradition, and are worked upon by divine grace.

A BRIEF NOTE ON NON-RELIGIOUS APPROACHES TO TRANSCENDING THE EGO

Today, there are a growing number of individuals who do not ground their metaphysical beliefs in any sort of a religious faith or doctrine (whether theistic or nontheistic), but who nonetheless strive to transcend the limiting boundaries of the ego as part of their regular spiritual practice. For the most part, the specific strategies used (e.g., mindfulness meditation, Vipassana meditation, and so forth) have been borrowed directly from the ancient Hindu yogic traditions or from the Buddhist meditative traditions. These practices do not require one to make any substantial leaps of faith, nor to endorse specific speculative assumptions about the nature of the universe in order to receive benefits. In essence, these disciplines have in common the goals of heightened awareness of the present moment of experience; a nonjudgmental, detached, observing stance toward one's intruding thoughts and feelings; and a gradually increasing identification with the conscious awareness "behind" one's thoughts and feelings. While this may sound easy, anyone who has actually tried such a discipline will know that it is anything but. Typically, it takes considerable time and regular, diligent practice to realize the fruits of mindfulness meditation, which include reduced rumination, stress reduction, boosts to focus and working memory, less emotional reactivity, more cognitive flexibility, enhanced self-insight, fear reduction, increased sense of morality, and enhanced capacity for compassion (Davis & Hayes, 2012). Many research studies have verified that those who practice meditation regularly can receive substantial benefits across many domains of mental and physical health (see Sedelmeir, Schwartz, Zimmerman, Haarig, & Jaeger, 2012 for a meta-analysis).

CHAPTER 17

Objectification's Antidote

The Enlightenment Spectrum

When you accept the non-dualistic nature of reality, your way becomes non-violent. . . .
If we really want peace to be possible, then we should try to look at reality in such a way
that there is no separation. . . . We know from our own experience that if the other person
is not happy, it is very difficult for us to be [truly] happy.

Thich Nhat Hanh *(2007, p. 63)*

To comprehend is to know a thing as well as that thing can be known.

John Donne *(1990, p. 150)*

THE ENLIGHTENMENT SPECTRUM

In Chapter 3, I proposed a model of objectification represented as a spectrum of misapprehension, typified by increasing rigidity of our psychological boundaries, creating an escalating potential for violence against others. At the low end of the spectrum, *casual indifference* represents the level of objectification most of us engage in most of the time, at which only a select few others register as precious Subjects. *Derivatization* represents the wide-ranging middle of the spectrum, on which others are seen as mere derivatives of our own needs, desires, fears, and wishes; we use them in a variety of ways to satisfy our own ends at their expense. Objectification's middle latitudes encompass a host of behaviors and attitudes, ranging from the seemingly trivial (e.g., featuring scantily clad women engaged in a "cat fight" over beer in a television commercial) to the blatantly hostile (e.g., engaging in systematic humiliation and torture of suspected combatants in an ongoing violent conflict). At the high end of the spectrum, *dehumanization* represents objectification in the extreme, where we deny the humanity of certain other human beings, seeing them as being not only subhuman, but nonhuman.

If this spectrum is an accurate depiction of human nature's propensity for evil, then it also makes sense to view our capacities for love, compassion, and perceived interconnectedness with the rest of the world as a continuum representing differing levels of enlightenment at the opposite end of the spectrum. Enlightenment has been defined in many ways, likely because it does not represent a fixed point of human experience. Its potential meaning depends not only on our level of analysis, but on one's expectations and unique cultural perspective. For example, His Holiness, the Dalai Lama (2009) defines enlightenment as "a state of freedom from counterproductive emotions. . . and the predispositions in the mind established by those emotions" (p. 256). Thich Nhat Hanh (1998) defines it as "the ability to go from the world of signs [i.e., perceiving only the external side of objects] to the world of true nature" (p. 125, explanation added). Zen master Charlotte Joko Beck describes enlightenment as ". . . no. . . separation [i.e., resistance] between myself and the circumstances of my life, whatever they may be—that is it" (Magid, 2009, p. 68, explanation added). Noted author and lecturer Andrew Cohen (2002) defines enlightenment as "a condition in which the individual has come to the end of a fundamentally self-centered relationship to life" (p. 1). Ken Wilber (2007) suggests that enlightenment is "the realization of oneness with all states and all stages that have evolved so far, and that are in existence at any given time" (p. 94). Eckhart Tolle defines enlightenment as being "one with life;" in other words, bringing full acceptance to the present moment as it is (Tolle, 2008, p. 115). Celebrated Indian mystic Osho Rajneesh defines enlightenment simply and enigmatically as "the reward for watching yourself in action" (Mehta, 2011).

Underlying any additional description would be the same fundamental assertion: A person experiencing enlightenment undergoes a radical shift in his or her level of conscious awareness that is inherently positive, deeply life-affirming, and blissfully self-transcendent. Given this, I suggest that enlightenment be understood as the opponent-process (i.e., mirror-opposite) of objectification. Just as objectification is typified by our misapprehension of others' subjectivity and our lack of perceived interconnectedness with the rest of existence, so enlightenment is typified by its opposite: a heightened awareness of our "self in other" and our fundamental interconnectedness with the rest of existence. When the two continuums are placed together end-to-end, they form a grand spectrum of human psychology and behavior, running from the very best of which we are capable (the right half) to the very worst (the left half) (see Figure 17.1).[1]

With respect to numbers, most human beings will—according to the basic statistical principle of central tendency—likely be represented by the

1. For purposes of clarity, I have shifted the objectification spectrum to the left half of the figure and have made it run to the left, rather than to the right as it did in Chapter 3.

SPECTRUM OF HUMAN CAPABILITY

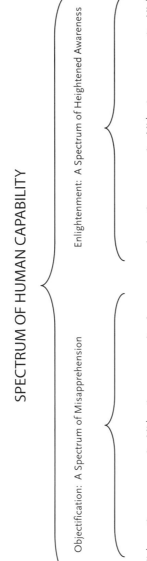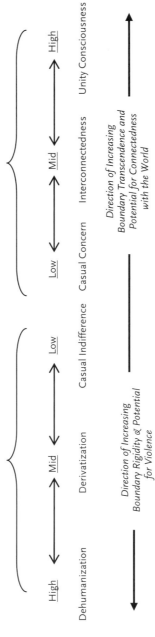

Objectification: A Spectrum of Misapprehension

Enlightenment: A Spectrum of Heightened Awareness

<u>High</u>　<u>Mid</u>　<u>Low</u>　<u>Low</u>　<u>Mid</u>　<u>High</u>

Dehumanization　Derivatization　Casual Indifference　Casual Concern　Interconnectedness　Unity Consciousness

Direction of Increasing Boundary Rigidity & Potential for Violence

Direction of Increasing Boundary Transcendence and Potential for Connectedness with the World

Figure 17.1: Spectrum of Human Capability

meridian of the figure, with the numbers becoming thinner toward the extremes. I assert, however, that the population curve at present would be skewed mildly to the left half rather than the right half of the figure. Though this may be less true of us now than it was in ages past, self-interest, clannishness, and a narrow circle of concern have always seemed to come quite easily to human beings, whereas progress on the right half of the spectrum requires sacrifice, directed work, and education to advance. As has already been mentioned, in order to attain the highest levels of the right half—to become truly loving, pure in heart, and pure in spirit—we must also engage in the paradox of self-surrender, a simple-sounding yet most difficult step. However, it also seems to be true that despite their drawbacks, relatively recent developments in communications technology, such as the telegraph, radio, telephone, television, and now the Internet and cellular technologies, are making it possible for unprecedented numbers of human beings to have practically unlimited access to information about the world. These innovations allow more of us than ever before to be vividly aware of the lives of distant others. How these developments—coupled with those highlighted by Steven Pinker (2011), discussed later in the chapter—will impact our perceived circles of concern remains to be seen, but there is remarkable potential for our collective sense of oneness to increase dramatically.

I now offer a tentative description of the right half of the spectrum's three demarcation points. I do so by describing what differing degrees of enlightenment might look like behaviorally and psychologically in a hypothetical person.

Casual Concern

At the low end of the enlightenment spectrum, *casual concern* typifies the state of mild awareness and appreciation of our basic kinship with the rest of humanity. This low level of enlightenment coexists alongside a predominantly self-centered state of awareness, which is capable of periodic occasions of mindfulness. Therefore, the casually concerned are capable of brief episodes of egolessness, which allows them to appreciate others and the world around them more fully than the casually indifferent. Casual concern has a set-point of general goodwill toward the world-at-large, regardless of others' nationality, ethnicity, color, sexual preference, political affiliation, or religious creed. Though they may support the need for "necessary military interventions" and may also feel considerable pride and identification with their particular culture, the casually concerned also have a dim underlying sense of the problematic nature of nationalism and of wars in general. Such individuals also have a basic concern for the environment and the experiences of other conscious creatures. The casually concerned have a vague sense that their own moment-to-moment experience of life is only one of billions going on at any given moment, and that their own view of reality, while practical and valid for themselves, may only be one of many, and may not necessarily represent "the truth." Such individuals also perceive, in a limited way, the vastness of the collective suffering of the planet; they realize that their own way of life represents only one mode of living, which may be much more privileged than most others. Yet, this casual interest in and concern for all other members of the species (and the planet as a whole) generally doesn't lead to consistent meaningful action on behalf of others or the environment.

Interconnectedness

At the middle of the enlightenment spectrum is *interconnectedness*, in which the realities only dimly perceived by those who are casually concerned come into clearer focus. For example, individuals at this level of enlightenment are more often centered in the present moment of experience due to regular engagement in various practices, such as meditation, yoga, certain religious rituals, prayer, tai chi, participation in the arts, or simply the attempt to practice mindfulness in small ways, numerous times each day. Thus, while still living under the ego, the interconnected are capable of recognizing when they are in the ego's grip, and they are therefore in a better position to shorten the duration or lessen the intensity of their egoic reactions. The interconnected also recognize that truth knows no national, religious, or cultural boundaries, that it comes from a variety of sources and methods of inquiry, and that no cultural construction has a monopoly on an accurate understanding of reality. However, such individuals also realize that not all cultural assumptions and values are created equally in terms of their capacities to map the universe accurately and to facilitate human flourishing. Having a heightened awareness of the commonalities that all human beings share (e.g., the desire to love and be loved, to commit oneself to meaningful purposes, and to have the capacity to provide for one's basic needs in a dignified way), individuals representing the middle of the enlightenment spectrum feel an ongoing, strong sense of kinship with all human beings. Therefore, they feel a strong desire for all human beings to have opportunities to live under benevolent, representative governments, the rule of law, and access to the provision of basic services that lay the foundation for human dignity (e.g., education, healthcare, adequate housing, sanitation, and clean air and water). The interconnected also have a heightened concern for other forms of life and the physical environment. Because of this, they are aware of their "ecological footprint" (Rees, 1992)—the impact that their personal lifestyle has on the earth and its limited resources. Such individuals thus strive to live the Golden Rule (which has variants in all cultures) on a more global scale—seeking to live more in accord with how they would want all human beings on the planet to live if all were living the same lifestyle. Such individuals are more highly conscious of the suffering of other sentient creatures than are the casually concerned, and are therefore likely to be either sparing in their consumption of meats, or to be vegetarian in their diet in an attempt both to minimize collective planetary suffering and to protect the planet's ecosystems. Finally, such individuals recognize the spiritually bankrupt and downwardly cyclical nature of violence as a means of solving human problems, and so are strongly committed to the ideals of nonviolence, appreciating its largely untapped potential to be a powerful force to diminish oppression and to generate social progress without destroying life.

However, for the interconnected, their basic reference point—the self—acts as a primary hindrance that keeps them from realizing an even fuller sense of unity in their lives. Because the self continues to be perceived as the center of existence, all things are known in reference to it, rather than as things in and of themselves. This is the final impediment separating those who have made substantial progress toward transcending objectification from those few who have actually achieved this end.

Unity Consciousness

Much has already been said about *unity consciousness* in Chapter 5 and elsewhere. In brief review, unity consciousness represents the pinnacle of human awareness extolled by the world's great wisdom traditions, and it is thus largely synonymous with enlightenment. In this state of awareness, we perceive that our identity does not stop at the boundary of our skin, but rather, that we are "one" with other human beings—indeed, with all of existence. Again, this does not represent a "break with reality" in a psychotic sense. The great contemplatives knew very well that on a practical level, they were individual persons with distinct location, needs, thoughts, feelings, and so forth. Yet, they experienced within themselves a spiritual reality of oneness with the rest of existence, which fundamentally transformed how they understood, interacted, and valued the world around them.

Unity consciousness represents the full flowering of realizations made in interconnectedness. Those few individuals who attain this highest level of awareness live lives typified by the acceptance of the present moment as it is. As a result, they are capable of engaging in almost any activity—be it walking, driving, washing dishes, making tea, communicating with others, or dealing with challenges—mindfully; that is, they stay centered in the present experience, rather than being lost in thought or reacting to their feelings. Moreover, as James Fowler (1981, 1984) stated of his analogous "stage six: *universalizing faith*," which represents the highest level of faith development human beings are capable of, unity consciousness represents the actualization of two tendencies developing over the course of the enlightenment spectrum. Speaking from the perspective of theism, Fowler asserts the first tendency involves *decentration from self*, literally "de-centering" from oneself as the center of existence. This occurs in two ways: (a) Our "circle of those who count as neighbor. . . expands outward from self to intimate family, extended family and friends, those who share our political and religious perspectives, and finally, beyond those to human kind or Being, in an inclusive sense" (1984, p. 68); and (b) We ". . . de-center in the valuing process to such an extent that we participate in the valuing of the Creator. . . [This is] a standpoint more nearly identified with the love of Creator for creatures than from the standpoint of a vulnerable, anxious creature (1984, p. 69).

The second actualized tendency for those achieving unity consciousness is captured by the Greek word *kenosis*, which literally means "to pour out the self." Often described as "detachment" or "disinterestedness," kenosis is the result of "having one's affections powerfully drawn beyond the finite centers of value and power in our lives that promise meaning and security. . . . [Kenosis] represents a person's total and pervasive response, in love and trust, to the radical love of God" (Fowler, 1984, p. 70). Experience shows that a theistic paradigm is not required in order to achieve such radical decentering of self. (One example among many would include the great mystical sages of the nontheistic Buddhist tradition.) Whether experienced in the context of theism or atheism, the end result is the same—the self paradoxically shrinks into nonexistence as we identify with a larger and larger portion of our world. These processes help explain why some of those in unity consciousness seem to create literal "zones of liberation" around themselves, which work to inspire others to transcend the social, political, economic, and ideological limits of their time and place. Such individuals often put their own lives on the line in order to advocate for the improved life and liveliness of complete strangers and so often run afoul of oppressive institutional interests. As a result, they sometimes die at the hands of those whom they hope to help change (Fowler, 1981, pp. 200–201).

Though they are few in number and often face untimely deaths, the great contemplatives' lives are as majestic clipper ships under full sail in life's vast ocean. They leave a substantial wake—initially narrow but gradually widening—behind them as they go. The rest of us are impacted by this passing wake. While many of us in our own small, rudimentary water crafts will simply notice a momentary rise and fall of the sea in terms of these contemplatives' influence (if we notice anything at all), the more sensitive among us will actually be conscious of the wake. Over time, as more of us experience such wakes and allow ourselves to be moved by them, the general consciousness of humanity progresses and deepens, albeit at a gradual pace. It is important to keep in mind that despite these remarkable developments, individuals in unity consciousness are not perfected human beings in a moral, intellectual, psychological, or social sense. While such individuals have experienced enlightenment (or have made remarkable progress toward this end), because they are human beings, they continue to struggle with certain weaknesses and "blind spots" until the end of their days.

Human Spiritual Growth: What Is Possible versus What Is Typical

Like Jack Kornfield's example from the last chapter, all of us remain in an "uncooked" or "unfinished" state; we will likely not reach the same heights of boundary transcendence that a Gandhi or a Mother Theresa did. It is also important to recognize that not all people are identical with respect to their basic approach to knowing the world and their capacity for discerning spiritual realities. As was suggested in Wilber's consciousness spectrum in Chapter 7, some of us are of a more Apollonian, intellectual bent, preferring controlled, analytical, "distant" approaches to truth. Others of us are more Dionesian in our outlook, leaning toward emotional, intuitive methods of truth discernment. Still others are of a more practical bent, preferring experientially based, pragmatic means to discovering intangible realities. Each approach has its strengths and weaknesses. For example, the Apollonian may achieve logical coherence in his paradigm, but he may also largely miss the fact that great spiritual truths tend to have a contradictory, paradoxical nature (Peck, 1978). The Dionesian may be more open to subtle, emotional, intuitive aspects of spiritual truth, such as, "Love can transcend and heal all barriers which separate and divide people." However, she may also be more prone to endorsing points of view that make inherently incompatible claims (e.g., that God is perfectly beneficent but also punishes the disobedient with suffering). The pragmatist may be adept at discovering methods that bring desired results, but he may fail to recognize that just because something "works" doesn't necessarily mean that it's true in an objective sense. For example, a woman may believe that a diamond the size of a refrigerator is buried in her backyard, and that routinely digging for this diamond brings her family together often, and provides them with a great deal of shared meaning, but of course, the refrigerator-sized diamond is a fiction (Harris, 2006).

Each of the world traditions reviewed in the last chapter realizes that in order to be successful, it must take human beings where they presently stand and provide for them basic stepping-stones to continue the process of spiritual growth. We must acknowledge, however, that if enlightenment can be understood by the well-worn metaphor of many paths leading to the pinnacle of an imposing but majestic mountain, many more people mill aimlessly about the various parking lots, trailheads, and lower parts of the path than ever actually reach the mountain's summit. The moral exhortations, teachings, precepts, and inspired directives that the wisdom traditions encourage their adherents to abide by, while necessary, are not sufficient in themselves to enlighten human beings. This is because—as the wisdom traditions make clear—humans are inherently flawed, imperfect, and fallible beings. We not only battle with a plethora of inner resistances to enlightenment, but for the vast majority of our species' history, the social structures in which we have lived have not been conducive to diminishing our tendencies to objectify one another. Indeed, in many cases, they have served to amplify these tendencies (the Roman Coliseum and the nearly ubiquitous institution of slavery are but a few examples).

However, despite occurrences of unspeakable human-created suffering and brutality occurring somewhere in the world each and every day, there is evidence that we are indeed making slow but inexorable progress toward gradually higher levels of enlightenment. For the overwhelming majority of our history, the only technology available for encouraging human beings to treat others as they might want to be treated themselves have been the indispensable teachings of the great sages. Only very recently in our history—thanks to the intellectual enlightenment of the seventeenth and eighteenth centuries and its offspring, the scientific method—have we added any additional tools to our toolkit.

"The Better Angels of Our Nature:" Why Increased Spirituality Is Not the Only Helping Factor

As mentioned in Chapter 7, many keen observers opine that the human race is moving slowly but inexorably in the direction of greater enlightenment. In a recent landmark book, renowned Harvard neurolinguist Steven Pinker argues convincingly that despite the common perception of the twentieth century as the bloodiest in human history (this likely due to two world wars occurring within 20 years of each other), violence has in fact declined precipitously over the past few hundred years, and there is no reason to assume that this is merely a random, momentary drop in an otherwise steady rate of mass destruction and mayhem (2011). While there is some dispute over Pinker's statistics of prehistoric hunter-gatherer male deaths due to warfare (Ryan and Jetha, 2010), the bulk of Pinker's argument focuses on more recent human history (e.g., the last 2,000 years). Pinker cites voluminous statistics that show the variety of ways in which humanity has indeed become less and less violent over time. He then goes on to posit a variety of "pacifying factors" (2011a) that combine together to play a substantial role in diminishing violence: (1) the "Leviathan" of the state, which includes the development of state system controls; (2) the development of "gentle commerce," or the perception that other people are much more valuable alive than dead; (3) the "expanding circle," or in other words, increasing empathy for those outside one's immediate family, and (4) the "escalator of reason," which makes reference to the calming effect of rational thought on one's approach to solving problems.[2] With some impressive but limited exceptions, such as Greece from 1100 B.C.E. to 450 B.C.E. (Bernstein, 2010), the modern era has been the sole beneficiary of these societal factors occurring together, and the numbers—according to Pinker—bear witness to the power of these factors to transform what we perceive as reasonable and acceptable policy and behavior in terms of how we treat one another.

Within the context of our discussion, the last two pacifying factors are especially relevant and deserve a bit more attention. The expanding circle is a concept that has been referred to numerous times in this book as an indicator of enlightenment. Pinker (2001a) gives the nod to both Charles Darwin and the contemporary ethicist Peter Singer for this idea. According to Singer (1981), altruism began as a genetically based drive to protect one's kin and community members, but has developed into a consciously chosen ethic with an expanding circle of moral concern. He asserts that human ethics cannot be explained by biology alone. Rather, it is our capacity for reasoning that makes moral progress possible. According to Darwin (1871), human evolution has endowed us with a sense of empathy for our immediate family and close friends because it has survival value. Over time, however, this circle has expanded outward—from village to clan, tribe, nation, other races, both sexes, children, and finally, to other species. Pinker (2011a) argues that this has occurred for a variety of reasons. First, increasing cosmopolitanism—an appreciation of history and literature, as well as the rise of mass media, journalism, and world travel—has encouraged us to mix and to see the world from the perspective of others. Second, the "escalator of reason"—reading literature, participating in the educational process, and engaging in public discourse—has encouraged us to think more abstractly and universally rather than provincially and tribally. Such factors encourage us to rise above our own parochial vantage point, making it harder to put our own interests above others. Such factors also help replace a morality based on tribalism, authority, and puritanism with a morality based on fairness and universal rules applicable to all.

2. A substantial caveat is in order with respect to the role of rational thought in the process of enlightenment. Though an incalculable boon to humankind, a plethora of research over the last 20 years has shown that, contrary to many people's assumptions about their own viewpoints and why they hold them, rational thought is generally not used by human beings as an unbiased probe of the self or the universe to discover truths to which we then subscribe. Rather, human beings' sense of morality comes from quick, intuitive flashes of emotion that are largely determined by our social agendas. Rationality is then brought to bear on the task of finding justifications for those feelings (apparently, we're all intuitive politicians, but few of us realize this [Lerner & Tetlock, 2003]). In other words, with respect to moral reasoning, "intuitions come first, strategic reasoning second" (Haidt, 2012, p. 92).

Pinker (2011a) concludes by asking why so many forces push in the same direction. In other words, "Why has history moved away not only from human sacrifices, drawing and quartering, breaking on the wheel, and burning at the stake, but also away from debtor's prisons, foot binding, eunuchism, lynching, bull-fighting, hunting, even the spanking of children?". Pinker asserts that violence has receded over time because human beings have been gradually "chipping away" at this problem, just as we have been chipping away at other important problems such as creating a safer, more abundant food and water supply, containing and extinguishing epidemics, and so forth. In short—and this is the heart of the matter—it is in our long-term best interest as human beings to transcend, as much as we possibly can, our tendency to objectify one another.

Some Practical Suggestions for Decreasing the Human Tendency to Objectify

We need systems that are wiser than we are. We need institutions and cultural norms that make us more honest and ethical than we tend to be. [This] project. . . is. . . even more important than an individual's refining his personal ethical code.

Sam Harris (2013)

In addition to the pacifying factors coming out of the Enlightenment mentioned above, recent social science research has illuminated some principles that can guide us in the implementation of small, practical strategies to increase people's tendencies to make pro-social choices in the present moment. Granted, these principles will not allow us to fast forward the processes of enlightenment, but they do suggest that there are some surprisingly low-tech ways to make more enlightened behaviors a bit easier for people to engage in, while at the same time, making selfish behaviors a little bit harder. As a result, these strategies act as small counterweights to our tendencies to objectify others.

In an important recent book, Heath and Heath (2010) boil the essence of these principles down to three heuristics that can be used in any situation where behavior change is desired. Using Jonathan Haidt's (2006) metaphor of human beings as large elephants (i.e., our more powerful emotional/intuitive side) with small human riders (i.e., our less powerful rational side), the Heaths (2010) suggest:

(1) *Direct the rider*: Give people good, clear, rational reasons for changing their behavior. What may look like resistance on their part is often a lack of clarity about exactly how to proceed.
(2) *Motivate the elephant*: When asking for behavior change, it is critical to engage people's emotions because their rational side can only get its way

in the face of powerful opposing emotions for so long. What looks like laziness on our part is often just exhaustion of our rational side trying to overcome our emotional side.

(3) *Shape the path*: What looks like a "people being resistant" problem is often a situational problem, where underappreciated environmental variables are complicating the performance of new behaviors. When the path is redirected or cleared of stumbling blocks, behavior change is much more likely to occur. (pp. 17–18)

These ideas can be utilized in various configurations to bring about desired behavior change. While the methods employed are not necessarily what I would call flashy or sexy, they can be potent. One shaping-the-path strategy involves structuring institutions in such a way that making "the moral choice"—at least in most people's minds—is the default condition that must be opted out of (otherwise known as "presumed consent"). To increase organ donations, for example, it is good to both direct the rider and motivate the elephant by increasing the public's awareness of the need for organs to be donated. This can be helped along by using compelling public service announcements highlighting specific, tragic cases to help motivate willingness to participate in the program. However, in this case, it's much more powerful to simply direct the path: On state's driver's licenses, if organ donation is the default choice that a driver has to specifically decline, then the number of individuals specified as organ donors goes up dramatically (Thaler, 2009; Thaler & Sunstein, 2009).

On the other hand, a powerful motivating-the-elephant strategy to encourage moral choices is to harness the passionate concern we all have to protect and enhance our social reputations. Many institutions—from universities and other large corporations, all the way down to individual grade school classrooms—have instituted some version of an honor code (a shape-the-path strategy) that constituents are required to sign at the onset of their tenure with the institution. So long as the institution has made the honor code an integral part of its identity, such codes do seem to influence behavior in the direction of less cheating, less stealing, and less of other forms of unfair advantage-taking, whether public or private (Leveille, 2012; Konheim-Kalkstein, 2006). This is because our reputations matter to us, both in terms of what others might think of us, and in terms of what we think of ourselves. A related motivating-the-elephant and shaping-the-path strategy is to ask employees to sign expense reports at the top of the form where a reminder to be honest is also placed. Doing this at the beginning of the form rather than at the end—after the employee has already filled in their claimed expenses and made self-rationalizations for these claims along the way—creates a big drop in the overclaiming of expenses (Ariely, 2008, as cited in Haidt, 2012, p. 336).

Again, these are small interventions that have the capacity to impact behavior in ways that can have substantial benefits to society (e.g., organ donation programs). Perhaps as we gain sophistication in utilizing such strategies, we can devise ways to not only increase pro-social behavior, but to impact people's underlying psychology, where the processes of enlightenment could actually be accelerated. This is not a call for an over-reach in the name of programming people's lives toward some glorious end. Rather, it's an acknowledgment that societies have long attempted to motivate and guide community member's behavior along prescribed paths toward valued ends. We have often seen these things as being influences for good. The rule of law, the Bill of Rights, governmental checks and balances, education, religion, even Boy Scouts and Girl Scouts—all these and more have been put in place to help human beings maximize their potential to impact their own and other's lives in positive ways. The perspective of *libertarian paternalism* (Thaler & Sunstein, 2009) can act as a guide in this endeavor: Society benefits when we are encouraged to make up our own minds and then act freely according to our conclusions. At the same time, it is legitimate for "choice architects" to try to influence people's behavior in ways that will make their lives longer, healthier, and better, *as judged by themselves* (Thaler & Sunstein, 2009, p. 5). It is important to keep in mind that in democratic systems, citizens are free to replace choice architects who introduce policies, procedures, or programs not to the majority of citizen's liking. In the United States, of course, this process takes place rapidly—every two to four years.

In addition to the small, practical strategies mentioned above, there are other more familiar, time-honored means of attempting to diminish human being's tendencies to objectify others. Reading "the great books" and other quality literature (as opposed to popular, "throw away" literature) has the capacity to enhance one's appreciation of what it means to be human. It encourages more compassion and empathy for others, so long as the reader becomes absorbed in the narrative (Bal & Veltcamp, 2013; Oatley, 2012; Gabriel & Young, 2011). Great literature endures because it deals with themes that transcend era and culture, and it depicts characters who have depth and contradictions. This makes it possible for the reader to identify with both protagonist and antagonist alike, illuminating the reader's own inner complexity, and her own angelic and shadow tendencies, which contributes to a more nuanced, deeper appreciation of self and others (Kidd & Castano, 2013; Mar, Oatley, & Petersen, 2009). In like manner, fostering an appreciation of the visual and performing arts encourages a greater sensitivity and awareness of our own and other's interior depths (Green, 2008; Kivy, 2002).

Though costly in terms of money and time, encouraging and participating in travel can enhance our capacities to be more tolerant and understanding. This is because observing and participating in the lives of culturally different others helps us to challenge our prejudices, to discover commonalities, and assists us in "trying on another person's life"—all key components of empathy (Krznaric, 2012).

Education itself has long been acknowledged to be the doorway through which human beings come to more fully know and appreciate themselves, others, and the world around them. A quick Internet search of the questions, "What are the purposes of education?" or "What's a liberal arts education good for?" will reveal literally tens of thousands of lengthy posts from amateur bloggers, college professors, university presidents, Nobel laureates, and even quotes from classical Greek philosophers expounding upon the absolute necessity for human beings to be exposed to—and to fully immerse themselves in—potentially transformative educational experiences in order that they maximize their potential to both perceive truth and to act freely.

What about Empathy Training?

While the subject of empathy is quite complex and could fill numerous books by itself, it deserves a mention here, given the role it plays in diminishing human beings' tendencies to objectify one another. In essence, empathy— the ability to understand and share the feelings of another—has two components: (1) *cognitive empathy*, which is the ability to accurately perceive and appropriately respond to the suffering of others; and (2) *affective empathy*, which is actually feeling another person's emotional state (Carkhuff & Truax, 1965; Hodges & Meyers, 2007). Many decades ago, the venerable Carl Rodgers asserted that empathy is an inherent human attribute that counteracts feelings of alienation and allows people to connect with others (Rogers, 1959). Rogers's prescient insight has been confirmed in numerous studies which show that indeed, human beings seem to come pre-wired for empathy (Zahn-Waxler, Yarrow, & King, 1979; Zahn-Waxler & Yarrow, 1990; Zahn-Waxler, Yarrow, Wagner, & Chapman, 1992; Iacoboni, 2008). There are good reasons for this. Given that human beings are highly social creatures, empathy is a powerfully adaptive trait: It helps our chances at survival by encouraging us to connect emotionally with others, especially those closest to us biologically, and to a lesser extent, those close to us geographically. These connections help us to strengthen the bonds of trust and affiliation that we have with others. When we have closer relationships with family and neighbors, not only are we more likely to survive, but we're more likely to thrive and be happy.

However, it is obvious that empathy is not equally distributed across the species, and that empathy is not a purely biological phenomenon—it can be influenced by our social environment. Empathic tendencies can be unlearned or extinguished through repeated exposure to abuse, neglect, or violence, which, as mentioned previously, can lead to empathy's opposite: emotional hardening (Glover, 1999). It also seems to be true that empathy can be enhanced through a variety of means, often referred to under the heading of "empathy training." Strategies used to enhance empathy are many—some tend toward the exotic, some less so—but the more standardly used methods include (Lam, Kolomitro, & Alamparambil, 2011):

1. *Experiential training*, in which subjects are exposed directly to live conflict scenarios or "dramas" between individuals for them to respond to. These responses are then discussed and analyzed.
2. *Didactic and experiential training*, in which a facilitator gives trainees information on empathy, then provides *in vivo* experiences for the participants to respond to through the use of games, live cases, and scenarios.
3. *Skill training*, in which a facilitator provides trainees with a description of specific skills to be learned, such as reflective listening, then demonstrates the effective use of the skill through modeling. Multiple practice opportunities are then provided for the trainees.
4. *Mindfulness training*, which involves teaching trainees to heighten their nonjudgmental awareness of the present moment, often through the use of basic meditational skills. This helps them to be more at ease and less critical.
5. *Video stimulus training*, in which trainees view their own or others' attempts at empathy, or they make attempts to infer the thoughts and feelings of others, which is followed by discussion and feedback.
6. *Writing training*, in which trainees attempt to write from another person's point of view as a strategy for enhancing empathy. (pp. 172–175)

Generally speaking, the results of meta-analytic studies on empathy training—single studies looking at overall findings of many studies on a particular subject—show that empathy is indeed trainable (Lam, Kolomitro, & Alamparambil, 2011; Butters, 2010). However, most studies show that those who have undergone empathy training show gains in cognitive empathy only, as many studies haven't attempted to measure affective empathy (Butters, 2010, p. 123). Unfortunately, no one is sure how long the gains derived from empathy training last (Butters, 2010, p. 124). Some researchers acknowledge, for example, that it will be meaningful to observe the degree to which the various branches of the US military—beset with high incidences of male-on-female and male-on-male sexual assaults—sees declines in reports of such violence resulting from broad-reaching and regularly repeated empathy trainings (Ellison, 2011; Ruiz, 2013).

So What? Why Diminishing Our Tendencies to Objectify Others Matters

On April 4, 2008, then Senator Barack Obama, speaking on the fortieth anniversary of the assassination of Dr. Martin Luther King, Jr., declared (Obama, 2008):

> Dr. King once said that the arc of the moral universe is long but it bends towards justice. It bends towards justice, but here is the thing: it does not bend on its own. It bends because each of us in our own ways put our hand on that arc and we bend it in the direction of justice. . . .

The words of both men ring true. If justice is to be realized, it is not because it materializes on its own, for justice is an abstract human ideal—a wish—which can only find realization through a condition of heightened awareness, not only of our own desires for full, abundant life, but of others' legitimate desires for the same. If we are to realize greater justice in the world, we must start by coming to see others more as we see ourselves. In other words, we must diminish our tendencies to objectify, which is in our best interest for a variety of reasons.

First, diminishing our tendency toward objectification will help us to become more moral, happy creatures. Each of us has had revealed to us, in fleeting, rare moments, the reality that we are more than mere isolates scratching on the surface of this planet. The splendor of nature, the rapturous embrace of our beloved, or the all-embracing grief at the death of a loved one disclose to us the great truth of our connectedness with the rest of existence. In moments such as these, we are most authentically ourselves, most fully alive. We feel ourselves at one with others and the world. From this place, we are most free to act, because our actions proceed from a position of clarity. Such remarkable states of awareness don't last long, but they provide us with glimpses of what is possible. When we quiet our minds and center ourselves in the present moment, we are better able to attend to that which is finest in ourselves—subtle impressions of our connectedness with humanity, our acceptance of our lives, and our desires to act in benevolent, nurturing ways toward others. When we transcend—even for brief moments—some of our limiting boundaries and come to see other people, other sentient forms of life, even the very planet itself more as we see ourselves, we have a greater capacity to bring what Itzhak Stern in *Schindler's List* (Spielberg, 1993) called "absolute good" into the world. Transcending limiting boundaries between ourselves and others allows us not only to be truly moral, but it expands our capacity for happiness, because happiness is an unintended byproduct of loving and being loved. Victor Frankl (1984) put it this way:

> Don't aim at success—the more you aim at it and make it a target, the more you are going to miss it. For success, like happiness, cannot be pursued; it must

ensue, and it only does so as the unintended side-effect of one's personal dedication to a cause greater than oneself or as the by-product of one's surrender to
a person other than oneself. Happiness must happen, and the same holds for
success: you have to let it happen by not caring about it. I want you to listen to
what your conscience commands you to do and go on to carry it out to the best
of your knowledge. Then you will live to see that in the long run—in the long
run, I say—success will follow you precisely because you had forgotten to think
of it. (pp. 12–13).

Second, reducing our tendencies to objectify others—striving to view
them as "Thous" rather than as "its"—will bring more peace and prosperity to the planet, and this has obvious benefits. Citizens of nations such as
Brazil, China, and India have seen a dramatic rise in their standards of living over the past few decades. While the reasons for this economic shift are
multifaceted and complex, one reason is the rise of gentle commerce (Pinker,
2011a). Human beings (speaking collectively and not individually) have realized that plunder and exploitation are "zero-sum games" in which one party's gain or loss is balanced by the losses or gains of another party. On the
other hand, when the two parties engage in trade with one another, everyone involved wins: "Others become more valuable alive than dead" (Pinker,
2011a). Granted, simply engaging in trade with other parties does not necessarily equate to viewing them as a "Thou" (for example, consider the relationship between the US and China), but it's a start. Thomas Friedman's (1999)
"Golden Arches theory of conflict prevention"—that no two nations with
McDonald's franchises within their borders have ever gone to war with each
other—has recently been disproved (e.g., Israel vs. Lebanon, 2006; Georgia
vs. Russia, 2008, etc.), but he now endorses "the Dell theory"—". . . that no
two countries that share stakes in a global market like Dell computers, will
ever fight a war against each other, as long as they are both part of the same
global supply chain" (2005, p. 421). It is probable that this theory will also
eventually fail, but the general idea has validity. Regardless of the reason,
when others matter to us—even for self-interested reasons—we are more
likely to engage in civil relations with them. Decades of research on the nature
of prejudice show that engaging in direct, positive interaction with different
others is one of the very best ways to diminish prejudicial attitudes about
them (Allport, 1954; Rothbart & John, 1985; Forsyth, 2009). Some recent
research shows that even just imagining direct, positive contact with culturally different others helps to diminish prejudicial attitudes against them
(Crisp & Turner, 2009). Ridding ourselves of prejudicial attitudes toward our
perceived adversaries will also help us avoid the downward spiral of retribu-
tory violence that has locked many cultures in seemingly perpetual conflict
(e.g., Israel and Palestine, India and Pakistan, Iran and Iraq, Sunni and Shia
Muslims).

Third, diminishing our limiting boundaries of self will also help us feel more oneness with the physical world, encouraging us to be better stewards of the planet. Decades ago, the great fear was that human beings, in their short-sightedness and fear, would destroy the planet in an atomic conflagration. While nuclear holocaust continues to remain a potential threat, it seems to have taken a back seat to concerns of global environmental fallout from more and more human beings adopting a "first-world" lifestyle. The earth is "closed system:" there is no "out" (unless we jettison our waste products into deep space); all the nonrenewable waste we produce stays right here with us in one form or another. There is only so much in terms of natural resources, such as farmable land and oxygen-producing rain forest, for us to draw from. More and more experts are becoming concerned that we are nearing a sort of "tipping point" with respect to population growth (especially in the developing world, which is becoming increasingly energy-hungry), food and fresh water supplies, the availability of fossil fuels, and climate change. If we are to secure the world for future generations, it will likely be because we have come to view the planet much as we view ourselves—incredibly rare, precious, limited, and worthy of gentle treatment and preventive care as time passes.

Finally, diminishing our tendencies toward objectifying others is necessary in order for us to continue to evolve, improve, and grow as a species. To paraphrase Abraham Maslow (1971, p. 35), one of the last century's most luminous minds, all of us have an impulse to better ourselves—an impulse toward bringing to fruition more of our potential for humanness, an inclination toward realizing our fully evolved, integrated, authentic self. This requires us to resolve dichotomies and transcend limiting boundaries, moving us toward higher, more inclusive unity. This is also an impulse to be the very best we are capable of becoming. If we content ourselves with being much less than we are capable of being, then we are likely to be unhappy. Settling for the status quo of a life lived in the depths of Plato's cave where we sit, fettered to the cave floor, encumbered with limiting boundaries, will not save us as a species.

The great contemplatives of every age have transcended the problem of objectification. They have shown us the various paths out of the cave of limited consciousness. Their lives suggest that we need not continue to repeat the greatest mistakes of the past, all of which result from our mistaking the shadows on the cave wall for the genuine article. While human beings continue to engage in brutality, depravity, and atrocities of all kinds on a scale that boggles the mind, we are also seeing some of the results of a slow but inexorable movement out of the cave. The circle of our concern has expanded to a point where we are now giving more thought than ever before to not just how we may live more peaceably and equitably with one another, but to how we should treat other forms of life, and even the very earth itself. While many of us may resist such questions or insist that the answers to these problems lie in returning to the past, others know that this goes against the general thrust of evolution, which is to transcend and include, rather than reverse and leave behind (Wilber, 1996). We may yet be far from coming to a consensus on such matters, but the fact that ever-increasing numbers of us are even asking these questions is indeed a good sign.

APPENDIX

The Narcissistic Personality Inventory (as used by D. Pinsky and S. Mark Young (see http://www.usatoday.com/news/health/2009-03-16-pinsky-quiz_ N.htm)

Instructions: Here you'll find a list of 40 statements, one in Row A and another in Row B. For each statement, choose the item from Row A or B that **best matches you,** even if it's not a perfect fit. Complete the quiz on your own and in one sitting. This takes most people between 5 and 10 minutes to finish.

1. A. I have a natural talent for influencing people.
   B. I am not good at influencing people.
2. A. Modesty doesn't become me.
   B. I am essentially a modest person.
3. A. I would do almost anything on a dare.
   B. I tend to be a fairly cautious person.
4. A. When people compliment me I sometimes get embarrassed.
   B. I know that I am good because everybody keeps telling me so.
5. A. The thought of ruling the world frightens the hell out of me.
   B. If I ruled the world it would be a better place.
6. A. I can usually talk my way out of anything.
   B. I try to accept the consequences of my behavior.
7. A. I prefer to blend in with the crowd.
   B. I like to be the center of attention.
8. A. I will be a success.
   B. I am not too concerned about success.
9. A. I am no better or worse than most people.
   B. I think I am a special person.
10. A. I am not sure if I would make a good leader.
    B. I see myself as a good leader.
11. A. I am assertive.
    B. I wish I were more assertive.

12. A. I like to have authority over other people.
    B. I don't mind following orders.
13. A. I find it easy to manipulate people.
    B. I don't like it when I find myself manipulating people.
14. A. I insist upon getting the respect that is due me.
    B. I usually get the respect that I deserve.
15. A. I don't particularly like to show off my body.
    B. I like to show off my body.
16. A. I can read people like a book.
    B. People are sometimes hard to understand.
17. A. If I feel competent I am willing to take responsibility for making decisions.
    B. I like to take responsibility for making decisions.
18. A. I just want to be reasonably happy.
    B. I want to amount to something in the eyes of the world.
19. A. My body is nothing special.
    B. I like to look at my body.
20. A. I try not to be a show off.
    B. I will usually show off if I get the chance.
21. A. I always know what I am doing.
    B. Sometimes I am not sure of what I am doing.
22. A. I sometimes depend on people to get things done.
    B. I rarely depend on anyone else to get things done.
23. A. Sometimes I tell good stories.
    B. Everybody likes to hear my stories.
24. A. I expect a great deal from other people.
    B. I like to do things for other people.
25. A. I will never be satisfied until I get all that I deserve.
    B. I take my satisfactions as they come.
26. A. Compliments embarrass me.
    B. I like to be complimented.
27. A. I have a strong will to power.
    B. Power for its own sake doesn't interest me.
28. A. I don't care about new fads and fashions.
    B. I like to start new fads and fashions.
29. A. I like to look at myself in the mirror.
    B. I am not particularly interested in looking at myself in the mirror.
30. A. I really like to be the center of attention.
    B. It makes me uncomfortable to be the center of attention.
31. A. I can live my life in any way I want to.
    B. People can't always live their lives in terms of what they want.
32. A. Being an authority doesn't mean that much to me.
    B. People always seem to recognize my authority.

33. A. I would prefer to be a leader.
    B. It makes little difference to me whether I am a leader or not.
34. A. I am going to be a great person.
    B. I hope I am going to be successful.
35. A. People sometimes believe what I tell them.
    B. I can make anybody believe anything I want them to.
36. A. I am a born leader.
    B. Leadership is a quality that takes a long time to develop.
37. A. I wish somebody would someday write my biography.
    B. I don't like people to pry into my life for any reason.
38. A. I get upset when people don't notice how I look when I go out in public.
    B. I don't mind blending into the crowd when I go out in public.
39. A. I am more capable than other people.
    B. There is a lot that I can learn from other people.
40. A. I am much like everybody else.
    B. I am an extraordinary person.

SCORING KEY

Assign one point for each response that matches the key.

1, 2 and 3: A
4, 5: B
6: A
7: B
8: A
9, 10: B
11, 12, 13, 14: A
15: B
16: A
17, 18, 19, 20: B
21: A
22, 23: B
24, 25: A
26: B
27: A
28: B
29, 30, 31: A
32: B
33, 34: A
35. B

36, 37, 38, 39: A
40: B

The average score for the general population is 15.3. The average score for celebrities is 17.8. Dr. Pinsky scored a 16.

Young says it is important to consider which traits are dominant. For example, an overall score that reflects more points on vanity, entitlement, exhibitionism, and exploitativeness is more cause for concern than someone who scores high on authority, self-sufficiency, and superiority, he says.

THE SEVEN COMPONENT TRAITS BY QUESTION

- Authority: 1, 8, 10, 11, 12, 32, 33, 36
- Self-sufficiency: 17, 21, 22, 31, 34, 39
- Superiority: 4, 9, 26, 37, 40
- Exhibitionism: 2, 3, 7, 20, 28, 30, 38
- Exploitativeness: 6, 13, 16, 23, 35
- Vanity: 15, 19, 29
- Entitlement: 5, 14, 18, 24, 25, 27

REFERENCES

INTRODUCTION

Buber, M. (1970). *I and Thou*. New York: Charles Scribner's Sons.

Cahn, S. M. (1995). The Republic. In S. M. Cahn (Ed.), *Classics of Western Philosophy*, 4th ed., 112–232. Indianapolis, Cambridge: Hackett Publishing.

Fowler, J. (1981). *Stages of Faith: The Psychology of Human Development and the Quest for Meaning*. San Francisco: Harper Collins.

Huxley, A. (1970) [1945]. *The Perennial Philosophy*, Perennial Library. New York: Harper & Row.

James, W. (1906). The Moral Equivalent of War. Retrieved from http://www.constitution.org/wj/meow.htm.

Jung, C. G. (1975). Psychology and religion. In S. R. Read & G. Adler (Eds.), & R. F. C. Hull (Trans.), *Psychology and Religion: West and East (The Collected Works of C. G. Jung, Vol. 11)*. Princeton, NJ: Princeton University Press, 131.

Smith, H. (1991). *The World Religions*. San Francisco: Harper Collins.

CHAPTER 1

Bandura, A. (2003). The role of selective moral disengagement in terrorism and counterterrorism. In F. M. Moghaddam and A. J. Marsella (Eds.), *Understanding Terrorism: Psychological Roots, Consequences, and Interventions*. Washington, DC: American Psychological Association, 121–150.

Cahill, A. J. (2011). *Overcoming Objectification: A Carnal Ethics*. New York: Routledge.

Chirot, D., & McCauley, C. (2006). *Why Not Kill Them All? The Logic and Prevention of Mass Political Murder*. Princeton, NJ: Princeton University Press.

Dupuy, R. E., & Dupuy, T. N. (1994). *The Collins Encyclopedia of Military History*, Glasgow: Collins, 1308.

Glover, J. (2001). *Humanity: A Moral History of the Twentieth Century*. New Haven, CT: Yale; Nota Bene.

Goldhagen, D. (2009). *Worse Than War: Genocide, Eliminationism, and the On-Going Assault on Humanity*. New York: Public Affairs.

Hasegawa, T. (2006). *Racing the Enemy: Stalin, Truman, and the Surrender of Japan*. Cambridge, MA: The Belknap Press of Harvard University Press.

Kelman, H. C. (1973). Violence without moral restraint: Reflections on the dehumanization of victims and victimizers. *Journal of Social Issues, 29* (4), 25–61.

Kressel, N. J. (2002). *Mass Hate: The Global Rise of Genocide and Terror*. Cambridge, MA: Worldview Press.

Lifton, R. J. (2011). *Witness to an Extreme Century: A Memoir*. New York: Free Press.

Neiman, S. (2004). *Evil in Modern Thought*. Princeton, NJ: Princeton University Press, 10.

Smith, D. L. (2011). *Less Than Human: Why We Demean, Enslave, and Exterminate Others*. New York: St. Martin's Press.

Stanton, G. H. (1998). The eight stages of genocide and preventing genocide. Paper presented to U.S. State Department, 1996. Retrieved from http://www.genocide-watch.org/aboutgenocide/8stagesofgenocide.html.

Wilson, W. (2007). The winning weapon? Rethinking nuclear weapons in light of Hiroshima. *International Security*, 31 (4), Spring, 162–179.

Zimbardo, P. G. (2008). *The Lucifer Effect: How Good People Turn Evil*. New York: Random House.

CHAPTER 2

Bartky, S. L. (1990). *Femininity and Domination: Studies in the Phenomenology of Oppression*. New York: Routledge.

Buber, M. (1970). *I and Thou*. New York: Charles Scribner's Sons.

Calogero, R. M. (2004). A test of objectification theory: Effect of the male gaze on appearance concerns in college women. *Psychology of Women Quarterly*, 28, 16–21.

Calogero, R. M., Tantleff-Dunn, S., & Thompson, J. K. (2011). *Self-Objectification in Women: Causes, Consequences, and Counteractions*. Washington, DC: American Psychological Association.

Csikszentmihalyi, M. (2008). *Flow: The Psychology of Optimal Experience*. New York: Harper Perennial Modern Classics.

Dworkin, A. (2000) [1985]. Against the male flood: Censorship, pornography, and equality. In Drucilla Cornell (Ed.), *Oxford Readings in Feminism: Feminism and Pornography*. Oxford: Oxford University Press, 19–44.

Fredrickson, B. L., & Roberts, T. A. (1997). Objectification theory: Toward understanding women's lived experiences and mental health risks. *Psychology of Women Quarterly*, 21 (2), 173–206.

Fredrickson, B. L., Roberts, T. A., Noll, S. M., Quinn, D. M., & Twenge, J. M. (1998). That swimsuit becomes you: Sex differences in self-objectification, restrained eating, and math performance. *Journal of Personality and Social Psychology*, 75, 269–284.

Jeffreys, S. (2005). *Beauty and Misogyny: Harmful Cultural Practices in the West*. New York: Routledge.

Kant, I. (1993) [1785]. *Grounding for the Metaphysics of Morals*, 3rd ed. (J. W. Ellington, Trans.). Indianapolis: Hackett, 30.

Kant, I. (1998) [1785]. *Groundwork of the Metaphysics of Morals*. Cambridge Texts in the History of Philosophy, Mary Gregor (Ed.), Cambridge: Cambridge University Press, 42.

Langton, R. (2009). *Sexual Solipsism: Philosophical Essays on Pornography and Objectification*. Oxford: Oxford University Press.

LeMoncheck, L. (1985). *Dehumanizing Women: Treating Persons as Sex Objects*. Lanham, MD: Rowman and Littlefield.

Moradi, B., & Huang, Y. P. (2008). Objectification theory and the psychology of women: A decade of advances and future directions. *Psychology or Women Quarterly*, *32*, 377–398.

Nussbaum, M. C. (1995). Objectification. *Philosophy and Public Affairs*, *24* (4) (Autumn), 249–291.

Nussbaum, M. C. (2000). *Sex and Social Justice*. Oxford: Oxford University Press.

Roberts, T., & Gettman, J. Y. (2004). Mere exposure: Gender differences in the negative effects of priming a state of self-objectification. *Sex Roles*, *51*, 17–27.

Schumacher, E. F. (1977). *A Guide for the Perplexed*. New York: Harper & Row.

Tiggemann, M., & Lynch, J. E. (2001). Body image across the life span in adult women: The role of self-objectification. *Developmental Psychology*, *37*, 243–253.

Tiggemann, M., & Kuring, J. K. (2004). The role of body objectification in disordered eating and depressed mood. *British Journal of Clinical Psychology*, *43*, 299–311.

Tiggemann, M., & Williams, E. (2012). The role of self-objectification in disordered eating, depressed mood, and sexual functioning among women: A comprehensive test of objectification theory. *Psychology of Women Quarterly*, *36*, 66–75.

Zubringen, E. L., & Roberts, T. A. (2012). *The Sexualization of Girls and Girlhood*. Oxford: Oxford University Press.

CHAPTER 3

Bandura, A. (1986). *Social Foundations of Thought and Action: A Social Cognitive Theory*. Englewood Cliffs, NJ: Prentice-Hall.

Bandura, A. (1990). Mechanisms of Moral Disengagement. In Reich, W. (Ed.). *Origins of Terrorism: Psychologies, Ideologies, Theologies, & States of Mind*. Cambridge: Cambridge University Press, 161–191.

Bandura, A. (2003). The role of selective moral disengagement in terrorism and counterterrorism. In Moghaddam, F. M., & Marsella, A. J. (Eds.). *Understanding Terrorism: Psychological Roots, Consequences, and Interventions*. Washington, DC: American Psychological Association, 121–150.

Bartky, S. (1990). *Femininity and Domination: Studies in the Phenomenology of Oppression*. New York: Routledge.

Benesch, S. (2004). Inciting genocide, pleading free speech. *World Policy Journal*, *21* (2), Summer. Retrieved from http://ics.leeds.ac.uk/papers/vp01.cfm?outfit=pmt&folder=193&paper=2022.

Borg, M. J. (2004) *The Heart of Christianity: Rediscovering a Life of Faith*. San Francisco: Harper.

Cahill, A. J. (2011). *Overcoming Objectification: A Carnal Ethics*. New York: Routledge.

Chang, I. (1997). *The Rape of Nanking: The Forgotten Holocuast of World War II*. London: Penguin Books.

Chirot, D., & McCauley, C. (2006). *Why Not Kill Them All? The Logic and Prevention of Mass Political Murder*. Princeton, NJ: Princeton University Press.

Goldberg, S. (2005, Jan. 26). Barber to the SS, Witness to the Holocaust. (Accessed May 24, 2011). Retrieved from http://articles.cnn.com/2005-01-26/world/auschwitz.barber_1_prisoners-ss-officers-auschwitz?_s=PM:WORLD.

Goldhagen, D. (2009). *Worse Than War: Genocide, Eliminationism, and the On-Going Assault on Humanity*. New York: Public Affairs.

Glover, J. (2001). *Humanity: A Moral History of the Twentieth Century*. New Haven, CT: Yale; Nota Bene.

Hedges, C. (2009). *Empire of Illusion: The End of Literacy and the Triumph of Spectacle*. New York: Nation Books.

Higham, S., & Stephens, J. (2004, May 21). New Details of Prison Abuse Emerge, *Washington Post*. Retrieved from http://www.washingtonpost.com/wp-dyn/articles/A43783-2004May20.html.

His Holiness the Dalai Lama (2009). *Becoming Enlightened*. New York: Atria Paperbacks.

Keen, S. (1986). *Faces of the Enemy: Reflections on the Hostile Imagination*. New York: HarperCollins.

Kelman, H. C. (1973). Violence without moral restraint: Reflections on the dehumanization of victims and victimizers. *Journal of Social Issues, 29* (4), 25–61.

Kressel, N. J. (2002). *Mass Hate: The Global Rise of Genocide and Terror*. Cambridge, MA: Worldview Press.

Lang, J. (2010). Questioning dehumanization: Intersubjective dimensions of violence in the Nazi concentration and death camps. *Holocaust and Genocide Studies. 24* (2), 225–246.

Lifton, R. J., & Humphrey, N. (1984). *In a Dark Time*. Cambridge, MA: Harvard University Press.

McEwan, I. (2011). Only love, and then oblivion. Love was all they had to set against their murderers. *The Guardian*, Sept. 15.

Morris, E. (Director). (2003). *The Fog of War: Eleven Lessons from the Life of Robert S. McNamara* [Film]. Available from Sony Picture Classics.

Muller, F. (1999). *Eyewitness Auschwitz: Three Years in the Gas Chambers*. New York: Ivan R. Dee.

Nussbaum, M. C. (1995). Objectification. *Philosophy and Public Affairs, 24* (4) (Autumn), 249–291.

Paulsky, S. (1996). *Rudolf Höss, Death dealer: Memoirs of the SS Kommandant at Auschwitz*. New York: Da Capo Press.

Quammen, D. (2003). *Monster of God: The Man-Eating Predator in the Jungles of History and in the Mind*. New York: W. W. Norton.

Scarry, E. (1998). The difficulty of imagining other persons. In E. Weiner (Ed.), *The Handbook of Interethnic Coexistence*. New York: Continuum Publishing, 40–62.

Sereny, G. (1974). *Into That Darkness: An Examination of Conscience*. New York: Vintage.

Singer, P. (1994). *Practical Ethics*, 2nd Ed. Princeton, NJ: Princeton University Press.

Smith, D. L. (2011). *Less Than Human: Why We Demean, Enslave, and Exterminate Others*. New York: St. Martin's Press.

Sofsky, W. (1997). *The Order of Terror: The Concentration Camp*. Princeton, NJ: Princeton University Press.

Stanton, G. H. (1998). The Eight Stages of Genocide and Preventing Genocide. Paper presented to US State Department, 1996. Retrieved from http://www.genocide-watch.org/aboutgenocide/8stagesofgenocide.html.

The Complete Text of the Poznan Speech (2004). Retrieved August 21, 2011, from http://www.holocaust-history.org/himmler-poznan/speech-text.shtml.

Todorov, T. (1999). *The Conquest of America: The Question of the Other*. Norman, OK: University of Oklahoma Press.

United Nations General Assembly (October 17, 2011). 1.5 Billion People Living in Absolute Poverty Makes Its Eradication Humankind's Most Significant Challenge, Second Committee Told. Retrieved August 2, 2013, from: http://www.un.org/News/Press/docs/2011/gaef3313.doc.htm.

Westra, H., Metsallar, M., van der Wal, R., & Stam, D. (2004). *Inside Anne Frank's House: An Illustrated Journey Through Anne's World*. New York: Overlook Duckworth.

Zernike, K. (2005, January 12). Detainees depict abuses by guard in prison in Iraq. *New York Times*. Retrieved from http://www.nytimes.com/2005/01/12/international/12abuse.html?_r=1.

Zimbardo, P. G. (2008). *The Lucifer Effect: How Good People Turn Evil*. New York: Random House.

CHAPTER 4

Bassiouni, M. C. (1997). Searching for peace and achieving justice: The need for accountability. *Law and Contemporary Problems. 9* (4), 9–28.

Brzezinski, Z. (1995). *Out of Control: Global Turmoil on the Eve of the 21st Century*. New York: Touchstone Books.

Buber, M. (1970). *I and Thou*. New York: Charles Scribner's Sons.

Dawkins, R. (2008). *The God Delusion*. Boston, MA: Mariner Books.

Dawkins, R. (2010). *The Greatest Show on Earth: The Evidence for Evolution*. New York: Free Press.

Dawkins, R. (2011). *The Magic of Reality: How We Know What's Really True*. New York: Free Press.

Dennett, D. (2004). *Freedom Evolves*. London: Penguin Books.

Dennett, D. (2007). *Breaking the Spell: Religion as a Natural Phenomenon*. London: Penguin Books.

Harris, S. (2005). *The End of Faith: Religion, Terror, and the Future of Reason*. New York: W. W. Norton.

Harris, S. (2011). *The Moral Landscape: How Science Can Determine Human Values*. New York: Free Press.

His Holiness the Dalai Lama (2009). *Becoming Enlightened*. New York: Atria Paperbacks.

Hitchens, C. (2008). *The Portable Atheist: Essential Readings for the Non-Believer*. Philadelphia: De Capo Press.

Huxley, A. (1970) [1945]. *The Perennial Philosophy*, Perennial Library. New York: Harper & Row.

Needleman, J. (2007a). *Why Can't We Be Good?* New York: Penguin Group.

Rogers, M. (2011). Death row inmate who stabbed prisoner 67 times says he had inadequate counsel. *Salt Lake Tribune*, June 6. Retrieved from http://www.sltrib.com/sltrib/news/51940093-78/kell-blackmon-prison-utah.html.csp.

Taylor, S. (2005). *The Fall: The Insanity of the Ego in Human History and the Dawning of a New Era*. Winchester, UK; New York: O Books.

Thich Nhat Hanh (1998). *The Heart of the Buddha's Teaching: Transforming Suffering into Peace, Joy, and Liberation*. New York: Broadway Books.

Tillich, P. (1964). *Theology of Culture*. Oxford: Oxford University Press.

Whitehead, A. N. (1979). *Process and Reality*. New York: Free Press.

CHAPTER 5

Blake, W. (1988). *The Complete Poetry and Prose of William Blake*. D. V. Erdman (Ed.). Anchor Books, New York, NY. 53.

Bucke, E. M. (1901). *Cosmic Consciousness: A Study in the Evolution of the Human Mind*. London: Penguin Books.

Dennett, D. (2009, June 27). What's a Deepity? Retrieved July 3, 2013 from http://www.youtube.com/watch?v=DKPhy03zNsU.

Eliot, G. (1994) [1871]. *Middlemarch*. Penguin Books, London, England.

Eves, H. W. (1977). *Mathematical Circles Adieu and Return to Mathematical Circles (Mathematical Circles, Vol. 3)*. Washington, DC: Mathematical Association of America.

James, W. (1958) [1902]. *The Varieties of Religious Experience*. New York: Mentor Books; New American Library.

Krulwich, R. (2010, November 11). My grandson, the rock. National Public Radio. Retrieved from http://www.npr.org/blogs/krulwich/2010/09/14/129858314/my-grandson-the-rock.

Maslow, A. (1970). *Religions, Values and Peak Experiences*. London: Penguin Books.

Otto, R. (1958). *The Idea of the Holy*. London: Oxford University Press.

Schwartz, T. (1995) *What Really Matters: Searching for Wisdom in America*. New York: Bantam Press.

Traherne, T. (1992) *Selected Poetry and Prose*. London: Penguin Books.

Wilber, K. (2001). *No Boundary: Eastern and Western Approaches to Personal Growth*. Boulder, CO: Shambhala.

Wilber, K. (2001a). *A Brief History of Everything*. Boulder, CO: Shambhala.

CHAPTER 6

CNN (2011, April 12). CNN: Hebah Ahmed, MuslimMatters Blogger, Debates Mona Eltahawy over French Niqab (Burka) Ban. Retrieved August 7, 2013 from http://muslimmatters.org/2011/04/12/cnn-hebah-ahmed-muslimmatters-blogger-debates- mona-eltahawy-over-french-niqab-burka-ban/.

Campbell, J. (1991). *Power of Myth*. New York: Anchor Books.

Erlanger, S. (2010, July 13). Parliament moves France closer to a ban on facial veils. *New York Times*. Retrieved August 7, 2013 from http://www.nytimes.com/2010/07/14/world/europe/14burqa.html.

Frost, R. (2012) [1915]. *Mountain Interval*. London: Forgotten Books.

Gerrig, R. J., & Zimbardo, P. G. (1989) Ways we can go wrong. [Table]. *Psychology and Life*, 12th ed. Glenview IL: Allyn & Bacon, 689.

Goddard, D. (1994). *A Buddhist Bible*. Boston: Beacon Press.

Hayes, S., Wilson, K. G., Gifford, E. V., & Follette, V. M. (1996) Experiential avoidance and behavioral disorders: A functional dimensional approach to diagnosis and treatment. *Journal of Consulting and Clinical Psychology, 64*, 1152–1168.

Hayes, S. C., & Smith, S. (2005) *Get Out of Your Mind and Into Your Life: The New Acceptance and Commitment Therapy*. Oakland, CA: New Harbinger Publications.

Hedges, C. (2009). *Empire of Illusion: The End of Literacy and the Triumph of Spectacle*. New York: Nation Books.

Huxley, A. (1970) [1945]. *The Perennial Philosophy*, Perennial Library. New York: Harper & Row.

Jones, J. M. (2007). Among religious groups, Jewish Americans most strongly oppose war. *Gallup News Service*, Feb. 23. Retrieved from http://www.gallup.com/poll/26677/among-religious-groups-jewish-americans-most-strongly-oppose-war.aspx.

Luoma, J. B., Hayes, S., & Walser R. D. (2007). *Learning ACT: An Acceptance and Commitment Therapy Skills Manual for Therapists*. Oakland, CA: New Harbinger Publications.

Maslow, A. (1970). *Religions, Values and Peak Experiences*. London: Penguin Books.

Namasivayam, D. (2011, April 11). For life, liberty, and the burqa: Muslim women defy France's ban on full-face veils. *Herald Sun*. Retrieved August 7, 2013 from http://www.sott.net/article/227091-For-life-liberty-and-the-burqa-Muslim-women-defy- Frances-ban-on-full-face-veils.

Newcomb, A. N. (2011, April 10). France to become first European country to ban burqa. *ABC News*. Retrieved August 7, 2013 from http://abcnews.go.com/International/burqa-ban-effect- france/story?id=13344555.

Smith, D. L. (2007). *The Most Dangerous Animal: Human Nature and the Origins of War*. New York: St. Martin's Griffin.

Thich Nhat Hanh, (2007). *Buddha Mind, Buddha Body: Walking Toward Enlightenment*. Berkeley, CA: Paralax Press.

Trouble in Trappes (2013, July 27). Violence erupts over the controversial burqa ban. *The Economist*. Retrieved August 7, 2013 from http://www.economist.com/news/europe/21582314-violence- erupts-over-controversial-burqa-ban-trouble-trappes.

Wilber, K. (1996). *A Brief History of Everything*. Boulder, CO: Shambhala Press.

Wilber, K. (1998). *The Marriage of Sense and Soul*. New York: Broadway Books.

Wilber, K. (2001). *No Boundary: Eastern and Western Approaches to Personal Growth*. Boulder, CO: Shambhala Press.

CHAPTER 7

Brach, T. (2003). *Radical Acceptance: Embracing Your Life with the Heart of a Buddha*. New York: Bantam Books.

Buber, M. (1913). *Daniel: Dialogues on Realization*. New York: Holt, Rinehart, and Winston.

Butler, A. C., Chapman, J. E., Forman, E. M., & Beck, A. T. (2006). The empirical status of cognitive-behavioral therapy: A review of meta-analyses. *Clinical Psychology Review*, 26, 17–31.

Fowler, J. (1981). *Stages of Faith: The Psychology of Human Development and the Quest for Meaning*. San Francisco: Harper Collins.

Huxley, A. (1970) [1945]. *The Perennial Philosophy*, Perennial Library. New York: Harper & Row.

Jung, C. G. (1960) *Synchronicity: An A causal Connecting Principle*. Bollingen Press.

Katz, S. T. (1978). *Mysticism and Philosophical Analysis*. Oxford: Oxford University Press.

Keck, L. R. (2000) *Sacred Quest: The Evolution and Future of the Human Soul*. West Chester, PA: Chrysalis Books.

Pinker, S. (2011). *The Better Angels of Our Nature: Why Violence Has Declined*. New York: Viking Adult.

Rogers, C. (1961). *On Becoming a Person: A Therapist's View of Psychotherapy*. Boston: Houghton Mifflin.

Schuler, N. (1985). Trying to change as denial. *California Association for Counseling and Development Journal*, 6, 49–51.

Sting (1991). All this time. *The Soul Cages* [CD]. New York: A&M Records.

Taylor, S. (2005). *The Fall: The Insanity of the Ego in Human History and the Dawning of a New Era*. Winchester, UK; New York: O Books.

Thich Nhat Hanh, (1991) *Peace Is Every Step*. New York: Bantam.

Tolle, E. (2004). *Power of Now*. Novato, CA: New World Library.

Tolle, E. (2008). *A New Earth: Awakening to Your Life's Purpose*. New York: Plume Books.

Wilber, K. (2001). *No Boundary: Eastern and Western Approaches to Personal Growth*. Boulder, CO: Shambhala.

CHAPTER 8

American Psychiatric Association (2013). *Desk Reference to the Diagnostic Criteria from DSM-5*. Washington, DC: Author.

American Psychological Association (2009). *Publication Manual of the American Psychological Association*, 5th ed. Washington, DC: Author.

Becker, E. (1974). *The Denial of Death*. New York: The Free Press.

Carroll, L. (1987). A study of narcissism, affiliation, intimacy, and power motives among students in business administration. *Psychological Reports*, *61*, 355–358.

Lively, W. J., Jang, K. L., Jackson, D. N., & Vernon, P.A (1993). Genetic and environmental contributions to dimensions of personality disorder. *American Journal of Psychiatry*, *150*, 1826–1831.

Mays, D. (Presenter) (2010). Personality disorders: Powerful techniques to overcome the frustrations and improve client outcomes [Tele-conference]. Eau Claire, WI: Pesi Productions.

Raskin, R., & Howard, T. (1988). A principle-components analysis of the Narcissistic Personality Inventory and further evidence of its construct validity. *Journal of Personality and Social Psychology*. *54* (5), 890–902.

Stinson F. S., Dawson, D. A., Goldstein. R. B., Chou, S. P., Huang, B., Smith, S. M., Ruan, W. J., Pulay, A.J., Saha, T. D., Pickering, R. P., & Grant, B. F. (2008). Prevalence, correlates, disability, and comorbidity of DSM-IV narcissistic personality disorder: Results from the wave 2 national epidemiologic survey on alcohol and related conditions. *Journal of Clinical Psychiatry*, *69* (7). 1033–1045.

CHAPTER 9

Adler, M. (2006). Behind the ever-expanding American dream house. National Public Radio. Retrieved from http://www.npr.org/templates/story/story.php?storyId=5525283.

Albert, P. J. (2009). The Integral Leadership of Saints Francis and Clare of Assisi: A Historical/Interpretive Biography Study. Unpublished doctoral dissertation, Fielding Graduate University, Santa Barbara, CA.

America's Homes Get Bigger and Better. (2005). Retrieved from http://abcnews.go.com/GMA/Moms/story?id=1445039.

Are Lottery Winners Really Less Happy? (2004). *Associated Press*. Retrieved from http://www.msnbc.msn.com/id/4971361/ns/health-health_care.

Are We Happy Yet? (2006). Pew Research Center. Retrieved from http://pewresearch.org/pubs/301/are-we-happy-yet.

Bhagavad-Gita (2002). *Signet Classics*. New York: New American Library.

Brickman, P., Coates, D., & Janoff-Bulman, R. (1978). Lottery winners and accident victims: Is happiness relative? *Journal of Personality and Social Psychology*, 36, 917–927.

Brown, J. (1970). Super bad. On *Super Bad* [LP]. King Records.

Frankl, V. (1984). *Man's Search for Meaning*. Boston: Beacon Press.

His Holiness the Dalai Lama (1986). *The Fullness of Emptiness*. In *Leaning on the Moment: Interviews from Parabola*. New York: Parabola Books, 231–249.

His Holiness the Dalai Lama (2009). *Becoming Enlightened*. New York: Atria Books.

Huxley, A. (1970) [1945]. *The Perennial Philosophy*, Perennial Library. New York: Harper & Row.

Needleman, J. (2007). *Why Can't We Be Good?* New York: Penguin Group.

Needleman, J. (2007a). Why Can't We Be Good? [Video file]. Retrieved from http://fora.tv/2007/04/24/Why_Can_t_We_Be_Good

Smith, H. (1991). *The World Religions*. San Francisco: Harper Collins.

Sting (1985). If you love someone, set them free. *Dream of the Blue Turtles* [CD]. New York: A&M Records.

Thich Nhat Hanh. (1998). *The Heart of the Buddha's Teaching: Transforming Suffering into Peace, Joy, and Liberation*. New York: Broadway Books.

Tolle, E. (2003). *Stillness Speaks*. Novato, CA: New World Library.

Tolle, E. (2004). *Power of Now*. Novato, CA: New World Library.

Tolle, E. (2008). *A New Earth: Awakening to Your Life's Purpose*. New York: Plume Books.

Tolle, E. (2009). *Guardians of Being*. Novato, CA: New World Library.

Vital Statistics of the Self-Storage Industry. (2011). Retrieved from http://www.selfstorageblog.com/vital-statistics-of-the-self-storage-industry/

Wilber, K. (2001). *No Boundary: Eastern and Western Approaches To Personal Growth*. Boulder, CO: Shambhala.

Wittgenstein, L. (2001) [1921]. *Tractatus Logico-Philosophicus*. New York: Routledge.

CHAPTER 10

Bernstein, W. (2010). *The Birth of Plenty: How the Prosperity of the Modern World Was Created*. New York: McGraw Hill.

Borg, M. J. (2004). *The Heart of Christianity: Rediscovering a Life of Faith*. San Francisco: Harper.

Brown, J. (1989). *Gandhi: Prisoner of Hope*. New Haven, CT: Yale University Press.

Carse, J. P. (2008). *The Religious Case Against Belief*. London: Penguin Press.

Cusa, N. (1990). *De Docta Ignorantia*, (Jasper Hopkins, trans.). Minneapolis: A. J. Banning Press.

Darley, J. M., & Batson, C. D. (1973). From Jerusalem to Jericho: A study of situational and dispositional variables in helping behavior. *Journal of Personality and Social Psychology*, 27 (1), 100–108.

Easwaran, E. (1978). *Gandhi the Man*. Petaluma, CA: Nilgiri Press.

Ferguson, N. (2010). Man charged with assault against census worker. *NewsChannel5.com*, Nashville, TN. Retrieved from http://www.newschannel5.com/story/12664886/man-charged-with-assault-against-census-worker?redirected=true.

Fowler, J. W. (1984) *Becoming Adult, Becoming Christian*. San Francisco: Harper & Row.

Frankl, V. (1984). *Man's Search for Meaning*. Boston: Beacon Press.

Fromm, E. (1976). *To Have or To Be?* New York: Harper & Row.

Gandhi, M. (1962). *Last Glimpses of Bapu*. Delhi: Shiva Lal Agarwala.

Huxley, A. (1970) [1945]. *The Perennial Philosophy*, Perennial Library. New York: Harper & Row.

Lifton, R. J. (1989). *Thought Reform and the Psychology of Totalism: A Study of Brainwashing in China*. Chapel Hill, NC: University of North Carolina Press.

Lifton, R. J. (2003). *Superpower Syndrome: America's Apocalyptic Confrontation with the World*. New York: Nation Books.

May, G. G. (2005). *The Dark Night of the Soul: A Psychiatrist Explores the Connection Between Darkness and Spiritual Growth*. San Francisco: HarperOne.

Nanda, B. R. (1997). *Mahatma Gandhi: A Biography*. Delhi: Oxford University Press.

Peck, M. S. (1978). *The Road Less Traveled: A New Psychology of Love, Traditional Values, and Spiritual Growth*. New York: Simon & Schuster.

Tolle, E. (2008). *A New Earth: Awakening to Your Life's Purpose*. New York: Plume Books.

CHAPTER 11

Bassiouni, M. C. (1997). Searching for peace and achieving justice: The need for accountability. *Law and Contemporary Problems. 9* (4), 9–28.

Becker, E. (1962). *Birth and Death of Meaning: An Interdisciplinary Perspective on the Problem of Man*. New York: The Free Press.

Becker, E. (1974). *The Denial of Death*. New York: The Free Press.

Berger, P. (1969). *The Sacred Canopy: Elements of a Sociological theory of Religion*. Garden City, NY: Doubleday.

Brzezinski, Z. (1995). *Out of Control: Global Turmoil on the Eve of the 21st Century*. New York: Touchstone Books.

Brown, N. (1959). *Life Against Death: The Psychoanalytical Meaning of History*. New York: Vintage Books.

Buber, M. (1970). *I and Thou*. New York: Scribner and Sons.

Burke, B. L., Martens, A., & Faucher, E. H. (2010). Two decades of Terror Management Theory: A meta-analysis of mortality salience research. *Personality and Social Psychology Review, 14*, (2), 155–195.

Campbell, J. (1949). *The Hero with a Thousand Faces*. Princeton, NJ: Princeton University Press

Coppola, F. F. (Writer), and Schaffner, F. J. (Director). (1970). *Patton*. [Film]. Hollywood, CA: Twentieth Century Fox Film Corporation.

Douglas, M. (2002). *Purity and Danger: An Analysis of Concepts of Pollution and Taboo*. London: Routledge Classics, Taylor Press.

Florian, V., & Milkulincer, M. (1998). Symbolic immortality and the management of the terror of death. *Journal of Personality and Social Psychology, 74*, 725–734.

Glover, J. (2001). *Humanity: A Moral History of the Twentieth Century*. New Haven, CT: Yale; Nota Bene.

Greenberg, J., Simon, L. Pyszczynski, T., Solomon, S., & Chatel, D. (1992). Terror management and tolerance: Does mortality salience always intensify negative reactions to others who threaten one's worldview? *Journal of Personality and Social Psychology, 63*, 212–220.

His Holiness the Dalai Lama (2009). *Becoming Enlightened*. New York: Atria Paperbacks.

Keen, S. (1986). *Faces of the Enemy: Reflections on the Hostile Imagination*. New York: HarperCollins.

James, W. (1958) [1902]. *The Varieties of Religious Experience*. New York: Mentor Books; New American Library.

Kierkegaard, S. (1957) [1844]. *The Concept of Dread*. Princeton, NJ: University Press Edition.

Landau, M., Solomon, S., Pyszczynski, T., & Greenberg, J. (2007). On the compatibility of terror management theory and perspectives on human evolution. *Evolutionary Psychology*, *5*, (3) 476–519.

Lewis, C. S. (1944). The Inner Ring. Memorial Lecture at King's College, University of London. Retrieved from http://www.lewissociety.org/innerring.php.

Milkulincer, M., & Florian, V. (2002). Exploring individual differences in reaction to mortality salience: Does attachment style regulate terror management mechanisms? *Journal of Personality and Social Psychology*, *79*, 260–273.

Miller, A. (1949). *Death of a Salesman*. New York: Penguin Books.

Montaigne, M. D. (2006). That to study philosophy is to learn to die. Quotidiana. Ed. Patrick Madden. Retrieved from <http://essays.quotidiana.org/montaigne/that_to_study_philosophy/>.

Nabokov, V. (1989). *Speak, Memory: An Autobiography Revisited*. New York: Vintage.

Orwell, G. (1949). *1984*. Toronto: S. J. Reginald Saunders.

Rank, O. (1932). *Art and Artist: Creative Urge and Personality Development*. New York: W. W. Norton.

Rank, O. (1958). *Beyond Psychology*. New York: Dover Publications.

Rank, O. (1968). *Art and Artist: Creative Urge and Personality Development*. New York: Agathon Press.

Roheim, G. (1971). *The Origin and Function of Culture*. New York: Anchor Books.

Shen, P. (Producer, Director), & Bennick, G. (Co-producer). (2005). *Flight from Death: The Quest for Immortality* [Film]. Available from http://www.flightfromdeath.com/index.htm.

Solomon, S. (Oct. 18, 2002). The structure of evil: History is a nightmare from which I'm trying to awaken: An introduction to the thought of Ernest Becker. *Ernest Becker Foundation*. Retrieved from http://www.ernestbecker.org/index.php?option=com_content&view=article&id=289:flight-from-death-20-dvd&catid=11:most-popular-items&Itemid=37.

Solomon, S., Greenberg, J., & Pyszczynski, T. (1991). A terror management theory of social behavior: The psychological functions of self-esteem and worldviews. *Advances in Experimental Social Psychology*, *24*, 93–159.

The Mahabharata, Book 3 of 18: Vana Parva. Forgotten Books, London, England.

Van Valin, V. (2009). *Casting Out Fear: Shedding Your Fictional Self and Awakening Your Authentic Self*. Denver, DO: Outskirts Press.

White, M. (2010). Historical Atlas of the Twentieth Century: Death by Mass Unpleasantness: Estimated Totals for the Entire Twentieth Century. Retrieved from http://users.erols.com/mwhite28/warstat8.htm.

CHAPTER 12

Arendt, H. (1963) *Eichmann in Jerusalem: A Report on the Banality of Evil*. London: Penguin Books.

Asch, S. E. (1955). Opinions and social pressure. *Scientific American*, *193* (5), 1–6.

Baumeister, R. F., & Bushman, B. J. (2010). *Social Psychology and Human Nature*. Independence, KY: Wadsworth Publishing.

Bellah, R., Madsen, R., Sullivan, W. M., Swindler, A., & Tipton, S. M. (1985). *Habits of the Heart: Individualism and Commitment in American Life*. New York: Harper & Row.

De Toqueville, A. (2001) [1838]. *Democracy in America*. New York: Signet Classics.

Goldhagen, D. (2009). *Worse Than War: Genocide, Eliminationism, and the On-Going Assault on Humanity*. New York: Public Affairs.

Haslam, S. A., & Reicher, S.D. (2007a). Beyond the banality of evil. *Personality and Social Psychology Bulletin*, *33*, 615–622.

Haslam, S. A., & Reicher, S. D. (2008). Questioning the banality of evil. *The Psychologist: Journal of the British Psychological Society*, *21*, 16–19. Retrieved from http://www.thepsychologist.org.uk/archive/archive_home.cfm/volumeID_21-editionID_155-ArticleID_1291.

Holocaust Studies (2011). The Eichmann Trial: 50 Years Later: A prosecutor and key witness reflect back on the even that transformed Israel. Retrieved from http://www.aish.com/ho/i/The_Eichmann_Trial_50_Years_Later.html.

Sherif, M, [Obituary] (1988). Musafer Sherif, Social Psychologist. *Los Angeles Times*, Oct. 30. Retrieved from http://articles.latimes.com/1988-10-30/news/mn-916_1_social-psychologist.

Smith, D. L. (2011). *Less Than Human: Why We Demean, Enslave, and Exterminate Others*. New York: St. Martin's Press.

Zimbardo, P. (2008). *The Lucifer Effect: How Good People Turn Evil*. New York: Random House.

CHAPTER 13

Bandura, A., Underwood, B., & Fromsons, M. E. (1975). Disinhibition of aggression through diffusion of responsibility and dehumanization of victims. *Journal of Research in Personality*. *9*, 253–259.

Carnaghan, T., & McFarland, S. (2007). Revisiting the Stanford prison experiment. *Personality and Social Psychology Bulletin*, *33*, 603–614.

Clemens, M. (2010). *The Secrets of Abu Ghraib Revealed: American Soldiers on Trial*. Dulles, VA: Potomac Books.

Haslam, S. A., & Reicher, S. D. (2008). Questioning the banality of evil. *The Psychologist: Journal of the British Psychological Society*, *21*, 16–19. Retrieved from http://www.thepsychologist.org.uk/archive/archive_home.cfm/volumeID_21-editionID_155-ArticleID_1291.

Milgram, S. (1963) Behavioral study of obedience. *Journal of Abnormal and Social Psychology*, *67* (4), 371–378.

Milgram, S. (1974). *Obedience to Authority: An Experimental View*. New York: Harper & Row.

Murray, H. R. & Cluckhohn, C. (1956). *Personality in Nature, Society, and Culture*. New York: Knopf.

Nietzsche, F. (1879). *Human, All Too Human: A Book for Free Spirits*.

Seligman, M. E. P., & Maier, S. F. (1967) Failure to escape traumatic shock. *Journal of Experimental Psychology*, *74*, 1–9.

Solzhenitsyn, S. (1976). *The Gulag Archipelago (1981–1956)*. New York: Harper Collins.

Zimbardo, P. (n.d.a). Stanford Prison Experiment. Retrieved September 16, 2011, from http://www.prisonexp.org.

Zimbardo, P. (n.d.b). The Lucifer Effect: Understanding How Good People Turn Evil. Retrieved September, 19, 2011, from http://www.lucifereffect.com/.

Zimbardo, P. (1969). The human choice: Individuation, reason, and order versus deindividuation, impulse, and chaos. In W. D. Arnold & D. Levine (Eds.), *Nebraska Symposium on Motivation*. Lincoln: University of Nebraska, 237–307.

Zimbardo, P. (2008). *The Lucifer Effect: How Good People Turn Evil*. New York: Random House.

CHAPTER 14

Buckley, C. (2007). Man is rescued by stranger on subway tracks. *The New York Times*, January 3. Retrieved from http://www.nytimes.com/2007/01/03/nyregion/03life.html.

Campbell, J. (1949). *The Hero with a Thousand Faces*. Princeton, NJ: Princeton University Press.

Darley, J. M., & Latane, B. (1970). *The Unresponsive Bystander: Why Doesn't He Help?* New York: Appleton-Century-Crofts.

Darley, J. M., & Batson, C. D. (1973). From Jerusalem to Jericho: A study of situational and dispositional variables in helping behavior. *Journal of Personality and Social Psychology*, 27 (1), 100–108.

Fowler, J. (1981). *Stages of Faith: The Psychology of Human Development and the Quest for Meaning*. San Francisco: Harper Collins.

If you move, sir, one of us is going to die (2007, March 1). *London Evening Standard*. Retrieved from http://www.thisislondon.co.uk/news/article-23380367-if-you-move-sir-one-of-us-is-going-to-die.do.

Moriarty, T. (1975) Crime, commitment, and the responsive bystander: Two field experiments. *Journal of Personality and Social Psychology*, 31, 370–376.

Rivera, R. (2009). In a split second, a pilot becomes a hero years in the making. *New York Times*. 01/16/09. Retrieved from http://www.nytimes.com/2009/01/17/nyregion/17pilot.html.

Seidler, V. J. (2009). *Kant, Respect and Injustice: The Limits of Liberal Moral Theory*. Routledge Revivals, New York, NY.

Zimbardo, P. G. (2007, April 2). The Lucifer Effect: Understanding How Good People Turn Evil." M.I.T. Retrieved from http://mitworld.mit.edu/video/459.

CHAPTER 15

Ardrey, R. (1970). *African Genesis,* 6th ed. New York: Dell Publishing Company.

Campbell, J. (1991). *Power of Myth*. New York: Anchor Books.

His Holiness the Dalai Lama (2009). *Becoming Enlightened*. New York: Atria Paperbacks.

Huxley, A. (1970) [1945]. *The Perennial Philosophy*, Perennial Library. New York: Harper & Row.

Maslow, A. (1970). *Religions, Values and Peak Experiences*. London: Penguin Books.

Koestler, A. (1960). *The Lotus and the Robot*. London: Hutchinson.

Laski, M. (1961). *Ecstasy*. London: Cresent Press.

Ross, S. (1994). *Art and Its Significance: An Anthology of Aesthetic Theory*. State University of New York Press, Albany, NY.

Schall, J. V. (1998). *At the Limits of Political Philosophy*. Catholic University of America Press, Washington, D.C.

Steindl-Rast, D. (1989). The mystical core of organized religion. *Revision, 12* (1), 11–14.

CHAPTER 16

Alexander, C. F. (1847). There Is a Green Hill Far Away. [Hymn]. *Hymns for Little Children*. Philadelphia: Herman Hooker.

Atran, S. (2002). *In Gods We Trust: The Evolutionary Landscape of Religion.*
    New York: Oxford University Press.

Becker, E. (1974). *The Denial of Death.* New York: Free Press.

Beit-Hallahmi, B. (1988). The religiosity and religious affiliation of Nobel Prize win-
    ners. Unpublished data.

Bono, J., & Remus, I. (2006). Charisma, positive emotions and mood contagion.
    Mendeley, 17, (4), 317–334. Retrieved from http://www.mendeley.com/research/
    charisma-positive-emotions-mood-contagion/.

Boyer, P. (2002). *Religion Explained: The Evolutionary Origins of Religious Thought.*
    New York: Basic Books.

Buber, M. (1966). *The Way of Man According to the Teaching of Hassidism.* Secaucus,
    NJ: Citadel Press.

Carson, D. A., Moo, D. J., & Morris, L. (1992). *An Introduction to the New Testament.*
    Grand Rapids, MI: Zondervan Publishing House.

Cragg, K. (1988). *Readings in the Koran.* London: Collins.

Diogenes, A. (2010). *Theology for a Troubled Believer: An Introduction to the Christian
    Faith.* Westminster: John Knoxx Press.

Frankl, V. (1984). *Man's Search for Meaning.* Boston: Beacon Press.

Gombrich, R. & Keegan, P. (1988). *Theravada Buddhism: A Social History from Ancient
    Benāres to Modern Colombo.* New York: Routledge.

Gould, S. J., McGarr, P., & Rose, S. P. R. (2007). Challenges to Neo-Darwinism and
    their meaning for a revised view of human consciousness. *The Richness of
    Life: The Essential Stephen Jay Gould.* New York: W. W. Norton.

Guenther, H. (1949). *The Problem of the Soul in Early Buddhism.* Curt Weller, Verlag,
    Constanz, Germany.

Guthrie, S. E. (1995). *Faces in the Clouds: A New Theory of Religion.* New York: Oxford
    University Press.

Haidt, J. (2009). *The Righteous Mind: How Good People Are Divided by Religion and
    Politics.* New York: Vintage.

His Holiness the Dalai Lama (2009). *Becoming Enlightened.* New York: Atria
    Paperbacks.

Huxley, A. (1970) [1945]. *The Perennial Philosophy,* Perennial Library.
    New York: Harper & Row.

Irenaeus of Lyons. *Against Heresies.* Create Space Independent Publishing Platform,
    March 28, 2012.

James, W. (1958) [1902]. *The Varieties of Religious Experience.* New York: Mentor
    Books; New American Library.

Joiner, T. E., & Katz, J. (1999). Contagion of depressive symptoms and
    mood: Meta-analytic review and explanations from cognitive, behavioral, and
    interpersonal viewpoints. *Clinical Psychology: Science and Practice, 6* (2), 149–164.

Kapogiannis D., Barbey, A. K., Su, M., Zamboni, G., Krueger, F., & Grafman, J. (2009).
    Cognitive and neural foundations of religious belief. *Proceedings of the National
    Academy of Sciences of the USA, 106,* 4876–4881.

Kirkpatrick, L. A. (2004). *Attachment, Evolution, and the Psychology of Religion.*
    New York: The Guilford Press.

Klausner, J. (1997). *Jesus of Nazareth: His Life, Times, and Teaching.* St. John's,
    FL: Bloch Publishing Company.

Koestler, A. (1960). *The Lotus and the Robot.* London: Hutchinson.

Laski, M. (1961). *Ecstasy.* London: Cresent Press.

Ledgerwood, G. (n.d.). Welcome to the Different Spiritual Paths of the World.
    Retrieved from http://www.spiritualworld.org/hinduism/spirit_perfect.htm.

Ledgerwood, G. (2010). A World of Yoga: Find More from Life Than You Ever Dreamed. *Mystic World Fellowship*. Retrieved from http://www.yogaworld.org/index.htm.

Matanga, K., & Gobharana (n.d.). Saying no. 41. The Sayings of the Buddha in Forty-Two Sections. Retrieved from http://www.fodian.net/english/42section.htm.

Michaelson, J. (2010). Jewish Enlightenment: Neo-Hasidism and Vedanta Hinduism. Retrieved from http://zeek.forward.com/articles/116715/.

Nasr, S. H. (1989). *Ideals and Realities of Islam*. Cairo: American University in Cairo Press.

Newberg, A. B., Alavi, A., Baime, M., Pourdehnad, M., Santanna, J., & d'Aquili, E. G. (2001). The measurement of regional cerebral blood flow during the complex cognitive task of meditation: A preliminary SPECT study. *Psychiatry Research: Neuroimaging 106*: 113–122.

Newberg, A., Pourdehnad, M., Alavi, A., & d'Aquili, E. (2003). Cerebral blood flow during meditative prayer: Preliminary findings and methodological issues. *Perceptual and Motor Skills, 97*: 625–630.

Osborne, E. (2005).*Founders and Leaders: Buddhism, Hinduism and Sikhism*. Dunstable, Great Britain: Folens, R. E. Limited.

Pascal, B. (1995). *Pense'es*, 149 (A. J. Krailsheimer, Trans.). Penguin Books, New York, NY.

Rector, J. M., & Rector, K. N. (2003). What is the challenge for LDS scholars and artists? *Dialogue: A Journal of Mormon Thought, 36*, (2), 33–46.

Religions ranked by number of adherents (n.d.). Retrieved October 20, 2011 from http://www.adherents.com/Religions_By_Adherents.html.

Schwartz, T. (1995) *What Really Matters: Searching for Wisdom in America*. New York: Bantam Press.

Sedlmeier, P., Eberth, J., Schwarz, M., Zimmermann, D., Haarig, F., Jaeger, S. (2012). The psychological effects of meditation: A meta-analysis. *Psychological Bulletin*. Retrieved from http://www.ashanamind.com/wp-content/uploads/2013/03/physiological-effects_Sedlmeier_12.pdf.

Shermer, M. (2012). *The Believing Brain: From Gods, Gods, Politics and Conspiracies—How We Construct beliefs and Reinforce Them as Truths*. New York: St. Martin's Griffin.

Smith, H. (1991). *The World Religions*. San Francisco: Harper Collins.

Sri Dhammananda, K. (1993). *What Buddhists Believe*, 5th ed. Kuala Lumpur, Malaysia: The Corporate Body of the Buddha Educational Foundation,.

Steadman, L., & Palmer, C. (2008). *The Supernatural and Natural Selection: The Evolution of Religion*. Boulder, CO: Paradigm Publishers.

Tertullian (1931). *Apology and De Spectaculis*. (G. R. Glover & G. H. Rendall, Trans.). Loeb Classical Library, No. 250 (English and Latin Edition) (Chap. 39, Sect. 7). Cambridge: Harvard University Press.

Thich Nhat Hanh. (1998). *The Heart of the Buddha's Teaching: Transforming Suffering into Peace, Joy, and Liberation*. New York: Broadway Books.

Thompson, J. A. (2011). *Why We Believe in Gods: A Concise Guide to the Science of Faith*. Charlottesville, VA: Pitchstone Publishing.

Vine, W. E. (1996). *Vine's Complete Expository Dictionary of Old and New Testament Words: With Topical Index*. Thomas Nelson.

Wade, N. (2009). *Faith Instinct: How Religion Evolved and Why it Endures*. New York: Penguin Press.

Wilber, K. (n.d.). An Integral Spirituality: The Silken Thread Which Unites the World's Great Wisdom Traditions. Retrieved from http://www.beliefnet.com/Wellness/2004/03/An-Integral-Spirituality.aspx.

Wilson, D. S. (2002). *Darwin's Cathedral: Evolution, Religion, and the Nature of Society*. Chicago: University of Chicago Press.

Allport, G. W. (1954). *The Nature of Prejudice*. Cambridge, MA: Perseus Books.

Ariely, D. (2008). *Predictably Irrational: The Hidden Forces That Shape Our Decisions*. New York: HarperCollins.

Bernstein, W. (2010). *The Birth of Plenty: How the Prosperity of the Modern World was Created*. New York: McGraw Hill.

Bal, P. M., & Veltkamp, M. (2013) How does fiction reading influence empathy? An experimental investigation on the role of emotional transportation. *PLOS ONE 8*(1): e55341. Retrieved from http://www.plosone.org/article/info%3Adoi%2F10.1371%2Fjournal.pone.0055341.

Butters, R. P. (2010). *A Meta-Analysis of Empathy Training Programs for Client Populations*. Ann Arbor, MI: ProQuest, UMI Dissertation Publishing.

Carkhuff, R. R., & Truax, C. B. (1965). Training in counseling and psychotherapy: An evaluation of integrated didactic and experiential approach. *Journal of Consulting Psychology, 29*, 333–336.

Cohen, A. (2002). *Living Enlightenment: A Call for Evolution Beyond Ego*. Lenox, MA: Mosksha Press.

Crisp, R. J., & Turner, R. N. (2009). Can imagined interactions produce positive perceptions? Reducing prejudice through simulated social contact. *American Psychologist, 64* (4), 231–240.

Darwin C. (2004) [1871]. *The Descent of Man*. London: Penguin Classics.

Donne, J. (1990). *Selections from Divine Poems, Sermons, Devotions, and Prayers*. J. Booty (Ed.). Paulist Press, Mahwah, NJ.

Ellison, J. (2011, April 3). The military's secret shame. *Newsweek*. Retrieved from http://www.thedailybeast.com/newsweek/2011/04/03/the-military-s-secret-shame.html.

Forsyth, D. R. (2009). *Group dynamics* (5th ed.). Pacific Grove, CA: Brooks/Cole.

Fowler, J. (1981). *Stages of Faith: The Psychology of Human Development and the Quest for Meaning*. San Francisco: Harper Collins.

Fowler, J. W. (1984). *Becoming Adult, Becoming Christian*. San Francisco: Harper & Row.

Frankl, V. (1984). *Man's Search for Meaning*. Boston: Beacon Press.

Friedman, T. L. (1999). *The Lexus and the Olive Tree: Understanding Globalization*. New York: Anchor Books.

Gabriel, S., & Young, A. (2011). Becoming a vampire without being bitten: The narrative collective assimilation hypothesis. *Psychological Science*. Retrieved from http://www.psychologicalscience.org/index.php/news/releases/becoming-a-vampire-without being-bitten-a-new-study-shows-that-reading-expands-our-self-concepts.html.

Glover, J. (2001). *Humanity: A Moral History of the Twentieth Century*. New Haven, CT: Yale; Nota Bene.

Green, M. (2008). Empathy, expression, and what artworks have to teach. In G. L. Hagberg (Ed.), *Art and Ethical Criticism*. Oxford: Blackwell Publishing, 95–122.

Haidt, J. (2006). *The Happiness Hypothesis: Finding Modern Truth in Ancient Wisdom*. New York: Basic Books.

Haidt, J. (2012). *The Righteous Mind: Why Good People Are Divided by Politics and Religion*. New York: Pantheon Books.

Hanh, T. N. (1998). *The Heart of the Buddha's Teaching: Transforming Suffering into Peace, Joy, and Liberation*. New York: Broadway Books.

Harris, S. (2006). Why religion must end: Sam Harris interviewed by Laura Shehan. *Third World Traveler—Beliefnet*. Retrieved from http://www.thirdworldtraveler.com/Sam_Harris/WhyReligionMustEnd.html.

Harris, S. (2013). The power of bad incentives. *Edge—The Edge Annual Question, 2013: What Should We Be Worried About?* Retrieved from http://www.samharris.org/media/the-power-of-bad-incentives.

Heath, C., & Heath, D. (2010). *Switch: How to Change Things When Change is Hard.* New York: Crown Business.

His Holiness the Dalai Lama (2009). *Becoming Enlightened.* New York: Atria Paperbacks.

Hodges, S. D., & Meyers, M. W. (2007). Empathy. *Encyclopedia of Social Psychology, 1,* 296–298.

Iacoboni, M. (2008). *Mirroring People: The New Science of How We Connect with Others.* New York: Farrar, Strauss, & Giroux.

Kidd, D. C., & Castano, E. (Oct. 18, 2013). Reading literary fiction improves theory of mind. *Science, 342* (6156), 377–380. Available at: http://www.sciencemag.org/content/342/6156/377.abstract

Kivy, P. (2002). *Introduction to a Philosophy of Music.* Oxford: Oxford University Press. 40–41.

Konheim-Kalkstein, Y. L. (2006). Use of a classroom honor code in higher education. *The Journal of Credibility Assessment and Witness Psychology, 7* (3), 169–179.

Krznaric, R. (2012, Nov. 27). Six habits of highly empathic people. *Greater Good: The Science of a Meaningful Life.* Retrieved from http://greatergood.berkeley.edu/article/item/six_habits_of_highly_empathic_people1.

Lam, T. C. M., Kolomitro, K., & and Alamparambil, F. C. (2011). Empathy training: Methods, evaluation practices, and validity. *Journal of MultiDisciplinary Evaluation, 7* (16), 162–200.

Lerner, J. S., & Tetlock, P. E. (2003). Bridging individual, interpersonal, and institutional approaches to judgment and decision making: The impact of accountability on cognitive bias. In S. L. Schneider and J. Shanteau (Eds.), *Emerging Perspectives on Judgment and Decision Research.* New York: Cambridge University Press, 431–457.

Leveille, L. (2012, Aug. 10). Sullivan: Honor code, communication cultivates culture of honor, integrity. *The Chautauquan Daily.* Retrieved from http://chqdaily.com/2012/08/10/sullivan-honor-code-communication-cultivates-culture-of-honor-integrity/.

Magid, B., & Beck, C. J. (2009). *Ordinary Mind: Exploring the Common Ground of Zen and Psychoanalysis.* Boston: Wisdom Publications.

Mar, R. A., Oatley, K, & Peterson, J. B. (2009). Exploring the link between reading fiction and empathy: ruling out individual differences and examining outcomes. *Communications 34:* 407–428.

Maslow, A. (1971). *The Farther Reaches of Human Nature.* New York: Viking Press.

Mehta, A. (2011). Interesting Osho quote on enlightenment. Retrieved from http://anmolmehta.com/blog/2008/01/08/osho-quote-on-enlightenment/

Oatley, K. (2012). Emotion and the story worlds of fiction. In M. C. Green, J. J. Strange, & T. C. Brock (Eds.), *Narrative Impact: Social and Cognitive Foundations.* Florence, KY: Psychology Press, 39–69.

Obama, B. (2008). Remembering Dr. Martin Luther King, Jr. Speech given April 4, 2008, Fort Wayne, IN. Retrieved from http://www.democraticunderground.com/discuss/duboard.php?az=view_all&address=132x5382479.

Peck, M. S. (1978). *The Road Less Traveled: A New Psychology of Love, Traditional Values, and Spiritual Growth.* New York: Simon & Schuster.

Pinker, S. (2011). *The Better Angels of Our Nature: Why Violence Has Declined.* New York: Viking Adult.

Pinker, S. (2011a). Lecture: The Better Angels of Our Nature: Why Violence Has Declined. Oct. 2011, Linda Hall Library. Retrieved from http://vimeo.com/30504043.

Rees, W. E. (1992). Ecological footprints and appropriated carrying capacity: What urban economics leaves out. *Environment and Urbanisation 4* (2): 121–130.

Rogers, C. (1959). A theory of therapy, personality, and personal relationships as developed in the client-centered framework. In S. Koch (Ed.), *Psychology: A Study of a Science: Vol. 3. Formulation of the Person and the Social Context.* New York: McGraw Hill, 184–256.

Rothbart, M., & John, O. P. (1985). Social categorization and behavioral episodes: A cognitive analysis of the effects of intergroup contact. *Journal of Social Issues, 41*, 81–104.

Ruiz, R. (2013, March 21). Training seeks to improve how military sexual assaults are investigated. *U.S. News on NBC News.com.* Retrieved from http://usnews.nbcnews.com/_news/2013/03/21/17375404-training-aims-to-improve-how-military-sexual-assaults-are-investigated?lite.

Ryan, C., & Jetha, C. (2010). *Sex at Dawn: The Prehistoric Origins of Modern Sexuality.* New York: HarperCollins.

Singer, P. (1981). *The Expanding Circle: Ethics and Sociobiology.* New York: Farrar Straus & Giroux.

Spielberg, S. (Director). (1993). *Schindler's List* [Film]. Universal City, CA: Universal Studios.

Thaler, R. H. (2009, Sept. 26). Opting in vs. opting out. *New York Times.* Retrieved from http://www.nytimes.com/2009/09/27/business/economy/27view.html?_r=0.

Thaler, R. H., & Sunstein, C. R. (2009). *Nudge: Improving Decisions about Health, Wealth, and Happiness.* New York: Penguin Books.

Wilber, K. (1996). *A Brief History of Everything.* Boulder, CO: Shambhala Press.

Wilber, K. (2007). *Integral Spirituality.* Boston: Integral Books.

Zahn-Waxler, C., Radke-Yarrow, M., & King, R. A. (1979). Child rearing and children's prosocial initiations toward victims of distress. *Child Development, 50*: 319–330.

Zahn-Waxler, C., & Radke-Yarrow, M. (1990). The origins of empathic concern. *Motivation and Emotion, 14*: 107–130.

Zahn-Waxler, C., Radke-Yarrow, M., Wagner, E., & Chapman, M. (1992). Development of concern for others. *Developmental Psychology, 28*: 126–136.

INDEX

Milgram, Stanley, 155, 161–163, 176, 180
Miller, Arthur, 146
Mislatch, Christina, 168
moral resources, 35, 43, *see also* empathy, human responses, Glover, Jonathan
Mother Teresa, 2, 16, 92, 180, 183, 221
motivate the elephant strategy, 236–237
mystical core of organized religion diagram(s), 190, 192–193, *see also* Steindl-Rast, David

Nabakov, Vladimir, 137
namasté, 4
narcissism
    as contributor to the problem of objectification, 93
    as part of the "blemding in" mode of heroism, 147
    Beckerian explanation of, 94–95
    case example, 96–100
    definition of, 93–94
    DSM-5 criteria, 95
    Narcissistic Personality Inventory, 95n, Appendix
    problem of, 5
    relationship to ego diagram, 103
    three types of, 96
nature and manifestations of ego, 101, *see also* ego, having versus being, tanha
    attachment, 110–111
    content, 107–108
    identification with objects, 109–110
    need to be right and for others to be wrong, 113–114
    self-enhancing mechanism, 102
    self-organizing mechanism, 102–103
    separateness, 112–113
    structure, 108–109
    wanting, 111–112
Needleman, Jacob, 48–49, 49n, 50, 93, 101, 105–107, 131, 133
Nicholas of Cusa, 135
Nietzsche, Friedrich, 173
nirvana, 201–202, 212
nunc fluens, 85, 115
nunc stans, 85

Nussbaum, Martha, 18–20, 22, 40, *see also* objectification, definition of

Obama, Barak, 240
objectification, *see also* casual indifference, derivatization, dehumanization
    antidote to, 225
    as perceptual error, 21
    author's definition of, 2, 9
    author's model of, 22, 225
    boundaried, separate self, cause of, 4, 23, 52, 73–74, 76, 88, 212
    boundaries, contribution to, 61, 69–72
    Buddhist method toward transcending, 209–212
    caused by perceived separation and distance from others, 4, 64, 103, 108, 112
    Christian methods toward transcending, 215
    classic examples of, 14
    contribution to human evil, 10
    deindividuation contributing to, 175
    dispositional factors contributing to, 59
    Dworkin, Andrea definition of, 15–16
    feminist definition of, 15, 17–18
    frequency of feminist reference to, 14
    Hindu method toward transcending, 200–201
    human tendencies toward, 4, 118, 163, 180
    "I am not that", as example of, 23, 74, 91, 118, 177
    Islamic method toward transcending, 218
    Judaism method toward transcending, 205
    Kantian bias about, 27
    Kantian definition of, 14–15
    language's contribution to, 61
    labels contributing to, 173, 175
    momentary transcendence of, 180
    Nussbaum, Martha definition of, 18–21, 40
    Plato's Allegory of the Cave as reference to, 3–4
    practical ways to reduce, 237–38